HIKING THE SAN FRANCISCO BAY AREA

A GUIDE TO THE BAY AREA'S GREATEST HIKING ADVENTURES

SECOND EDITION

Linda Hamilton

FALCONGUIDES

GUILFORD, CONNECTICUT

For Doug, Ben, and Max, all my hiking friends, and all those who dedicate
their time and efforts to protecting and nurturing our open spaces.

FALCONGUIDES®

An imprint of The Rowman & Littlefield Publishing Group, Inc.
4501 Forbes Blvd., Ste. 200
Lanham, MD 20706
www.rowman.com

Falcon and FalconGuides are registered trademarks and Make Adventure Your Story is a
trademark of The Rowman & Littlefield Publishing Group, Inc.

Distributed by NATIONAL BOOK NETWORK

Copyright © 2018 by The Rowman & Littlefield Publishing Group, Inc.

A previous edition of this book was published by Falcon Publishing, Inc. in 2003.

Maps: © The Rowman & Littlefield Publishing Group, Inc.

All photos by Linda Hamilton unless otherwise noted

British Library Cataloguing in Publication Information Available

Library of Congress Cataloging-in-Publication Data Available

ISBN 978-1-4930-2983-9 (paperback)

ISBN 978-1-4930-2984-6 (e-book)

∞™ The paper used in this publication meets the minimum requirements of American
National Standard for Information Sciences—Permanence of Paper for Printed Library
Materials, ANSI/NISO Z39.48-1992.

Printed in the United States of America

The author and Rowman & Littlefield assume no liability for accidents happening to, or
injuries sustained by, readers who engage in the activities described in this book.

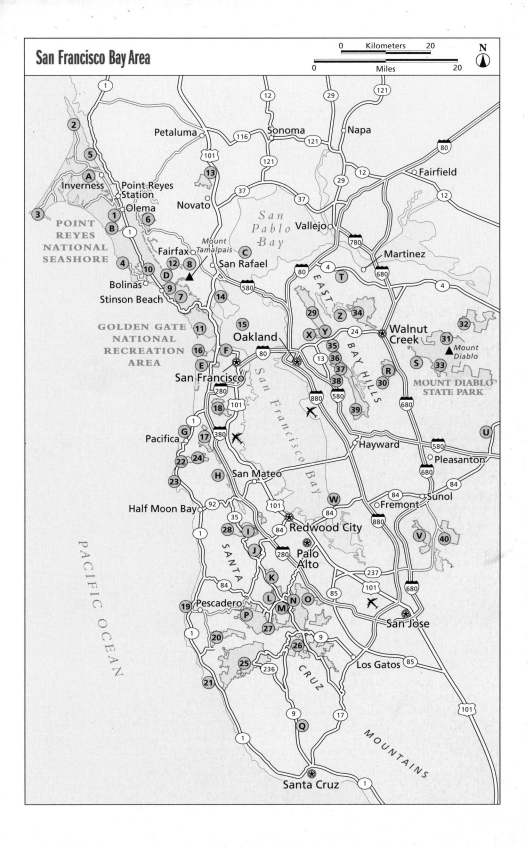

THE HIKES

MEET YOUR GUIDE   ix

FIVE BAY AREA HIKING TIPS   x

MAP AND ICON LEGENDS   xiii

TRAIL FINDER   xiv

TOP FIVE HIKES   xviii

BEFORE YOU HIT THE TRAIL   xx

THE HIKES

Point Reyes   *1*

1. Point Reyes National Seashore: Mount Wittenberg and Bear Valley to the Sea Loop   2
2. Point Reyes National Seashore: Tomales Point   7
3. Point Reyes National Seashore: Lighthouse and Chimney Rock Trails   12
4. Point Reyes National Seashore: Palomarin Trailhead to Alamere Falls   17
5. Tomales Bay State Park: Heart's Desire Beach to Shell Beach   22
6. Samuel P. Taylor State Park: To the Top of Barnabe Peak   27

BONUS HIKES: POINT REYES
A. Point Reyes National Seashore: Inverness Ridge   32
B. Kule Loklo & the Earthquake Trail   35

Mount Tamalpais and Its Foothills   *36*

7. Muir Woods: Bootjack Trail to Dipsea Trail Loop   37
8. Phoenix Lake: Tucker and Bill Williams Trails   43
9. Steep Ravine Loop to Stinson Beach   48
10. Mt. Tamalpais: East Peak Loop   54
11. Marin Headlands: Miwok Trail to Point Bonita   60
12. Marin Municipal Water District: Kent Trail along Alpine Lake   66

13. Mount Burdell Open Space Preserve 71
14. Ring Mountain Open Space Preserve 76

BONUS HIKES: MOUNT TAMALPAIS AND ITS FOOTHILLS
C. China Camp State Park: Shoreline-Bayview
   Loop Trail 82
D. Cataract Trail 83

San Francisco and the Bay 84

15. Angel Island State Park: Mt. Livermore 85
16. Golden Gate National Recreation Area:
   San Francisco's Lands End 90
17. Sweeney Ridge: San Francisco Bay Discovery Site 95
18. San Bruno Mountain State Park: Summit Loop Trail 100

BONUS HIKES: SAN FRANCISCO AND THE BAY
E. Golden Gate Park 105
F. The Presidio: Lovers' Lane and the Ecology Trail 106

San Mateo County Coastline 107

19. Pescadero Marsh Trail 108
20. Butano State Park 113
21. Año Nuevo State Park 119
22. McNee Ranch at Montara State Beach 124
23. James V. Fitzgerald Marine Reserve: The Tide
   Pool Loop 129
24. San Pedro Valley County Park 135

BONUS HIKES: SAN MATEO COASTLINE
G. Mori Point 140
H. Crystal Springs Regional Trail 141

The Northern Santa Cruz Mountains 144

25. Big Basin Redwoods State Park: Berry Creek
   Falls Trail Loop 145
26. Castle Rock State Park: Saratoga Gap/Ridge
   Trail/Castle Rock Trail 152
27. Portola Redwoods State Park: Slate Creek/
   Summit/Iverson Loop 158

28. Purisima Creek Redwoods Open Space Preserve:
Craig Britton and Purisima Creek Loop   164

BONUS HIKES: THE NORTHERN SANTA CRUZ MOUNTAINS
  I. Huddart County Park and Phleger Estate   169
  J. Wunderlich County Park   171
  K. Windy Hill Open Space Preserve   172
  L. Russian Ridge Open Space Preserve   173
  M. Skyline Ridge Open Space Preserve   176
  N. Monte Bello Open Space Preserve   177
  O. Rancho San Antonio Open Space Preserve
     and County Park   180
  P. Pescadero Creek County Park   181
  Q. Henry Cowell Redwoods State Park   182

Mount Diablo and Las Trampas Foothills   *184*
29. Las Trampas Regional Wilderness   186
30. Mount Diablo State Park: Donner Canyon
    to the Falls Trail   191
31. Black Diamond Mines Regional Preserve   196
32. Mount Diablo: Rock City to the Summit   201

BONUS HIKES: MOUNT DIABLO AND LAS TRAMPAS FOOTHILLS
  R. Las Trampas Regional Wilderness: The Eugene
     O'Neill Loop   208
  S. Mount Diablo State Park: Wall Point—Pine
     Canyon Loop   210
  T. John Muir National Historic Site: Mount Wanda   211
  U. Brushy Peak Regional Preserve   214

*Three Ridges: San Pablo, the Oakland/Berkeley Hills,
and Sunol Ridge*   *215*
33. Tilden Regional Park: From Jewel Lake to
    Wildcat Peak   216
34. Briones Regional Park   222
35. Robert Sibley Volcanic Regional Preserve   227
36. Huckleberry Botanic Regional Preserve   233

37. Redwood Regional Park: Stream Trail, from East
    Ridge to West Ridge   239
38. Joaquin Miller Park: Sequoia Bayview Trail and
    Big Trees Loop   245
39. Anthony Chabot Regional Park   249
40. Sunol Regional Wilderness   255

BONUS HIKES: THREE RIDGES: SAN PABLO, THE OAKLAND/
BERKELEY HILLS, AND SUNOL RIDGE
 V. Mission Peak Regional Preserve   260
 W. Coyote Hills Regional Park   262
 X. Claremont Canyon Regional Preserve   265
 Y. Tilden Regional Park—Greater Tilden   266
 Z. Briones Reservoir   267

LOCAL INTEREST TRAIL FINDER   271

HIKE INDEX   275

MEET YOUR GUIDE

Day hiking was our most frequent family activity when I was a child, mostly in the Sierras during summer. Then, one Saturday during my high school years, I drove to below the South Gate of Mount Diablo and hiked to the peak. It was my rite of passage, having grown up in the mountain's rolling foothills and shadowed valley. But it wasn't until my adult life that I really started to explore the incredible open spaces around the Bay Area. I was amazed at the diversity and vastness and stories of the land, which were so like the people who live here.

Raising a family of my own, we've created many treasured memories in our Bay Area parklands: the first kiss with my to-be-husband on Mount Tam, our preschoolers awed by thousands of undulating ladybugs in Redwood Regional Park, the kids and their friends counting over 300 banana slugs along the trail in Butano State Park, walking through history on Angel Island, and laughing together with our growing young men creekside down Steep Ravine to Stinson Beach.

I hope you too will enjoy discovering the forests, marshes, streams, lakes, beaches, canyons, and hillsides of this rich landscape, along with all its flora and fauna and intriguing history.

Linda Parker Hamilton is also the author of *Best Hikes Near San Francisco, Camping Northern California,* and the *Camping Activity Book for Families: The Kid-Tested Guide to Fun in the Outdoors.*

FIVE BAY AREA HIKING TIPS

Since my first Bay Area hiking guidebook in 2003, people have asked me these questions: Where can I find a trail away from people? How do I get my kids into hiking? What is your favorite Bay Area hike? How do I get the most out of this book? How do I get the most out of each hike?

Here are the answers, my five tips for hiking in the Bay Area:

1. Where can I find a trail away from people?

To boldly hike where no man has hiked before—or at least feel that way—try watershed land. The East Bay Municipal Utility District, or EBMUD (www.ebmud.com/recreation/east-bay/east-bay-trails/), requires a reasonably priced permit, which makes trail users more infrequent. The San Francisco Public Utilities Commission (www.sfwater.org/index.aspx?page=134) offers docent-led hikes on the Fifield-Cahill Ridge Trail (10 miles) between CA 92 and Sweeney Ridge above Crystal Springs, with plans for expansion and possibly more open trails.

Try the spaces in between. The Bay Area Ridge Trail (over 375 miles and growing) connects our Bay Area parklands as well as those in the North Bay and South Bay (http://ridgetrail.org).

Sunol Regional Wilderness
MIGUEL VIEIRA (FLICKR.COM/
PHOTOS/MIGUELVIEIRA/)

Set your alarm and hike early in the day. You will see fewer people, have better parking, see more wildlife, and have the rest of your day to go to nearby restaurants and attractions.

Don't let a little bad weather stop you! A light rain will keep less hearty hikers at home, making the trail yours. An added benefit is the presence of colorful fungi that arise in the moisture overnight.

2. How do I get my kids into hiking?
Here are the golden rules for positive family hiking experiences:

Exploring on Mount Tam

- Don't hike too far. Go the kids' pace, giving them time to explore. (See the Trail Finder chart for family-friendly hikes and "Alternate routes" at the end of longer feature hikes in this book for shorter versions.)

- For goodness' sake, don't call it a hike. Call it an adventure or family outing or nature trip, anything that doesn't imply lots of walking.

- Bring snacks, snacks and more snacks, and fun ones at that. Stop often along the way to distribute water and snacks. Think Hansel and Gretel, without the wicked witch, of course.

- Choose hikes with cool features or destinations: rocks to climb, hollow trees to enter, labyrinths, ruins, fossils, geocaching, wading and swimming holes and beaches are among the many features discoverable in the Bay Area.

- Remember the journey is the experience. Start with a fun car ride (music, road games, books-on-tape) and consider songs, conversation, and games on the trail. You'll find lots of ideas in the *Camping Activity Book for Families: The Kid-Tested Guide to Fun in the Outdoors.*

3. What is your favorite Bay Area hike?
I adore the Oakland Hills hikes, Steep Ravine, Berry Creek Falls Trail, Butano, the Craig Britton Trail in Purisima, and anywhere on Point Reyes. Most important is to find your favorites and repeat them at different times of the day and year for entirely new experiences (see the "Top Five Hikes" section).

4. How do I get the most out of this book?

Stories are powerful: They create connections to people, to history and to the land. I've tried to include both human and ecological stories for each of the featured hikes in this book. Hopefully this enhances your hiking experience. It does mine.

Also, use each suggested trail, including the many Bonus Hikes, as a guide to finding even more trails in that area or adjoining areas and ones that best suit your mood. We are so fortunate to have the Golden Gate Recreational Area, the largest urban park in the world, as well as all the national, state, and well-managed regional parks in the Bay Area.

5. How do I get the most out of each hike?

Come prepared. In the Bay Area, you can go from 50 degrees and foggy to 80 degrees and sunny in a matter of an hour. Poison oak is common, so be alert, wear long pants, or bring products like Technu to wash on the trail. Bring a map or this book. Carry plenty of water (for you and your dog), sunscreen, and snacks, especially for longer hikes.

Take pictures, bring friends, print out online bird or flower or nature guides, give yourself extra time on the trail to look around, take in details, vistas, and imagine this beautiful land in its past. Really take advantage of hiking in the Bay Area by coupling your hike with a new restaurant, bookstore, museum, or attraction in this vibrant and diverse Bay Area.

Finally, we are all caretakers of our open spaces. Feel the ownership. Stay on developed trails. Mutt-mitt your dog's waste to a garbage can. Leave no trace. And bring an extra feel-good bag in your backpack to pick up any garbage you see along the trail.

Map Legend

Municipal

≡⟨80⟩≡ Interstate Highway

≡⟨101⟩≡ US Highway

≡⟨1⟩≡ State Road

——— Local Road

—·—·— State Boundary

Trails

------- Featured Trail

------ Trail or Fire Road

·········· Optional Trail Route

▮▮▮▮▮ Steps/boardwalk

Water Features

⬭ Body of Water

Marsh

River/Creek

Intermittent Stream

Waterfall

Spring

Land Management

National Park/Forest

National Monument/
Wilderness Area

State/County Park

National Seashore/
Marine Reserve

Symbols

✈ Airport

)(Bridge

■ Building/Point of Interest

▲ Campground

† Cemetery

•—• Gate

⌂ Inn/Lodging

⚲ Lighthouse

◇ Mileage Marker

🅿 Parking

)(Pass

▲ Peak/Elevation

⊞ Picnic Area

Ranger Station/Park Office

Restroom

Scenic View

Stables

☎ Telephone

○ Town

① Trailhead

⊢==⊣ Tunnel

❓ Visitor/Information Center

Water

♿ Wheelchair Accessible

ICON LEGEND

BEST PHOTOS

FAMILY FRIENDLY

WATER FEATURES

DOG FRIENDLY

FINDING SOLITUDE

TRAIL FINDER

	BEST PHOTOS	FAMILY FRIENDLY	WATER FEATURES	DOG FRIENDLY	FINDING SOLITUDE
POINT REYES					
1. Point Reyes National Seashore: Mount Wittenberg and Bear Valley to the Sea Loop	•		•		•
2. Point Reyes National Seashore: Tomales Point	•				•
3. Point Reyes National Seashore: Lighthouse and Chimney Rock Trails	•	•	•		
4. Point Reyes National Seashore: Palomarin Trailhead to Alamere Falls	•		•		
5. Tomales Bay State Park: Heart's Desire Beach to Shell Beach	•	•	•		•
6. Samuel P. Taylor State Park: To the Top of Barnabe Peak					•
BONUS HIKES POINT REYES					
A. Point Reyes National Seashore: Inverness Ridge					•
B. Kule Loklo & the Earthquake Trail		•			
MOUNT TAMALPAIS AND ITS FOOTHILLS					
7. Muir Woods: Bootjack Trail to Dipsea Trail Loop	•	•			
8. Phoenix Lake: Tucker and Bill Williams Trails	•	•	•	•	
9. Steep Ravine Loop to Stinson Beach	•	•	•		
10. Mt. Tamalpais: East Peak Loop	•			•	
11. Marin Headlands: Miwok Trail to Point Bonita	•	•	•	•	
12. Marin Municipal Water District: Kent Trail along Alpine Lake	•		•	•	•
13. Mount Burdell Open Space Preserve				•	•
14. Ring Mountain Open Space Preserve	•			•	

	BEST PHOTOS	FAMILY FRIENDLY	WATER FEATURES	DOG FRIENDLY	FINDING SOLITUDE
BONUS HIKES MOUNT TAMALPAIS AND ITS FOOTHILLS					
C. China Camp State Park: Shoreline-Bayview Loop Trail			●		
D. Cataract Trail	●		●	●	
SAN FRANCISCO AND THE BAY					
15. Angel Island State Park: Mt. Livermore	●	●	●		
16. Golden Gate National Recreation Area: San Francisco's Lands End	●	●	●	●	
17. Sweeney Ridge: San Francisco Bay Discovery Site				●	
18. San Bruno Mountain State Park: Summit Loop Trail		●			
BONUS HIKES: SAN FRANCISCO AND THE BAY					
E. Golden Gate Park	●	●	●	●	
F. The Presidio: Lovers' Lane and the Ecology Trail		●		●	
SAN MATEO COUNTY COASTLINE					
19. Pescadero Marsh Trail	●	●	●		
20. Butano State Park	●	●	●		●
21. Año Nuevo State Park	●	●	●		
22. McNee Ranch at Montara State Beach			●	●	●
23. James V. Fitzgerald Marine Reserve: The Tide Pool Loop	●	●	●		
24. San Pedro Valley County Park	●	●	●		
BONUS HIKES: SAN MATEO COUNTY COASTLINE					
G. Mori Point		●	●	●	
H. Crystal Springs Regional Trail		●	●	●	

	BEST PHOTOS	FAMILY FRIENDLY	WATER FEATURES	DOG FRIENDLY	FINDING SOLITUDE
THE NORTHERN SANTA CRUZ MOUNTAINS					
25. Big Basin Redwoods State Park: Berry Creek Falls Trail Loop	●		●		●
26. Castle Rock State Park: Saratoga Gap/Ridge Trail/ Castle Rock Trail	●				●
27. Portola Redwoods State Park: Slate Creek/Summit/Iverson Loop			●		●
28. Purisima Creek Redwoods Open Space Preserve: Craig Britton and Purisima Creek Loop	●		●		●
BONUS HIKES: THE NORTHERN SANTA CRUZ MOUNTAINS					
I. Huddart County Park and Phleger Estate	●	●			
J. Wunderlich County Park	●	●			
K. Windy Hill Open Space Preserve					●
L. Russian Ridge Open Space Preserve					●
M. Skyline Ridge Open Space Preserve	●	●	●		●
N. Monte Bello Open Space Preserve		●			●
O. Rancho San Antonio Open Space Preserve and County Park		●			●
P. Pescadero Creek County Park	●	●			●
Q. Henry Cowell Redwoods State Park	●	●	●	●	
MOUNT DIABLO AND LAS TRAMPAS FOOTHILLS					
29. Las Trampas Regional Wilderness		●		●	●
30. Mount Diablo State Park: Donner Canyon to the Falls Trail	●		●		●
31. Black Diamond Mines Regional Preserve	●	●		●	
32 Mount Diablo: Rock City to the Summit	●	●			

	Best Photos	Family Friendly	Water Features	Dog Friendly	Finding Solitude
BONUS HIKES: MOUNT DIABLO AND LAS TRAMPAS FOOTHILLS					
R. Las Trampas Regional Wilderness: The Eugene O'Neill Loop			•		
S. Mount Diablo State Park: Wall Point—Pine Canyon Loop	•				
T. John Muir National Historic Site: Mount Wanda	•	•		•	
U. Brushy Peak Regional Preserve				•	•
THREE RIDGES: SAN PABLO, THE OAKLAND/BERKELEY HILLS, AND SUNOL RIDGE					
33. Tilden Regional Park: From Jewel Lake to Wildcat Peak	•	•	•	•	
34. Briones Regional Park			•	•	
35. Robert Sibley Volcanic Regional Preserve	•	•		•	
36. Huckleberry Botanic Regional Preserve		•			•
37. Redwood Regional Park: Stream Trail, from East Ridge to West Ridge	•	•	•	•	
38. Joaquin Miller Park: Sequoia Bayview Trail and Big Trees Loop		•		•	
39. Anthony Chabot Regional Park			•	•	•
40. Sunol Regional Wilderness	•	•	•	•	•
BONUS HIKES: THREE RIDGES: SAN PABLO, THE OAKLAND/BERKELEY HILLS, AND SUNOL RIDGE					
V. Mission Peak Regional Preserve				•	
W. Coyote Hills Regional Park	•	•	•		
X. Claremont Canyon Regional Preserve				•	
Y. Tilden Regional Park—Greater Tilden	•		•	•	•
Z. Briones Reservoir	•	•	•	•	•

One of many bridges on Steep Ravine Trail

Ladybugs on the Stream Trail in Redwood Regional Park

20. BUTANO STATE PARK

Butano has it all: redwoods and banana slugs, knobcone pine ridges with views, and even a bat house, and it can be coupled with a drive to Pescadero Marsh and State Beach (with a stop in the town of Pescadero for signature artichoke bread or artichoke soup).

9. STEEP RAVINE LOOP TO STINSON BEACH

It's entrancing: the bridges crisscrossing Webb Creek through the redwoods, the unique ladder descent (or climb), vast coastal views, and ending up at Stinson Beach to play in the surf and have a nice lunch.

37. REDWOOD REGIONAL PARK: STREAM TRAIL, FROM EAST RIDGE TO WEST RIDGE

With the descent into a serene redwood forest, the views along the ridge, rabbits scurrying across the trail, seasonal ladybugs, and hidden geocaches, this dog-friendly and kid-friendly trail is an East Bay favorite.

On Six Bridges Trail in Butano State Park

23. JAMES V. FITZGERALD MARINE RESERVE: THE TIDE POOL LOOP

To be able to hike through wind-leaning cypress trees and then see so much colorful, moving aquatic life makes you grateful for the earth and oceans—and wishing to do everything you can to protect them.

25. BIG BASIN STATE PARK: BERRY CREEK FALLS TRAIL LOOP

You have to earn these waterfalls with the out-and-back hike, but Berry Creek Falls in the spring will leave you smiling for a mile and feeling like you just visited a mini Yosemite.

Anemone in the tide pools at James V. Fitzgerald Marine Reserve

Berry Creek Falls, Big Basin National Park
DESKTOPRESS.COM

BEFORE YOU HIT THE TRAIL

STATE/REGION OVERVIEW

The San Francisco Bay Area is home to more parks, beaches, and open spaces—an estimated 1.1 million acres—than any other major urban area in the United States. No other metropolis in the world offers so much open space so close to a major city. This is the result of over one hundred years of advocacy by park lovers, hikers, and environmental groups. Few areas offer such a variety of ecosystems to explore as the Bay Area, from riparian, forest, and canyon environments to pastoral hillsides, marshes, coastal ridges, and sandy beaches. Whether you like it wet, dry, high, low, perfectly level, or mountain goat steep, there's something here for you. Diversity is a Bay Area theme, in its land and its people.

The trails in this book lead you to roaring waterfalls, silent glades, and wind-whipped mountaintops. They'll show you quiet meadows covered with wildflowers, swarming with butterflies, or crawling with ladybugs, and deep, verdant forests where ferns grow lush and colossal trees stand like pillars holding up the sky. And they'll take you to places to breathe, beyond the daily commute, beyond the sleepy suburbs, and beyond the familiar tourist attractions. You can also experience flora and fauna found only in and around the Bay Area. There are hikes here for every level of experience, with options for families, longer hikes, and even backpacking.

Hiking Bay Area parklands is also a great way to discover the human history of the area, from our native Ohlone and Miwok past, to the land's stint as Mexican rancheros, to the gold rush that changed everything and still defines this area, to wars, industrial revolution, reaching for the American Dream through immigration, and all the way to the present day.

And, of course, this is an urban center, so after hiking there are fun attractions and shops and museums to take in and opportunities for great places to eat or stay the night. You can create an entire multifaceted adventure starting with a hike in this book.

It was hard to create a perimeter for the featured hikes. The beauty of Northern California continues in all directions from the Bay Area, one of the many reasons people love to live here. Nonetheless, the epicenter, if you will, is the San Francisco Bay Bridge, and all the hikes, with only a couple exceptions, are within an hour and a half's weekend drive. Within this range, this book features some of the most diverse, exhilarating, and beautiful hikes around the bay, hikes that do justice to the history, natural diversity, stories, and character of this region. Enjoy your hike!

The Golden Gate Bridge from Lands End
M. TOYAMA (INSTAGRAM@MPTOYAMA)

BAY AREA OPEN SPACE AND PARKLAND

Here's a rundown on some of the major agencies in the Bay Area featured in this book:

Golden Gate Recreational Area

It is one of the most visited national park areas in the United States and one of the largest urban parks in the world, hosting more than 15 million visitors a year. It protects 82,027 acres, nineteen distinct ecosystems, over 2,000 plant and animal species, and hundreds of miles of trails.

Point Reyes National Seashore

This is a 71,028-acre park preserve with over 1,500 species of plants and animals.

California State Parks

Within the greater Bay Area (extending a bit north and south beyond the boundaries of this book), the state park system contains all these types of parkland with hundreds of miles of trails:

- 3 national wildlife refuges
- 1 state forest
- 1 national seashore
- 3 state reserves
- 2 state wildlife areas

- 25 state parks
- 2 national historic sites
- 2 historic buildings
- 1 national recreation area

East Bay Regional Park District
The system comprises 121,030 acres in seventy-three parks, including over 1,250 miles of trails.

San Mateo County Parks Department
This county system encompasses 17,000 acres and numerous trails.

Midpeninsula Regional Open Space District
This growing open space includes 63,000 acres of public land and twenty-six open-space preserves with over 220 miles of trails.

SAN FRANCISCO BAY AREA WEATHER
Possibly no other region in this country displays as many varieties of weather simultaneously as does the San Francisco Bay Area. With the area's diverse landscape, sharp topography, and maritime surroundings, the area experiences numerous microclimates. It can be sunny on the Las Trampas Ridge, raining on Mount Tamalpais, snowing on Mount Diablo, foggy on Sweeney Ridge, and windy on Montara Mountain all at once. On any one hike you can experience severe changes in temperature and humidity as trails take you abruptly from one ecosystem to the next. Atmospheric forces and geologic formations come together to form the area's unique combination of forest, river, ocean, bay, and hills, one of the most prominent phenomena being the jet stream, which causes the famous summer fog that pours over the Golden Gate Bridge.

Coastal fog over the bay
MIGUEL VIEIRA (FLICKR.COM/
PHOTOS/MIGUELVIEIRA/)

The green hills of winter and spring
MIGUEL VIEIRA (FLICKR.COM/
PHOTOS/MIGUELVIEIRA/)

Overall, the area is said to have a Mediterranean climate, generally characterized by moist mild winters and dry summers.

Summertime in San Francisco is characterized by cool marine air and persistent coastal stratus (low-level clouds) and fog, with average high temperatures between 60 and 70 degrees F, and lows between 50 and 55 degrees F. It gets warmer the farther east you go into the wind-sheltered valleys east of the Coastal Range. Trails in Oakland and Berkeley, for example, may experience some of that morning fog, but then clear to temperatures 5 to 10 degrees higher than San Francisco. East of the Las Trampas range, in the San Ramon and Silicon Valleys, there is little to no summer fog, and temperatures are 10 degrees higher still, with highs into the 90s (and more frequently, with global warming, into the low 100s).

Winter temperatures in San Francisco are rather temperate, with highs between 55 and 60 degrees F and lows in the 45- to 50-degree F range. The range is similar inland, but a few degrees warmer generally. Skies are often cloudy in this rainiest time of year, but it can be crisp and clear in winter.

Over 80 percent of San Francisco's seasonal rain falls between November and March, occurring over about ten days per month. Only about 5 percent of the annual rainfall occurs between May and September. The yearly average is between 21 and 24 inches in the San Francisco Bay Area. However, with California being a drought state and subject to El Niño weather every few years or so, this varies.

The golden hills of summer and fall

Spring and fall produce the most cloud-free days in the San Francisco Bay Area, with the hottest days typically in the spring and especially in the fall. The entire region is subject to heat waves and periodic windstorms in the autumn.

Snow is rare, with only ten documented instances of measurable snow in the past 143 seasons. However, there may be a very temporary thin covering of white on top of Mount Diablo and Mission Peak once every few winters.

You can find up-to-date weather forecasts for the Bay Area at www.nbcbayarea.com/weather/?zipCode=95141 or https://weather.com (enter the nearest city or zip code).

And for tide information, visit tidesandcurrents.noaa.gov or tides.net.

FLORA AND FAUNA

With the many microclimates and ecosystems in the Bay Area, it's no wonder the vegetation and wildlife are abundant and varied here. This may seem even more amazing for an area touching so much human development.

Of the over 6,300 native plants in California, more than a third of them are endemic to the state, a high percentage of those occurring in the Bay Area. The coast is famous for its redwood trees—the tallest living things on earth. Under the thick canopies of these giants, varieties of ferns carpet the forest floor, occasionally making room for clover-like redwood sorrel. Shady hills may feature a mixture of madrone, California bay, many types of oak, bigleaf maple, and pungent California laurel trees. The coastal bluffs alternate between brushy chaparral, coastal scrub, and forested headlands, depending very much on the local microclimates. In Point Reyes National Seashore alone, over 700 plants have been identified. South-facing sunny slopes often host oak savanna with wildflower-filled, grassy meadows. Sagebrush, manzanita, and knobcone pines are characteristic of dry sandstone ridges, where plants must be able to tolerate the meager precipitation and intense summer heat. Common flowers in spring include California poppies, Douglas iris, blue flax, cow parsnip, common star lily, calypso orchid, and crimson columbine.

Rare and endangered plants found only in the San Francisco Bay Area include—among others—the coast rock cress, Franciscan and Presidio manzanitas, the hairy San Francisco gumplant, coast iris, Michael's Rein orchid, and Francisco thistle.

Wildlife in the region is more diverse than almost anywhere in the United States, giving the Bay Area a reputation, according to the Audubon Society, "as an international biodiversity hotspot." Invertebrates, many endemic, are abundant in the muddy bottom sediments of the San Francisco Bay estuary. The wetlands provide critical feeding and breeding grounds for migratory birds traveling the Pacific Flyway, as well as some 500 species of fish, mammals, and plants, which are either threatened or endangered.

Of the more than 600 bird species that have been spotted in California—making up two-thirds of all bird species in North America—most make appearances in the Bay Area. Sandhill cranes, snow geese, and American coots all stop here on their travels. You may readily spy a Canada goose, pied-billed grebe, double-crested cormorant, great blue heron, acorn woodpecker, California towhee, dark-eyed junco, and Anna's hummingbird. The marbled murrelet and spotted owl are limited to old-growth forests. Grassy hillsides all over the Bay Area support raptors like red-shouldered hawks and golden eagles and the small mammals and birds upon which they feed.

Pacific false bindweed on Ring Mountain
MIGUEL VIEIRA (FLICKR.COM/PHOTOS/MIGUELVIEIRA/)

Mushrooms along the Skyline-to-the-Sea Trail in Big Basin
MIGUEL VIEIRA (FLICKR.COM/PHOTOS/MIGUELVIEIRA/)

Cattail reed on Alpine Lake, Marin County

Western wood pewee on Mount Burdell
BECKY MATSUBARA
(FLICKR.COM/PHOTOS/
BECKYMATSUBARA/)

Tule elk, once numbering in the tens of thousands, were hunted to near extinction before being protected. They now survive on Tomales Point in Point Reyes. Mountain lions, seldom seen, roam throughout the area, wherever deer are abundant. Bobcats, ravens, gray foxes, raccoons, and skunks are also common. Mammals most commonly seen on the trail include the brush rabbit, eastern fox and western gray squirrels, coyotes, California ground squirrels, and black-tailed deer.

This region of the Pacific Ocean is home to diverse and abundant marine life. Seals and sea lions are a common sight along the coast and in coastal estuaries. Harbor seals are the most visible, but California and northern sea lions are also abundant. The largest of the lot, northern elephant seals, hang out and breed on the beaches of Año Nuevo. Whale watchers can observe the yearly migrations of the gray whale from a high spot along the coast, like Point Reyes and Bodega Head. Fitzgerald Marine Preserve has some of the best tide pools on the West Coast, full of sea anemones, sea stars, crabs, and even octopi.

While threatened by logging, agricultural runoff, dams, and overdevelopment, a few of the Bay Area's rivers still host seasonal trout and salmon runs. Coho salmon and steelhead trout make their way from the ocean up rivers and streams to spawn in the headwaters where they were born. Many of the reservoirs and lakes in the area host bigmouth and other bass, bluegill, and catfish. A few are annually stocked with rainbow trout.

Among the area's endangered species are the San Francisco garter snake, the California clapper rail, the California least tern, the San Joaquin kit fox, the salt marsh harvest mouse, the western snowy plover, the Mission blue butterfly, and the red-legged frog. Spotting these creatures—from afar so as not to disturb their habitats—is a real treat when hiking the San Francisco Bay Area.

A coyote spotted on the Round Valley Regional Preserve Miwok Trail
MIGUEL VIEIRA (FLICKR.COM/PHOTOS/MIGUELVIEIRA/)

San Francisco from San Bruno Mountain
SEROUJ

WILDERNESS RESTRICTIONS/REGULATIONS

The San Francisco Bay Area has a combination of city, county, state, and national parks, preserves and reserves, and open space. These lands have important biological, cultural, economic, and recreational value. Permits, access quotas, and fees are part of the effort to balance human use without compromising the health and wild character of the wilderness.

Dogs are restricted in preserves and delicate wildlife areas, but most parks have made paved roads and some trails accessible for dog-walkers. The East Bay Regional Park allows dogs on most of their trails. Please respect the wilderness and other users by cleaning up

Elephant seal on
Año Nuevo Beach

after your pets—even when it's tempting to leave their waste—and keep your dogs on leash (maximum 6-foot) unless in areas designated for your pets to run free. Service dogs are always allowed.

In this highly populated area, it is important to stay on designated trails. There could be sensitive plant life and wildlife off-trail. Don't disturb any animals you may see, and never feed them human food.

Our dry forests are prone to wildfires, so most parks do not allow smoking, limit fires to designated fire pits when deemed safe, and never allow weapons.

Most parks in the San Francisco Bay Area do not allow drones, but a few have designated areas, so call each agency or research online before flying one.

Regulations vary, so it's important to check out restrictions and rules for the different park agencies concerning dogs, parking, fees, and trail use and closures before departing. Help keep the wilderness wild.

The southern section of Great Beach,
eleven miles of undeveloped beach in
Point Reyes NATIONAL PARK SERVICE
DIGITAL IMAGES ARCHIVES

POINT REYES

You can feel far away from the Bay Area at Point Reyes National Seashore, whether camping on the beach, staying in a quaint cottage, or visiting for the day. In one hike, it is possible to walk through thick forests of redwoods or Bishop pines and over shrub-speckled hillsides, see the ocean crashing through over rocks, and watch deer grazing on open grasslands. You may observe in one day hundreds of the 1,500 distinct species of plants and animals in Point Reyes, including giant elephant seals sunbathing on Drakes Beach, sandpipers scurrying along daintily over foamy, wet sand at the mouth of Abbotts Lagoon, and gangs of native tule elk roaming on Tomales Point. Rocks protect pools that at low tide reveal millions of sea creatures: starfish, anemones, and clams that cling to the watery stones and hide in crevices in this co-op home. Chimney Rock hosts one of the most spectacular wildflower displays on the West Coast.

And everywhere there is human history too. Driving in, you can blink and imagine the dairy ranches in 1870 covering the entire Point Reyes Peninsula with 10,000 cows, the largest "Butter Rancho" in the country. You can stand on the epicenter of the great 1906 San Francisco earthquake where the North American Plate meets the Pacific Plate (the narrow peninsula shifts northward a few inches each year). You can wander into a recon-structed Miwok village and glimpse pre-European California. And you can enter a Vic-torian lighthouse and stand outside in the foggiest and windiest place on the Pacific coast and, perhaps, on a clear day, spot a gray whale spouting on its long, semiannual migration.

Even with over 2 million visitors every year, you don't feel crowded here or rushed. Artisans are drawn to Point Reyes for its living watercolors. Outdoor enthusiasts come for the hiking, kayaking, and bird-watching. But mostly, people travel to Point Reyes for serenity, contemplation, and the sheer beauty of the place.

Wildcat Beach from the Coast Trail
MIGUEL VIEIRA (FLICKR.COM/PHOTOS/
MIGUELVIEIRA/)

1. POINT REYES NATIONAL SEASHORE: MOUNT WITTENBERG AND BEAR VALLEY TO THE SEA LOOP

WHY GO?

The hike starts in a lush forest of Douglas fir and oak trees. You then follow the ridgeline, with views of Drakes Bay and the Pacific Ocean. The trail descends to the treeless, stark beauty of coastal bluffs. Have lunch on a tiny, idyllic beach. Then walk through wind-manicured scrub, with views of blue-rippled ocean. Head inland through a fairy-tale woodland of chalk-white alders, following a meandering stream. End up back at the Bear Valley Visitor Center.

THE RUN DOWN

Start: 0.2 mile up Bear Valley Trail from the end of the Bear Valley parking lot
Elevation gain: 1,300 feet
Distance: 12.3-mile loop
Difficulty: Strenuous due to length and elevation gain
Hiking time: About 6 hours
Seasons/schedule: Sunrise to sunset year-round
Fees and permits: None
Trail contact: Point Reyes National Seashore, 1 Bear Valley Visitor Center

Access Rd., Point Reyes Station 94956; (415) 464-5100; www.nps.gov/pore/index.htm
Dog-friendly: No dogs allowed
Trail surface: Steep and flat double- and single-track dirt trail
Land status: National seashore
Nearest town: Olema
Nat Geo TOPO! Map: Inverness
Nat Geo Trails Illustrated Map: Mount Tamalpais, Point Reyes #266
Other trail users: Equestrians; bikers on Bear Valley and Coast Trails

FINDING THE TRAILHEAD

From US 101 take Sir Francis Drake Boulevard west to Olema. Turn north on CA 1, then make an almost immediate turn west onto Bear Valley Road. Continue on Bear Valley Road for less than a half mile to the Bear Valley Visitor Center. **GPS:** N38 2.23' / W122 48.3'

WHAT TO SEE

After taking off from the Bear Valley Visitor Center, a brief meadow jaunt brings you to the Mount Wittenberg Trail, the only uphill portion of the hike and your 1,300-foot climb. At 1,407 feet, Mount Wittenberg is the highest point on the Point Reyes

Looking back at Bear Valley from the Coast Trail
MIGUEL VIEIRA (FLICKR.COM/PHOTOS/MIGUELVIEIRA/)

Peninsula. It was named for a father and son who leased land here for a large—and hilly—dairy ranch in the 1860s.

Thick, lush Douglas fir and oak forest—with the occasional endangered Bishop pine—canopies a dirt trail textured with angular roots and surrounded by maidenhair, chain, and five-fingered ferns. It's a fairly popular weekend trail, but less so than the flat, wide, and easy Bear Valley Trail.

Sky Trail takes you along the ridge where you get your first glimpse of ocean to the northwest with Drakes Bay and the Estero de Limantour hugging the Limantour Spit. Tall Bishop pine trunks charred by the 1995 Mount Vision fire stand on hills to the west. But here and on Woodward Valley Trail, you can see young Douglas firs and Bishop pines reinvigorating the forest. Bishops, like Monterey and knobcone pines, are fire pines. It takes fire to "hatch" the seeds from their cones and start new growth. To identify them, note that Bishop pines have two long needles per cluster and large cones. Douglas firs have short needles that poke out from the branch like a bottlebrush and small, waxy-looking cones.

The Woodward Valley Trail takes you through hillside valleys bathed with afternoon sunlight and a woodland of mostly new-growth Douglas fir. It opens up to a breathtaking view of the Pacific Ocean.

The Coast Trail offers the stark beauty of the bluffs, the contemplative view of the Pacific, the salty smell of the sea, and the mesmerizing sound of the waves. Yellow and blue-purple coast bush lupine adds color in the spring, along with golden-yellow lizard-tail, coast fiddleneck, and gumplant. Pink bursts of sea thrift color the early summer.

A short detour to Sculptured Beach offers a great lunch spot if the wind is calm. Winter rains feed two creeks, which stream across the sand into the ocean, creating a wet barrier that isolates the little coarse-sand beach that takes its name from the jutting, water-carved rocks exposed at low tide.

The Coast Trail section of the hike ends near Arch Rock, which collapsed in 2015. Over the past 10,000 years or so, the ocean level has risen to inundate former valleys, leaving behind sea stacks, sea caves, and arches like the one that used to be here. That same rise is also wearing down the bluffs. Please keep your distance from the edge, as the area is unstable.

Cliffs from the Coast Trail
MIGUEL VIEIRA (FLICKR.COM/PHOTOS/
MIGUELVIEIRA/)

The Bear Valley Trail heads inland, following Coast Creek, with its chalk-white alder trees, to Divide Meadow with picnic tables, log seats, and restrooms. In late August the far end of the meadow displays bright pink "naked ladies," old-world amaryllis lilies probably planted by owners of the hunting lodge that once stood here. In the early 1900s, Bear Valley Road brought travelers from Olema by horse-drawn carriage to hunt. Presidents William H. Taft and Theodore Roosevelt belonged to the hunting club, which disbanded when Point Reyes became a preserve in 1976.

Bear Valley beyond Divide Meadow is probably the single most traveled trail in Point Reyes, but near dusk, most tourists have already gone to town for cocktails and oysters. The path follows Bear Valley Creek, bordered with oak, bay, and Douglas fir, back to the visitor center.

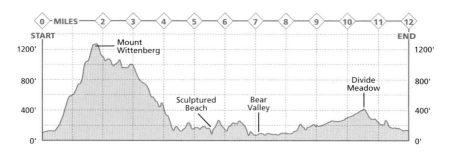

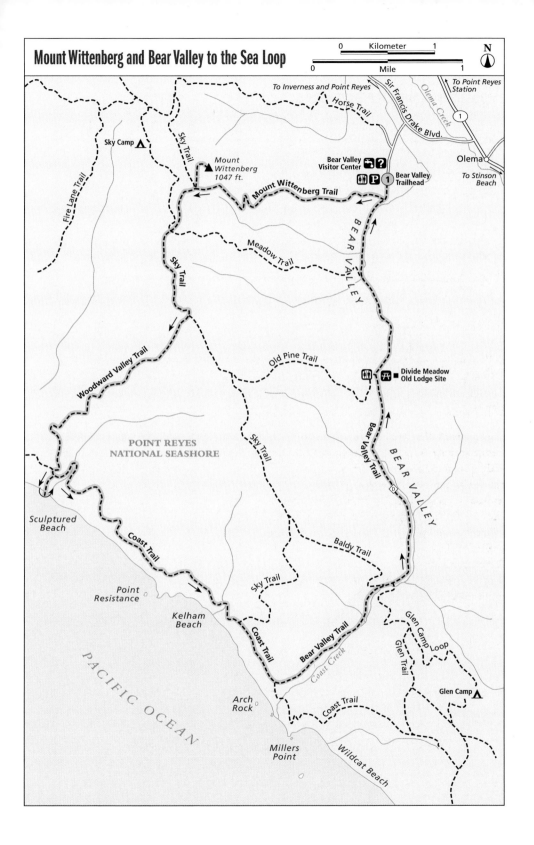

MILES AND DIRECTIONS

0.0 START from the parking lot at Bear Valley Visitor Center. Walk to the end of the lot, west toward the driveway to the old Morgan Ranch. The double-track Bear Valley Trail heads west across the meadow.

0.2 Turn right onto Mount Wittenberg Trail.

2.0 To continue on Mount Wittenberg Trail, turn left. It becomes Sky Trail toward Woodward Valley Trail.

2.4 Trailhead for Sky Trail and Meadow Trail. Continue straight on Sky Trail.

3.1 At the Woodward Valley trailhead, turn right.

4.9 Turn left onto Coast Trail.

5.4 Detour to Sculptured Beach. Turn left onto a single-track trail that leads to the beach.

5.6 Reach Sculptured Beach. Return on the same path to Coast Trail.

5.8 Turn right on Coast Trail. After the second wooden bridge, watch for Arch Rock. Pass the trailhead for Sky Trail.

8.3 Trailhead for Bear Valley Trail. Turn left, heading inland along Coast Creek.

10.7 Come to Divide Meadow. Continue on Bear Valley Trail.

12.1 Bear Valley trailhead; continue to visitor center and parking lot.

12.3 Arrive back at the Bear Valley Visitor Center and parking lot.

Alternative route: For a pleasant family hike of 3.2 miles in Divide Meadow, take Bear Valley Trail to Bear Valley Creek Trail, returning to the visitor center on Earthquake Trail.

Fallen Arch Rock along the Coast Trail
MIGUEL VIEIRA (FLICKR.COM/PHOTOS/MIGUELVIEIRA/)

2. POINT REYES NATIONAL SEASHORE: TOMALES POINT

WHY GO?

The stark beauty of this narrow coastal bluff, the ocean often appearing and disappearing in sheets of wispy fog, can be otherworldly and humbling in its implied vastness. Springtime wildflowers add bursts of color along the trail, and the tule elk, a timelessness. Though hikers, as a rule, are generally unsatisfied with a return-trip single trail, the crashing of the Pacific against the shore and the majestic rocky sculptures and sea cliffs offer a contemplative view that's worth revisiting.

THE RUN DOWN

Start: Right of the historic Pierce Point Ranch at the end of Pierce Point Road
Elevation gain: 390 feet
Distance: 9.2 miles out and back
Difficulty: Moderate
Hiking time: About 4.5 hours
Seasons/schedule: Sunrise to sunset year-round
Fees and permits: None
Trail contact: Point Reyes National Seashore, 1 Bear Valley Visitor Center Access Rd., Point Reyes Station 94956; (415) 464–5100; www.nps .gov/pore/index.htm
Dog-friendly: No dogs allowed

Trail surface: Mostly double-track, some single-track dirt trail
Land status: National seashore
Nearest town: Inverness
Nat Geo TOPO! Map: Tomales
Nat Geo Trails Illustrated Map: Mount Tamalpais, Point Reyes #266
Other trail users: Hikers only
Special considerations: There are no facilities at the ranch. A short drive will take you to restrooms and the trailhead to McClures Beach. A short, steep, downhill 0.6-mile walk brings you to this small cove with its intense surf.

FINDING THE TRAILHEAD

From US 101 take Sir Francis Drake Boulevard west to Olema. Turn north on CA 1, then make an almost immediate turn west onto Bear Valley Road. At the end of Bear Valley Road, turn left on Sir Francis Drake Boulevard. Pass the town of Inverness. Turn right on Pierce Point Road, where you see the sign for Kehoe and McClures Beaches and Tomales Point. Take it to the Pierce Point Ranch.
GPS: N38 11.23' / W122 57.15'

WHAT TO SEE

Tomales Point's rich pasture caught the eye of a farmer named Solomon Pierce, who began a dairy here in 1858. Pierce and his son Abram produced fine butter, which was

Endangered tule elk
OLEG ALEXANDROV

shipped to San Francisco from a wharf they built on Tomales Bay. In post–gold rush San Francisco, if a proprietor displayed the sign "Point Reyes Butter," shoppers knew they were getting the best. For seven decades, the point remained in the Pierce family.

The walk begins at Upper Pierce Point Ranch at the Pierce family house, barn, and outbuildings, now maintained by the National Park Service. The path, the old ranch road, wanders over the green hills, which are seasonally sprinkled with yellow-orange poppies and tidy tips, orange fiddleneck, and purple iris.

Tomales Point, the northernmost boundary of Marin County and Point Reyes National Seashore, can make you feel as if you've reached the end of the world. The point is literally splitting away from the Bolinas Ridge, separated by Tomales Bay, which follows the San Andreas Fault line. The fault is where the Pacific and the North American tectonic plates move past each other in opposite directions.

Views from this trail are superb, starting with the beach and surf to the west, with an occasional fishing vessel bobbing on the ocean. In February and March you can spot molting elephant seals on isolated beaches below the cliffs. As you crest the ridge, you can see little Hog Island to the east in the bay, and the village of Dillon Beach, oyster central. The old ranch road descends to the site of Lower Pierce Ranch, marked by a pond and a eucalyptus grove. The narrowing trail takes you out to a high vista point that looks down on Bird Rock, occupied by cormorants and white pelicans. From there, you'll reach the very top of Tomales Point for stirring views of Bodega Head and Tomales Bay.

If you are trekking with children or are short on time, you can turn around at any point on the hike and still see the highlight of this trail: the tule elk. For thousands of years, as many as 500,000 tule elk thrived in California. The Miwok Indians lived peacefully with the herds on Tomales Point, but following the gold rush of 1849, the new settlers hunted the elk nearly to extinction and took over their habitat for agriculture and livestock grazing. By 1870, fewer than ten tule elk survived.

In 1874 ranch workers draining a marsh to create new agricultural fields near San Luis Obispo discovered a last remaining herd. Initially protected by a private landowner near San Luis Obispo, the state awarded the elk complete protection in 1971. In the spring of 1978, two bulls and eight cows were brought into Point Reyes from the San Luis Island Wildlife Refuge. They obviously liked their new coastal views; six of the cows

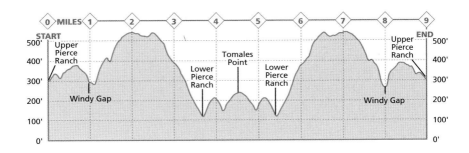

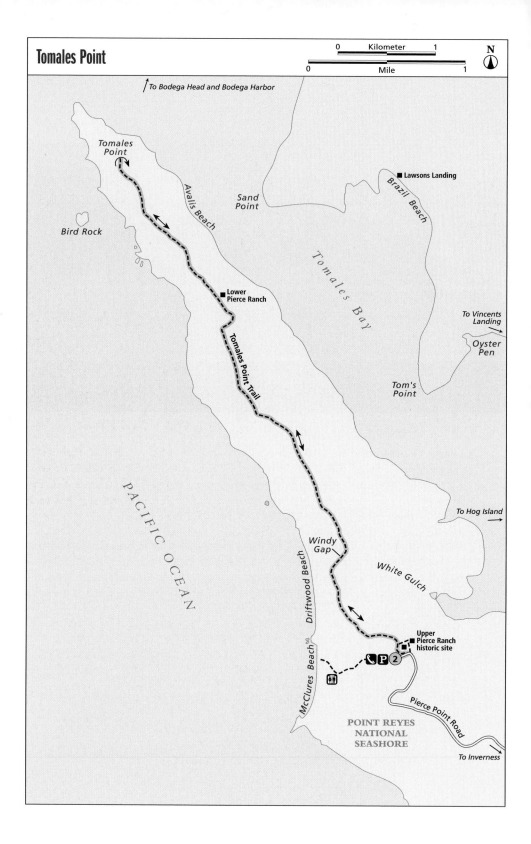

Tomales Point

0 — Kilometer — 1
0 — Mile — 1

N

To Bodega Head and Bodega Harbor

Tomales
Point

Bird Rock

Avalis Beach

Sand
Point

Tomales Bay

Lawsons Landing

Brazil Beach

Lower
Pierce Ranch

Tomales Point Trail

To Vincents
Landing

Oyster
Pen

Tom's
Point

PACIFIC OCEAN

Windy
Gap

To Hog Island

White Gulch

Driftwood Beach

Upper
Pierce Ranch
historic site

McClures Beach

P 2

POINT REYES
NATIONAL
SEASHORE

Pierce Point Road

To Inverness

Tomales Point . . . the end of the world
OLEG ALEXANDROV

bore calves that summer. By 1998, over 500 elk lived on the bluffs and more than 3,000 in different parts of California. The Point Reyes herd is one of the largest in the state.

The point is also home to an amazing number of hawks and falcons that rest on the scrub looking for moles and rabbits. Big black ravens sit in pairs on the blanched rock outcroppings that give the grassy ridgetop a sort of Stonehenge feel.

MILES AND DIRECTIONS

0.0   START from the parking lot at Upper Pierce Point Ranch.

1.0   Reach Windy Gap; Driftwood Beach is below.

2.0   The highest point on the hike is at 535 feet. To the east is Tom's Point, jutting out into Tomales Bay; to the north, Brazil Beach.

3.0   Come to Lower Pierce Ranch. A sign leads to Tomales Bay. To the east is Sand Point, with the town of Dillon Beach just north. Between the two is the University of Pacific Marine Station of Biological Science.

4.0   Trail to western edge of point overlooking Bird Rock. Several faint trails heading northwest lead to Tomales Bluff, the tip of the point.

4.6   Reach Tomales Point (255 feet above sea level) and a view of Bodega Bay. Turn around and head back the way you came.

9.2   Arrive back at Upper Pierce Point Ranch's parking lot.

3. POINT REYES NATIONAL SEASHORE: LIGHTHOUSE AND CHIMNEY ROCK TRAILS

WHY GO?

The Chimney Rock Trail is a short, easy hike that boasts one of the best wildflower displays on the coast and is the site of shipwrecks dating to 1585. The trail traces a bluff above 500-foot cliffs, providing spectacular coastline scenery. Add a visit to the Point Reyes Lighthouse, full of history, great whale watching, and 310 steep steps, for additional exercise.

THE RUN DOWN

Start: Two short hikes start at the end of Sir Francis Drake Highway in Point Reyes National Seashore.
Elevation gain: 250 feet
Distance: 1.2 miles out and back and 1.8-mile loop
Difficulty: Easy
Hiking time: About 2 hours for both
Seasons/schedule: Sunrise to sunset year-round
Fees and permits: None for parking or hiking; fee for shuttle bus December 30 to mid-April (ages 16 and over)
Trail contact: Point Reyes National Seashore, 1 Bear Valley Visitor Center

Access Rd., Point Reyes Station 94956; (415) 464-5100; www.nps.gov/pore/index.htm
Dog-friendly: No dogs allowed
Trail surface: Paved road, lighthouse stairs, single-track dirt trail
Land status: National seashore
Nearest town: Point Reyes Station
Nat Geo TOPO! Map: Drakes Bay
Nat Geo Trails Illustrated Map: Mount Tamalpais, Point Reyes #266
Other trail users: Hikers only
Special considerations: Wind and fog are likely.

FINDING THE TRAILHEAD

From US 101 take Sir Francis Drake Boulevard west to Olema. Turn north on CA 1, then make an almost immediate turn west onto Bear Valley Road. At the end of Bear Valley Road, turn left on Sir Francis Drake Boulevard. Continue on Sir Francis Drake Boulevard for about 20 miles until it ends at the lighthouse parking lot. The driving time from the Bear Valley Visitor Center is about 45 minutes.
Chimney Rock GPS: N37 59.43' / W122 58.46'
Lighthouse GPS: N37 59.52' / W123 0.43'

December 30 through mid-April on weekends and holidays, you'll need to park at Drakes Beach and take the shuttle to Chimney Rock and the lighthouse. The migration of gray whales and return of mating elephant seals on the beaches bring more travelers to Point Reyes. Weekdays and all days the rest of the year, you can drive to the

Stairs to the lighthouse
MADISONGARDEN, STOCK FREE IMAGES

trailheads. To reach Drakes Beach, follow Sir Francis Drake Boulevard toward the lighthouse, but turn left onto Drakes Beach Road. Follow it to the parking lot and Kenneth C. Patrick Visitor Center at the end. Check details and the schedule at (415) 464-5100, ext. 2 (then press 3 and then 1); www.nps.gov/pore/planyourvisit/shuttle.htm.
Drakes Beach GPS: N38 1.41' / W122 57.42'

WHAT TO SEE

The lighthouse is known as the foggiest place on the West Coast and one of the windiest, so check the weather before you go. The lighthouse walk starts with the Lighthouse Visitor Center offering some fascinating history of the building and facts about whales. Those strange cement domes across from the visitor center were built in 1870 for catching and storing rain for drinking water and steam for energy up here when lightkeepers kept their lonely watch.

The sea adventures of Henry Dana, Jules Verne, and Robert Louis Stevenson come to mind as you descend the 310 stairs to the isolated whitewashed lighthouse on its narrow precipice. There is more learning to be had inside before the return climb.

On the Chimney Rock bluffs along the trail, especially in spring, you will see a beautiful West Coast wildflower display. Yarrow, baby blue eyes, cobweb thistle, flowering flax, purple Douglas iris, yellow footsteps of spring, violet and yellow bush lupine, orange

Chimney Rock trail view
MIGUEL VIEIRA (FLICKR.COM/PHOTOS/
MIGUELVIEIRA/)

California poppy, red Indian paintbrush, large star linanthus, and seaside daisy grow in thick clumps on the hillsides sloping to the sea.

To your left as you face the Chimney Rock trailhead is Drakes Bay, named for sixteenth-century explorer Sir Francis Drake. An easy walk on the single-track trail to the end of the bluff brings you to Chimney Rock, a rock outcrop resembling a chimney stack that marks the meeting point of Drakes Bay, the headlands, and the sea. On isolated beaches below, you can observe elephant seals molting or mating.

This bluff and the nearby lighthouse platform are among the best places in Northern California to see migrating whales. When whale spotting, look for spouting (that's when a whale exhales air through its blowhole and the air rises 10 to 15 feet, condensing into a white vapor). Or, if you're lucky, you may see a whale 30 to 50 feet in length breaching, hurling itself out of the water and landing smack on its back. Bring binoculars.

Along the Pacific side of the bluff, waves crash against the cliffs below you. You are at times only 5 feet from the edge. Be safe and stay on the trails. Hiking on the Overlook Trail on a clear day offers views of the Farallon Islands 20 miles off the point. The 948-nautical-mile area between the point and the islands became the Gulf of the Farallones National Marine Sanctuary in 1981. It includes marshes, mudflats, a tidal zone, and deep ocean waters, and is home to numerous seabirds, diving birds, Steller and California sea lions, elephant seals, porpoises, dolphins, whales, harbor seals, flounder, halibut, Pacific herring, and invertebrate species.

These shores have also known many shipwrecks during the last few centuries, dating back to the first reported wreck, the San Agustin in 1595. Despite the dangers, a lot of trade and commerce used to take place here. Ships would motor or sail over the sandbar during high tide into Limantour and Drakes Bay to a little inlet called Scooter Bay. Area dairy workers would meet the ships on scooters, carrying butter, cheese, and dairy products that the vessels would take back to San Francisco.

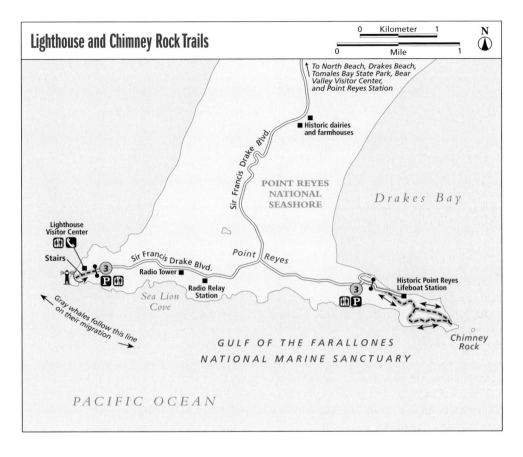

Lighthouse and Chimney Rock Trails

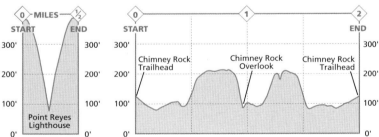

The Lifeboat Station on the beach of Drakes Bay is available for touring and worth visiting. The US Life Saving Service built the first fully equipped station in Point Reyes in 1889. The station moved to its current site on Drakes Beach in 1912.

MILES AND DIRECTIONS

0.0 START at the lighthouse parking lot. Walk uphill past the gate on the paved road to the lighthouse.

0.1 Point Reyes Beach is below (not accessible from the paved trail).

0.5 Explore the Lighthouse Visitor Center, then head down the stairs to the lighthouse.

0.6 Arrive at the lighthouse. Head back up the stairs.

0.7 Back to the visitor center. Head back down the service road to the parking lot.

0.8 Interpretive sign about local plant life.

1.2 Arrive back at your car. Drive to Chimney Rock Trail. To reach the trailhead, drive out the way you came about 1.5 miles and turn left, following the signs to Chimney Rock.

0.0 START at the Chimney Rock trailhead.

0.3 Junction with Underhill Road. Continue straight. The US Coast Guard Lifeboat Station is below.

0.9 End of the bluff, overlooking Chimney Rock. Head back on Overlook Trail.

1.4 Overlook area. Turn right onto trail toward Drakes Bay.

1.5 Junction with Chimney Rock Trail. Turn left and follow it back to your car, or continue down to tour the Lifeboat Station, then take the road back to the trailhead.

1.8 Arrive back at the parking lot.

Alternate routes: Consider adding a 1.9 mile out and back along Drakes Beach.

View of Point Reyes Beach on the way to the lighthouse

4. POINT REYES NATIONAL SEASHORE: PALOMARIN TRAILHEAD TO ALAMERE FALLS

WHY GO?

The trail from Palomarin on the southwestern edge of Point Reyes National Seashore takes you through coastal bluffs and woodland with Pacific views. There are two lakes on the featured hike. The highlight of this hike is 40-foot Alamere tidal falls. During low tide, you can take the beach all the way back. Otherwise, travel back the way you came on gently graded trails. Bring plenty of water, binoculars for marine and coastal wildlife, and long pants to protect from poison oak on the narrow trail to the top of the falls.

THE RUN DOWN

Start: Palomarin trailhead for the Coast Trail at the end of Mesa Road
Elevation gain: 600 feet
Distance: 8.8 miles out and back
Difficulty: Moderate due to a strenuous 0.1-mile climb down to the beach at the falls and back up
Hiking time: 5 hours
Seasons/schedule: Sunrise to sunset year-round
Fees and permits: None
Trail contact: Point Reyes National Seashore, 1 Bear Valley Visitor Center Access Rd., Point Reyes Station

94956; (415) 464-5100; www.nps .gov/pore/index.htm
Dog-friendly: No dogs allowed
Trail surface: Double-track dirt trail, narrow single-track trail, shale and sandstone bluffs down to the falls
Land status: National seashore
Nearest town: Bolinas
Nat Geo TOPO! Map: Bolinas; Double Point
Nat Geo Trails Illustrated Map: Mount Tamalpais, Point Reyes #266
Other trail users: Equestrians

FINDING THE TRAILHEAD

Take CA 1 north past Stinson Beach. Turn left (west) on Bolinas/Fairfax Road. In 0.1 mile turn left (south) onto Olema Bolinas Road. In 1.2 miles turn left again to stay on Olema Bolinas Road. Turn right (west) on Mesa Road for about 4 miles; it becomes a gravel road and passes the Point Reyes Bird Observatory–Palomarin Field Station. At the end of Mesa Road is the gravel parking lot for the Palomarin trailhead. **GPS:** N37 56.3' / W122 44.58'

WHAT TO SEE

The Palomarin trailhead is well marked on the right side of the parking lot past the Point Reyes Bird Observatory–Palomarin Field Station. Here at the field station, scientists band more than 5,000 birds and monitor over 100 nests in the area annually.

The view on Coast Trail
MIGUEL VIEIRA (FLICKR.COM/PHOTOS/MIGUELVIEIRA/)

The hike starts in grassland between tall, soldier-like rows of eucalyptus. The Australian natives were probably planted as windbreakers for a ranch built on this spot, though there is a colorful but unlikely legend that people planted patches of eucalyptus around the Bay Area to create a habitat for imported koalas.

Past the turnoff for Palomarin Beach (with tide pools at low tide), you walk stark coastal bluffs through fields of yellow lupine, peach-orange monkeyflowers, broom, coffeeberry, coyote brush, and California sagebrush. Binoculars help you see the sea lions and various seabirds bobbing above a kelp bed in the surf below. In February or March, those binoculars may even help you spot gray whales as they migrate north along the coast. If it's clear, the Farallon Islands seem only a long leap away. Farther south you may see fishing vessels or freighters making their way into the San Francisco Bay.

The Coast Trail heads inland, passing over numerous seasonal finger creeks. You enter a forest of mature Douglas firs that shadow out most plants except moisture-loving ferns. Where sunlight gets through, you can see wild strawberries and manroot. Branches of Alamere Creek are on either side of the path. Seasonally you may see a series of still ponds with green lily pads growing on their surface.

Bass Lake, a popular swimming hole in summer, may be overrun on warm weekends, but in winter and on some weekdays, it is quiet and invites long gazing. Ducks often skim the water, making silver streaks on the black mirror surface.

Pelican Lake offers a wonderful illusion. The freshwater lake is backed by two hillsides, called Double Point, that slope down in a V and kiss just at the lake's surface, revealing the Pacific backdrop. It looks like the lake is suspended just above the sea.

Alamere Falls is an amazing sight, especially after rains. It is one of two coastal falls in California. (Its sister, McWay Falls, is at Big Sur.) Wide Alamere Creek tumbles over the bluff in tiers, then drops straight off the edge of a cliff onto exposed rock and Wildcat Beach. At its heaviest flow, the falls are 25 feet across. During drier times, it may split into

Alamere Falls
RENE DRIVERS

two narrower falls. As the tide rises, the salty surf comes up to meet the fresh water flowing in. From Wildcat Camp, past serene Ocean Lake and the narrow end of Wildcat Lake, you can hike the beach the entire way within an hour of low tide. But that takes careful planning. From the Coast Trail, keep your eye open for the narrow, marked single-track

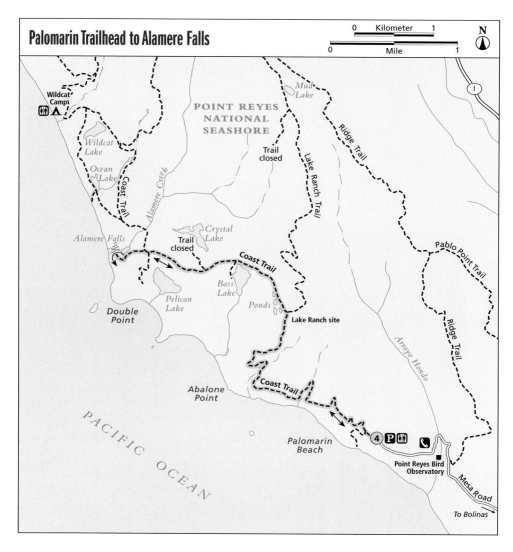

Palomarin Trailhead to Alamere Falls

Wildcat Camp

POINT REYES NATIONAL SEASHORE

Mud Lake

Wildcat Lake

Ocean Lake

Trail closed

Lake Ranch Trail

Ridge Trail

Coast Trail

Alamere Creek

Alamere Falls

Crystal Lake

Trail closed

Coast Trail

Pablo Point Trail

Bass Lake

Ponds

Lake Ranch site

Pelican Lake

Double Point

Ridge Trail

Arroyo Hondo

Abalone Point

Coast Trail

Palomarin Beach

4

Point Reyes Bird Observatory

PACIFIC OCEAN

Mesa Road

To Bolinas

1

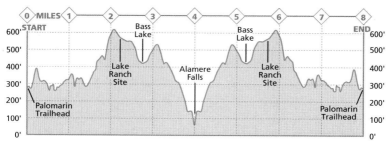

dirt trail to the falls. Scrub threatens to overgrow the path, and there is plenty of poison oak here.

To get to the bottom of the falls on the beach, follow the tiered falls down and climb down the water-rutted cliff wall north of the falls. It is manageable but not entirely stable, and the rock can be slippery when wet. But it is well worth it.

After your hike, consider a meal or drink in Bolinas. Charming, quirky, and somewhat reclusive, the coastal town is born of old hippies, young surfers, artists, and naturalists. The lagoon supports an amazing variety of waterbirds. The Audubon Canyon Ranch has more information and guided bird-watching.

MILES AND DIRECTIONS

0.0　START from the parking lot for the Palomarin trailhead. The trailhead is on the east side of the parking lot next to the restrooms. Climb the stairs and turn left onto Coast Trail.

0.1　Pass the trailhead for Palomarin Beach (0.6 mile to beach). Continue on Coast Trail.

2.2　At the junction with Lake Ranch Trail, stay to your left on Coast Trail.

2.8　Reach Bass Lake.

3.1　Pass the trailhead for Crystal Lake Trail. Stay on Coast Trail.

3.6　Reach Pelican Lake. Continue on Coast Trail.

3.9　Trailhead for Alamere Falls Trail. Turn left onto single-track trail.

4.3　Top of Alamere Falls. Cross the stream below second falls for the trail down to the beach. Be careful of loose rock.

4.4　View of falls from Wildcat Beach. Return by the same trail.

4.5　Return to Coast Trail via Alamere Falls Trail.

4.9　Turn right on Coast Trail, and retrace your steps past the lake to Palomarin.

5.2　Pass Pelican Lake.

6.0　Pass Bass Lake.

6.6　Stay on Coast Trail past the junction with Lake Ranch Trail.

8.8　Arrive back at the Palomarin trailhead and parking lot.

Alternate routes: Time your hike so you reach the falls just before low tide and continue on Coast Trail. Take the left (west) loop of Ocean Loop Trail past Ocean Lake and Wildcat Lake and down to the beach. Follow the beach back to Alamere Falls, and hike up the trail just before the falls. Return to Coast Trail on Alamere Falls Trail.

5. TOMALES BAY STATE PARK: HEART'S DESIRE BEACH TO SHELL BEACH

WHY GO?

The hike encompasses three of the park's four beaches that offer swimming. An extra mile gets you to Indian Beach as well. Between beaches, each more isolated than the last, the trail takes you through a thick, damp woodland. It's an excellent trail year-round to see birds and California sea lions, botanical variety, and seashells and learn about the native Miwok.

THE RUN DOWN

Start: Johnstone trailhead at Heart's Desire Beach, past the main entrance of Tomales Bay State Park
Elevation gain: 670 feet
Distance: 8-mile partial loop
Difficulty: Moderate
Hiking time: 4 hours
Seasons/schedule: 8 a.m. to sunset year-round
Fees and permits: Vehicle entrance fee, payable by credit or debit card only
Trail contact: Tomales Bay State Park, Star Rte., Inverness 94937; (415) 669-1140; www.parks.ca.gov/?page_id=470

Dog-friendly: No dogs allowed, except in picnic areas on leash
Trail surface: Single-track dirt trail from beach to beach
Land status: State park
Nearest town: Inverness
Nat Geo TOPO! Map: Tomales
Nat Geo Trails Illustrated Map: Mount Tamalpais, Point Reyes #266
Other trail users: Mountain bikers and equestrians
Special considerations: Fishing, nonmotorized boating, and swimming is available along the hike. Restrooms are located at each beach.

FINDING THE TRAILHEAD

From US 101 take Sir Francis Drake Boulevard west until it ends at CA 1 in Olema. Turn right (north) on CA 1 and take the first left on Bear Valley Road (toward the Bear Valley Visitor Center). Continue past the visitor center. At the stop sign, Bear Valley once again meets up with Sir Francis Drake Boulevard. Turn left (north) and follow the boulevard until it splits again. Stay right on Pierce Point Boulevard (signed to Tomales Bay State Park). Turn right at the main entrance to Tomales Bay State Park (signed to Heart's Desire Beach) until you reach the Heart's Desire parking lot. The Johnstone trailhead is at the southeast end of the beach.
GPS: N38 07.53' W122 53.41'

Indian Beach
TOM HILTON (FLICKR.COM/PHOTOS/TOMHILTON/)

WHAT TO SEE

The Coast Miwok people lived around Tomales Bay for 3,500 years, fishing, digging for clams and oysters, collecting edible and medicinal plants, and hunting game for food and clothing. The Támal-ko, the Indians of the Tomales, had more than one hundred village sites on the Point Reyes Peninsula. Eleven of them were at Shell Beach and Indian Beach. The self-guided Indian Beach Nature Trail (a 0.9-mile wheelchair-accessible loop trail) tells some of the Coastal Miwok story.

The Támal-ko ate Washington clams and used basket or heart cockles and bay mussels for tools and jewelry as well as food. They made other items out of chert, obsidian, and fired clay. As you walk the trail, you can imagine the Miwok going about their daily routines in the sheltered coves, beaches, tidal marshes, and Bishop pine forests on these western shores of Tomales Bay.

Fast-forward through exploration of the area by the Portuguese, Spanish, British, Germans, and Russians to the 1940s. Real estate developers began to purchase large areas of beachfront land here, but local residents and conservation groups said, "No way!" As a result of their grassroots efforts, Tomales Bay was formally dedicated and opened to the public in 1952.

Each of the four beaches accessed on this hike has its own character. Heart's Desire Beach, at the trailhead and most accessible, tends to get crowded on summer weekends. Pebble Beach, a mile past the Vista Point group picnic area, is a secluded cove aptly named for its colorful stones decorating the sand. Shell Beach, the final destination of the hike, consists of two small beaches separated by rock outcrops covered with black-shelled mussels and white barnacles.

California sea lions frequent the bay waters, as do a variety of waterfowl. Brandt's cormorants can be spotted drying themselves on the rocks. Puffins, great blue herons, and sandhill cranes add a more exotic feel to the bay view.

The thick woodland, wet ravines, and pastoral meadows that you glimpse are home to foxes, raccoons, badgers, chipmunks, rabbits, bobcats, wood rats, coyotes, and black-tailed deer. You may see coveys of quail in the brush, goldfinches, or towhees hopping from branch to branch, and spotted owls at dusk. The hammer of a woodpecker often echoes through the trees as a meadowlark whistles a favorite melody. Lizards skitter over stumps in summer, as monarch butterflies stretch their wings around blossoming wildflowers. Many kinds of edible berries grow here—woodland strawberries, huckleberries, gooseberries, thimbleberries, currants, salal, native blackberries, and madrone and Toyon berries. Rain and cooler weather create an awesome mushroom display along the trail. Collecting or destroying anything in the park, including mushrooms, is prohibited.

The two adjoining trails that make up this hike are named for two lovers and protectors of plants. Botanist professor Willis Linn Jepson (1867–1946) founded the School of Forestry and funded the Jepson Herbarium at the University of California–Berkeley. The author of the esteemed *Manual of the Flowering Plants of California* is honored by the Jepson Trail. Way ahead of his time, he wrote an article in 1893 describing how native California plants were being crowded out by alien plants. You walk through one of the finest remaining virgin groves of Bishop pine in California in the park's Jepson Memorial Grove.

Conservationist Bruce Johnstone, a Marin County planner, and his wife, Elsie, worked long and hard to preserve Tomales Bay and place part of it in a state park. Johnstone Trail leads from Pebble Beach to Shell Beach. A plaque trailside pays them tribute.

MILES AND DIRECTIONS

0.0 START from Heart's Desire Beach at the Johnstone trailhead.

0.1 Pass the picnic area for Heart's Desire Beach.

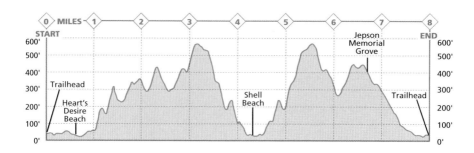

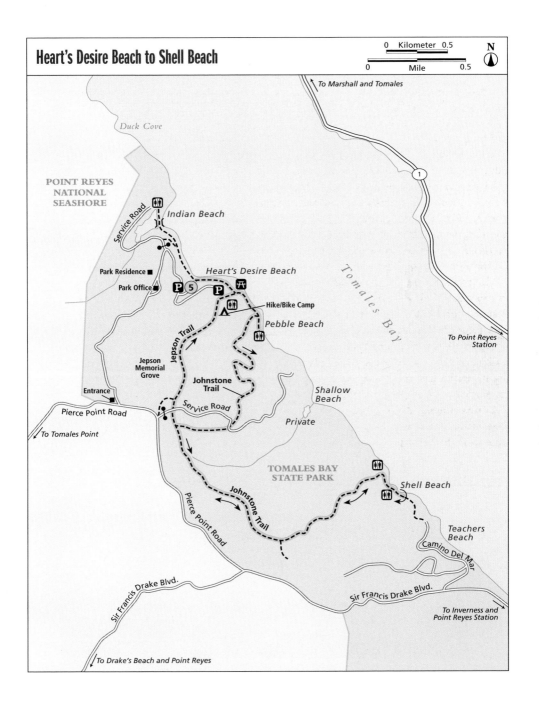

Heart's Desire Beach to Shell Beach

0   Kilometer   0.5

0   Mile   0.5

N

To Marshall and Tomales

Duck Cove

POINT REYES
NATIONAL
SEASHORE

Service Road

Indian Beach

Park Residence ■

Park Office ■

P 5

P

Heart's Desire Beach

Hike/Bike Camp

Pebble Beach

Tomales Bay

Jepson Trail

Jepson
Memorial
Grove

Johnstone
Trail

Shallow
Beach

To Point Reyes
Station

Entrance

Service Road

Private

Pierce Point Road

To Tomales Point

TOMALES BAY
STATE PARK

Shell Beach

Johnstone Trail

Pierce Point Road

Johnstone Trail

Teachers
Beach

Camino Del Mar

Sir Francis Drake Blvd.

Sir Francis Drake Blvd.

To Inverness and
Point Reyes Station

To Drake's Beach and Point Reyes

0.2 Come to the Vista Point group picnic area. Follow Johnstone Trail to Pebble Beach.

0.4 Bear left to Pebble Beach. Return to single-track Johnstone Trail to Shell Beach.

0.5 Turn left, continuing on Johnstone Trail to Shell Beach. A bridge crosses the creek. The trail heads uphill at a moderate grade. Lawson's Landing is to the east.

1.5 Trailhead and junction with paved fire road. Cross the paved road, staying on the single-track dirt trail, now Johnstone/Jepson Trail.

1.7 Trailhead for Jepson Trail (to take on the way back). Go straight, continuing on Johnstone Trail (to Shell Beach, 2.5 miles). Look for wild strawberries, lilies, mushrooms, and rare western leatherwood scrub. The flat trail starts to rise moderately. Viewing benches are scattered along the way.

4.2 Wooden steps and a path lead to Shell Beach, your final destination. (Beyond that is a 0.2-mile trail to Camino del Mar Drive.)

6.7 Back to Jepson Trail. Turn left. In less than 0.1 mile, pass over a paved access road and continue on Jepson Trail to Jepson Memorial Grove.

7.7 Jepson Trail ends at the parking lot for Vista Point. Walk across the parking lot to the Vista Point picnic area.

7.8 In Vista Point picnic area, turn left onto single-track Johnstone Trail.

8.0 Arrive back at Heart's Desire Beach and the parking lot.

Alternate routes: Families will enjoy the nature hike and a swim at Indian Beach (0.9–mile loop).

From Heart's Desire Beach make Pebble Beach your destination, or reach Shell Beach from the dirt parking lot off Pierce Point Road (3.2 miles out and back), or walk 0.5 mile each way to Shell Beach from the end of Camino Del Mar Road.

Heart's Desire Beach

6. SAMUEL P. TAYLOR STATE PARK: TO THE TOP OF BARNABE PEAK

WHY GO?

Starting off in redwoods on a flat trail, you ascend steadily to the top of Barnabe Peak, with its 360-degree view taking in Tomales Bay to the Pacific Ocean, the towns of San Geronimo and Lagunitas, and isolated Kent Lake and Peters Dam in the Marin watershed. Then it's downhill on grasslands back into the woods.

THE RUN DOWN

Start: Camp Taylor parking lot in Samuel P. Taylor State Park on Sir Francis Drake Boulevard
Elevation gain: 1,350 feet
Distance: 6-mile loop
Difficulty: Moderate to strenuous due to elevation gain
Hiking time: 3 hours
Seasons/schedule: Sunrise to sunset year-round
Trail surface: Single-track dirt trail and dirt and gravel fire road
Trail contact: Samuel P. Taylor State Park and Camp Taylor, 8889 Sir Francis Drake Blvd., Lagunitas 94938; (415) 488-9897; www.parks .ca.gov/?page_id=469

Dog-friendly: No dogs allowed
Fees and permits: Vehicle entrance fee
Land status: State park
Nearest town: Lagunitas
Nat Geo TOPO! Map: San Geronimo
Nat Geo Trails Illustrated Map: Mount Tamalpais, Point Reyes #266
Other trail users: Mountain bikers and equestrians on fire roads
Special considerations: Camping and cabins are available. In warm weather, enjoy a dip in the swimming hole—a favorite for over half a century.

FINDING THE TRAILHEAD

From US 101 North, take Sir Francis Drake Boulevard west past the town of Lagunitas into a wooded area. Turn left (south) into the main entrance of Samuel P. Taylor Park and Camp Taylor (about 18 miles from US 101). Start at the Cross Marin trailhead, at the end of the parking lot. **GPS:** N38 01.04' / W122 43.4'

WHAT TO SEE

Samuel Penfield Taylor (1827–1896) was ahead of his time, with many firsts and as an advocate for the combination of responsible land use and recreation. On this site he started the first paper mill on the West Coast and the first overnight camp for city dwellers. He established one of the first major towns on the Point Reyes Peninsula (Taylorville, long gone), built the first fish ladder in the West, and developed the first "modern"

Looking north from Barnabe Fire Road
MIGUEL VIEIRA (FLICKR.COM/PHOTOS/
MIGUELVIEIRA/)

grocery bag as we know it today. He was entrepreneurial and innovative, practiced recycling, and once rescued a mule he named Barnabe. Now that's Bay Area spirit.

Barnabe, the mule in question, was a retired army animal that had crossed the plains with General John C. Fremont and his troops. Taylor found the old, white burro at the San Francisco Presidio and brought him back to Camp Taylor, where he became a favorite pet of the children and guests. Barnabe often escaped his corral and trekked to the top of the mountain to graze on the plentiful grasslands. And so the peak takes the burro's name.

Taylor purchased this land with gold dust, the rare successful 49er. But this was after profiting from his own food stand on the beach in San Francisco and co-owning a lumberyard. Along with the paper mill, in 1874 Taylor built a rustic hotel to house friends and business associates (the site is now the Redwood Grove picnic area). With the opening of a narrow-gauge railroad to serve the isolated Tomales Bay region, the general public started showing up. Taylor enlarged the hotel and added tent cabins and a dance pavilion big enough for a thirty-piece brass band. He and his wife called it Camp Taylor, and it was the first campground for city children and their parents in the state of California. By 1888 over 3,000 people were coming to Camp Taylor each year.

Taylor's son James took over management of Camp Taylor in 1888 and added more facilities and a third floor to the hotel, renaming it Hotel Azalea for the blooms covering the banks of Lagunitas Creek, then called Papermill Creek. The hotel burned down in the early 1900s and was not reconstructed. But the state park service purchased the land in 1946. Samuel P. Taylor was one of the first parks in the United States to offer camping as part of its recreation program.

It's hard to believe all this bustle took place here as you walk through the quiet forests and up the grass-covered hillsides.

The featured hike starts on flat, shaded ground beside Lagunitas Creek, with the sound of traffic nearby. A footbridge on Cross Marin Trail takes you to the other side of Sir Francis Drake Boulevard, still along the creek until you reach Barnabe Fire Road. A few endangered coho salmon and steelhead trout spawn here in the late fall and winter. Fishing is prohibited.

It's a steady climb through forest and then open grassland to the Dickson Fire Lookout tower (Marin County Fire Department) on the top of Barnabe Peak (1,466 feet). Here you can enjoy lovely views of rolling hills, Tomales Bay—on a clear day—and the town of Lagunitas. At the junction of Riding and Hiking Trail and Barnabe Trail on your way back, you'll see Taylor's grave site.

Samuel P. Taylor's grave marker
STEPHENG3

Red-tailed and red-shouldered hawks, kestrels, vultures, and ravens circle the skies. You may spot a fox, bobcat, or badger. Skunks, gophers, squirrels, mice, and snakes also make this home. Black-tailed deer are the most commonly seen big animals.

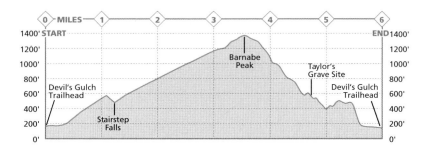

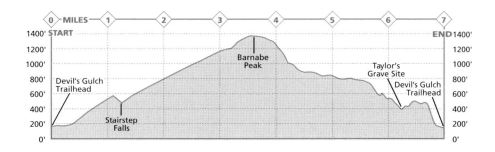

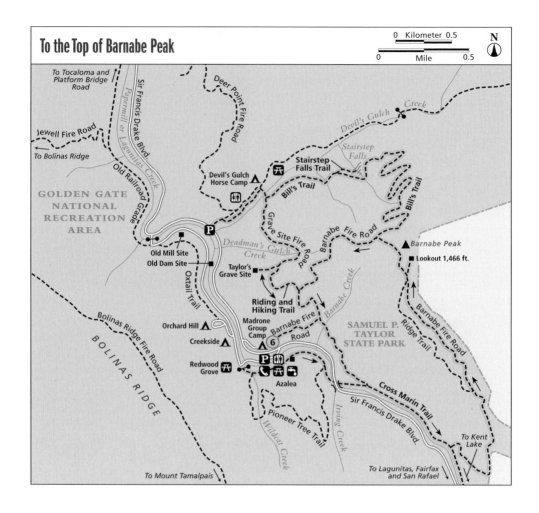

To the Top of Barnabe Peak

MILES AND DIRECTIONS

0.0 START at the Camp Taylor parking lot.

0.2 Cross the auto bridge and turn left. Cross Marin Trail starts at the end of the road.

0.8 Take the footbridge across Sir Francis Drake Boulevard and continue on Cross Marin Trail next to Lagunitas Creek.

1.6 Take the Barnabe Fire Road on the left up to the peak.

3.5 Reach Dickson Fire Lookout and Barnabe Peak. After taking in the view, continue on Barnabe Fire Road.

3.8 Pass the junction to Bill's Trail (closed until 2020) and stay on Barnabe Fire Road.

4.8 Turn right onto Gravesite Road/Riding and Hiking Trail to see Taylor's grave site.

5.0 Arrive at Samuel P. Taylor's grave. Turn back the way you came.

5.2 Continue on the Riding and Hiking Trail.

5.6 Take the trail toward the Madrone Group Campsite and Madrone Campsite Road toward Sir Francis Drake Boulevard.

5.8 Be careful crossing Sir Francis Drake Boulevard. On the other side, take the marked access trail to North Creek Trail, near the campground. Turn left onto North Creek Trail.

6.0 Arrive back at the Camp Taylor parking lot.

Alternate routes: Though Bill's Trail is closed for reconstruction until about 2020, watch for its reopening to access the 35-foot Stairstep Falls.

Families may enjoy the 2.5-mile loop Pioneer Tree Trail, where you can walk through a fire-scarred redwood tree.

Laguintas Creek

Bonus Hikes: Point Reyes

A. POINT REYES NATIONAL SEASHORE: INVERNESS RIDGE

WHY GO?

This 7-mile loop over Inverness Ridge takes you into fairly new forest and to expansive views. All growth has occurred since the 1995 Mount Vision fire. Bishop pines grow in fast, healthy crowds on the hillsides, but you'll likely still see some charred remains of their ancestors. You can look out at hillsides and valleys all the way to the sea.

Several loop hikes are accessed by Muddy Hollow Road/Trail. This one goes from Muddy Hollow Trail to the Bayview Trail, onto Drake's View Trail to the Inverness Ridge. Down Bucklin Trail, you'll see views of Drakes Bay and the ocean, before returning to Muddy Hollow Road.

THE RUN DOWN

Start: On Limantour Road, at Muddy Hollow Trail. GPS: N38 2.53' / W122 52.49'
Elevation gain: 700 feet
Distance: 7-mile loop
Difficulty: Moderate due to elevation gain
Hiking time: 3.5 hours
Seasons/schedule: Sunrise to sunset year-round
Fees and permits: None
Trail contact: Point Reyes National Seashore, 1 Bear Valley Visitor Center Access Rd., Point Reyes Station

94956; (415) 464–5100; www.nps.gov/pore/index.htm
Dog-friendly: No dogs allowed
Trail surface: Double-track and single-track dirt trail
Land status: National park
Nearest town: Inverness
Nat Geo TOPO! Map: Inverness; Drakes Bay
Nat Geo Trails Illustrated Map: Mount Tamalpais, Point Reyes #266
Other trail users: Equestrians
Special considerations: No facilities available at trailhead or on trail. Can be muddy in winter.

Wild iris in Point Reyes

On the paved earthquake trail

B. **KULE LOKLO & THE EARTHQUAKE TRAIL**

WHY GO?

Looking for a fun family hike in Point Reyes? Need accessibility? Or are you out for a walk in heavy rain?

Park at the Bear Valley Visitor Center, take in the slide show, then head across the parking lot to the Earthquake Trail. A 0.6-mile loop starts near the epicenter of the great San Francisco earthquake of 1906 (which may have been just off the coast). Interpretive signs along the way show you how the right slip San Andreas Fault line works and illustrates how Point Reyes is traveling north on the Pacific Plate, while the North American Plate moves west at the speedy rate of several feet per century. Next, walk 0.5 mile to Kule Loklo, a modern rendering of a Miwok village. Along the way you pass a meandering creek, pretty wooden farm fences, scrub oaks and shrubs, meadows, and grassy hills.

THE RUN DOWN

Start: Bear Valley Visitor Center. GPS: N38 2.23' / W122 48.3'
Elevation gain: 36 feet
Distance: 1.6-mile loop and out and back
Difficulty: Easy
Hiking time: 1 hour
Seasons/schedule: Sunrise to sunset year-round
Fees and permits: None
Trail contact: Point Reyes National Seashore, 1 Bear Valley Visitor Center

Access Rd., Point Reyes Station 94956; (415) 464-5100; www.nps .gov/pore/index.htm
Dog-friendly: No dogs allowed
Trail surface: Paved path and dirt trail
Land status: National park
Nearest town: Point Reyes Station
Nat Geo TOPO! Map: Inverness
Nat Geo Trails Illustrated Map: Mount Tamalpais, Point Reyes #266
Other trail users: Hikers only

MOUNT TAMALPAIS AND ITS FOOTHILLS

Mount Tamalpais is an important part of the Bay Area's western skyline. Its foothills rise from the towns of Fairfax, Mill Valley, and San Anselmo to the east and end at the Pacific Ocean and the resort town of Stinson Beach to the west. Traveling up the mountain and down to the sea, a hiker can find a little bit of everything.

Fifty miles of trails within the park connect to a larger, 200-mile-long trail system. On the slopes are deep canyons with redwoods and Douglas firs, cascading creeks, grassland meadows, and ridges of manzanita and sandstone. An outdoor amphitheater hidden in the trees hosts musicals for the public every summer. The friendly Mount Tam watershed offers hiking near pristine lakes. Also within the mountain's folds is Muir Woods, the nature lover's cathedral, with redwoods 500 years old covering 560 acres, filling the area with a rich aroma of citrusy needles and moist earth.

The Marin Headlands, just south of Mount Tam, is one of the best places in Northern California to watch raptors. Trails lead you through not only pretty countryside but also the rich history of the vaqueros (cowboys), Portuguese dairy farmers, military movements, and early seafarers. From Point Bonita Lighthouse, the cityscape and Golden Gate Bridge prompt lots of picture taking.

Mount Burdell, a distant cousin above Novato, gives the hiker a smaller mountain to climb, with meadows and a view into quarrying days. Nearby Olompali State Park is the site of a major Miwok Indian village that dates from AD 1100 to 1300.

Miwok Indians once inhabited the valleys and foothills of the mountain. New settlers were drawn to Mount Tam too, making their way up to the East Peak on the "world's crookedest railroad," to dance and drink or just admire the views. The rails gone, the route of the train is now a trail for hikers and mountain bikers, who are also drawn up the canyons and hillsides as the "Sleeping Maiden" emerges out of the fog and everyone in the valleys below seems to sigh.

Mount Tamalpais State Park
OSCAR VASQUEZ (CALIFORNIA DEPARTMENT
OF PARKS AND RECREATION)

7. MUIR WOODS: BOOTJACK TRAIL TO DIPSEA TRAIL LOOP

WHY GO?

On the first mile of your hike in Muir Woods, you'll contend with lots of camera-swinging tourists, awe-inspired by the giant, ancient trees. Venturing past the milling masses, you are rewarded with solitude. There for your discovery are ridge trails lined with young pine trees dripping with grandfather's beard, bay and alder woodlands with flitting bushtits and hammering woodpeckers, sunny meadows, bridged streams with feathery ferns, hills full of huckleberries, and panoramic views of the Pacific.

THE RUN DOWN

Start: Muir Woods National Monument main entrance
Elevation gain: 1,200 feet
Distance: 6.3-mile loop/lollipop
Difficulty: Moderate to strenuous
Hiking time: About 3.5 hours
Seasons/schedule: 8 a.m. to sunset year-round
Fees and permits: Entrance fee for adults, children 15 and under free; no charge for parking. Reservations are required.
Trail contact: Muir Woods National Monument, 1 Muir Woods Rd., Mill Valley 94941; (415) 561-2850; www.nps.gov/muwo/index.htm

Dog-friendly: No dogs allowed
Trail surface: 1 mile of paved pathway, then well-maintained, mostly single-track dirt trail
Land status: National monument
Nearest town: Mill Valley
Nat Geo TOPO! Map: San Rafael
Nat Geo Trails Illustrated Map: Mount Tamalpais, Point Reyes #266
Other trail users: Equestrians
Special considerations: Rangers and volunteers present 15-minute talks and guided tours of Muir Woods. The Muir Woods Cafe prepares meals and snacks throughout the day.

FINDING THE TRAILHEAD

From US 101 exit at Mill Valley/CA 1/Stinson Beach. Follow signs to CA 1 and then to Muir Woods. Parking is limited. **GPS:** N37 53.34' / W122 34.21'

WHAT TO SEE

This is the best tree lover's monument that could possibly be found in all the forests of the world.

—John Muir

Muir Woods Ocean View Trail
MIGUEL VIEIRA (FLICKR.COM/PHOTOS/MIGUELVIEIRA/)

Early in the 1850s on Mount Tamalpais came the crashing sound of felled virgin red-woods and giant Douglas fir trees. Lumber was in high demand for the booming new metropolises around San Francisco and Sacramento following the 1849 California gold rush. But because of its inaccessibility, caused by the steep slopes around it, the majestic old-growth forest in Redwood Canyon—now Muir Woods—survived. It is the only stand of virgin redwoods left in the Bay Area.

In the twentieth century, water shortages in the ever-growing Bay Area resulted in plans to dam Redwood Creek, which flows down from Mount Tam. The huge trees were to be logged, then the canyon flooded to form a reservoir. Hearing this disturbing news, Mount Tam landowner and avid outdoorsman William Kent asked his wife, Elizabeth, "If we lost all the money we have and saved the trees, it would be worthwhile, wouldn't it?" In 1905 they bought 611 acres and in 1908 donated 295 acres, the heart of the canyon, to the American people. They insisted that the grove be named for their friend John Muir, champion of the nation's environmental movement. Agreeing, President Theodore Roosevelt proclaimed it a national monument in 1908 (the seventh in history, and the first created from land donated by a private individual).

Now the monument attracts a million admirers every year. On summer weekends, the visitor center is packed, the roads are slow, and the parking lot is an obstacle course. (Try a weekday, or arrive before 10 a.m. for a day hike or after 4 p.m. for a sunset stroll.) But even with the crowds, these giants, the oldest 1,200 years old and the tallest 258 feet tall, inspire and amaze even those averse to crowds. Traveling beyond the paved pathways, you may feel as if you know some great secret.

Summer is the season of fog, azaleas, and aralias. Elk clover shrubs stretch their stalks and sprout tiny white flowers. Gray squirrels scamper everywhere, enjoying an abundance of nuts and flowering plants. Wilson's warblers and chestnut-backed chickadees preen and chirp.

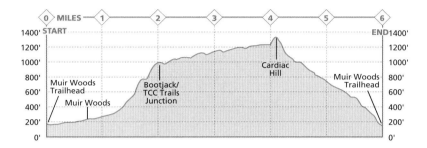

Fall tends to be the warmest time of year, attracting ladybugs on the horsetail ferns and crayfish in Redwood Creek. Monarch butterflies pass through on their migration to the central coast of California and Mexico, where they winter. Purple thistles appear in golden grasslands. Turning maple leaves and red-leafed poison oak bring fall colors to the trail. When rains start to fall, more than one hundred kinds of mushrooms appear on the soaked forest floor, some popping up overnight and lasting only a few hours, others growing slowly and remaining for weeks.

During winter the endangered steelhead and coho salmon spawning in Redwood Creek guard their nests for a week or so, then die. Juvenile salmon live in the stream for over a year, feeding on insects, unhatched salmon eggs, and each other before the ocean calls them. According to park naturalists, Muir Woods salmon are unique, representing one of the last truly wild, genetically distinct populations of salmon in California. Best viewing occurs a few days after a heavy storm.

Coming out of the canyon up Cardiac Hill, the open ocean view is startling and expansive when clear. Rolling fog provides an equally dramatic sight. This is a great area to enjoy a trail snack before the descent back into woodland. Facilities are available only at the start of the hike.

MILES AND DIRECTIONS

0.0   START at the Muir Woods parking lot. Follow the Main Trail along Redwood Creek. Bohemian Grove has some of the tallest trees in the park. Pass three bridges.

0.9   Take Bootjack Trail along Redwood Creek, where the path narrows, turns to dirt, and begins to climb. Steps help with the ascent.

2.3   At Van Wyck Meadow, look for the large rock centerpiece. Take the trail to the left of the meadow (signed To Stapleveldt Trail), the TCC (Tamalpais Conservation Club) Trail. A bridge crosses the creek.

2.8   Manzanita stand and a view of Mount Tam.

3.7   Go left to stay on TCC Trail. Cross a bridge and stay on the TCC Trail.

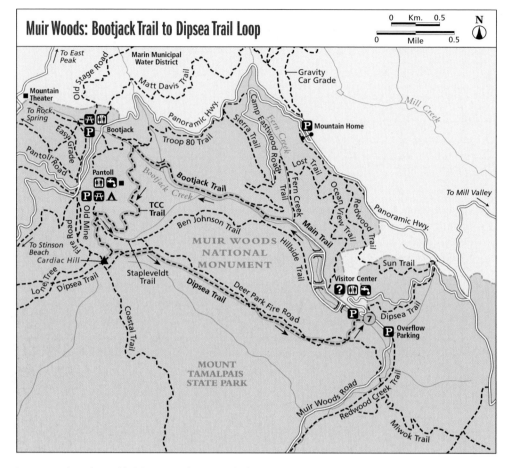

Muir Woods: Bootjack Trail to Dipsea Trail Loop

4.1   Junction with Dipsea Trail. Turn right for there-and-back side trip up Cardiac Hill (about 200 feet) for an ocean view. (Options: If you have more time, head down the Coastal Trail to Stinson Beach. If you want to skip Cardiac Hill, go to the next direction marker.) Backtrack to the junction of Dipsea and the TCC Trails.

4.5   Continue on Dipsea Trail past the TCC Trail. In 630 feet, Dipsea merges with the Deer Park Fire Road. In another 400 feet, bear right to stay on Dipsea Trail.

4.7   Dipsea Trail crosses over a grassy hillside called Hogsback.

5.9   Dipsea Trail crosses over Deer Park Fire Road and continues. Dipsea Trail continues to cross over Deer Park Fire Road several times. Stay on Dipsea Trail.

6.2   Dipsea Trail Bridge. Cross the creek and turn left, staying on Dipsea Trail.

6.3   Cross Redwood Creek on footbridge and arrive back at the parking lot of Muir Woods.

Muir Woods redwoods,
old and new

Alternate routes: Avoid the crowds in the Muir Woods parking lot and having to make an advance reservation by starting at Pantoll Station. The 4-mile loop takes you on Alpine Trail to the Bootjack Trail descending into Muir Woods. Cross Bridge 4 and hike up the Ben Johnson Trail and the Stapleveldt Trail back to Pantoll. Another road less traveled within Muir Woods is the Canopy View Trail, also known as the Ocean View Trail. Make it a 3.5-mile loop by taking the Lost Trail, which connects with the Fern Creek Trail to Redwood Creek Trail back into the central part of Muir Woods.

THE MAGIC OF REDWOODS

Walking through a grove of the giant, straight, red-barked trees can be a magical experience. But other than their obvious height, which is humbling in itself, what is it about these trees that captures the imagination and creates a sense of awe?

The coastal redwoods (*Sequoia sempervirens*) are the tallest living things on earth (some over 360 feet tall) and grow only in the Northwest, from Monterey County along the coast to Curry County in southwestern Oregon. But this was not always the case. In the age when dinosaurs roamed the earth, redwood forests covered the Northern Hemisphere. Imagine a brontosaurus lumbering through them, and their large scale makes sense. One of the amazing things about coastal redwoods is that, while the earth has shifted and re-formed all around them, these trees have barely changed at all since the Jurassic period 170 million years ago. They are a link to an ancient past, well before humans set foot on soil.

Glacial advances created a cooler, drier climate than the redwoods could tolerate, everywhere but here, where the fog keeps them cool and moist in summer, and mild, wet winters keep the freeze away. The needles of the tree collect the moisture and drop it onto their roots like rain. Redwoods have two ways of reproducing. One is by seed from their small cones. But just as often, a new trunk begins as a sprout from the base of an old tree. These redwood sprouts create a burl ring, a dense mass of living shoots. The burl settles into the soil and grows wider with the new trunk, awaiting some sort of biological signal before shooting upward to the sun. If we measured the age of a redwood by its roots, it could be 8,000 years old. Unidentified under the needle-carpeted floor in Muir Woods may be the oldest living woody plant on earth.

The rings of new trees are called family or fairy circles. Some people claim a spiritual connection standing in the middle of one. What we know for certain is that the trees in the circle are not separate individuals. All the trees make up one single living entity, and you are standing in the middle of it.

Repeated wind and fire do sometimes bring the trees crashing down, but not time. Unlike higher animals and other plants, redwoods do not seem to suffer physiological aging. They change as they get older, their growth slows down, but there is no inevitable deterioration like we experience as humans. They may be as close to immortal as anything on earth.

The height, the majesty, the contrasting red and green, how the canopy shelters a soft floor of shade-loving and moisture-loving plants, the ancient stillness, our tendency to personify the trees—all these characteristics help to create the magic we often feel in the redwoods. People who feel it strongly will go to any means to keep that magic alive.

8. PHOENIX LAKE: TUCKER AND BILL WILLIAMS TRAILS

WHY GO?

Beside a sparkling lake, admire a Victorian log cabin and watch anglers trying to land big-mouth bass. Below the branches of madrones, redwoods, bays, maples, and oaks, meander along a pleasant trail with wildflowers most of the year, wild iris in spring. Under the shade of the redwoods in Bill Williams Ravine, discover a dam built in 1886, and feel in this deepest part of the canyon very much "away" from it all.

THE RUN DOWN

Start: Parking lot of Natalie Greene Park in Ross
Elevation gain: 735 feet
Distance: 3.5-mile loop/lollipop
Difficulty: Easy
Hiking time: About 1.5 hours
Seasons/schedule: Sunrise to sunset year-round
Fees and permits: None
Trail contact: Marin Municipal Water District, 220 Nellen Ave., Corte Madera 94925; (415) 945-1180; www .marinwater.org

Dog-friendly: Dogs on leash
Trail surface: Dirt and gravel fire road and single- and double-track dirt trail
Land status: Municipal water district
Nearest town: Ross
Nat Geo TOPO! Map: San Rafael
Nat Geo Trails Illustrated Map: Mount Tamalpais, Point Reyes #266
Other trail users: Mountain bikers and equestrians around the lake

FINDING THE TRAILHEAD

From US 101 take Sir Francis Drake Boulevard into the town of Ross. In Ross turn left on Lagunitas Road. It will become Dibblee Road and take you to the Phoenix Lake parking lot in Natalie Coffin Greene Park. The parking lot holds about twenty cars, and it fills up fast. Back out near the tennis club is additional street parking. If you end up parking here, take the Ross Trail on the left side of the street to the parking lot and trailhead. **GPS:** N37 57.28' / W122 34.22'

WHAT TO SEE

In 1905 dairy ranchers damned the Phoenix Dam that eventually created the reservoir. Built across the old Shaver stagecoach road, the dam would cut ranches off from Ross Station, so that milk had to be taken on the more tedious trip over the hill to Fairfax. Legend has it that, in resistance, one of the ranchers threatened the builders with a gun. As a compromise, the Marin County Water Company built a road over the dam and up the canyon. This is the road that parallels the Ross Trail and continues beside Phoenix Lake.

A shared moment at Phoenix Lake
LEEANN WALLACE

The Marin Municipal Water District (MMWD) now maintains the little 25-acre lake and its surrounding lakes and trails (for more on the MMWD, see Hike 12, Kent Trail along Alpine Lake).

The first part of this hike takes you to see a redwood log cabin erected around 1893 by estate owner Janet Porteous and her husband, James, for their coachman, Martin Grant. It predates the lake by twelve years. Notice the Queen Anne–style turret over the front porch and the window and door frames made of an uncommon ribbon burl of wavy grain. In the 1920s it was the only building spared in a fire that destroyed the rest of the Porteous estate. It served as a gathering and meeting place for many years, undergoing renovation in 1940, 1989, and 2017. A trail and interpretive signs at the cabin offer insights into the history and architectural significance of the site.

On the lake you may see pied-billed grebes, mallard ducks, and cormorants. Ospreys and hawks hunt from the trees. Anglers compete with the birds, shore fishing for bass and bluegill.

The single-track Allen Trail takes you into a small ravine with oak, bay, and buckeye trees. In spring it hosts pink shooting star, blue hound's tongue, and white zigadene. In early summer, white modesty, blue dicks, and wood rose border the trail. Late fall, maple leaves turn golden and paprika red, and the buckeye trees drop their leaves, leaving round buckeyes hanging like Christmas ornaments from bare branches. Manzanitas add striking color on gray days with their burgundy-stained, gnarled branches. The creek below the hillside trail gurgles after rains. There is a wonderful cool, green smell of woodland that gets even better on the Bill Williams Trail.

In the 1860s Bill Williams lived in a cabin upstream from the dam in the gulch that now bears his name. Some say he was a Confederate Army deserter. The biggest mystery, however, is where in the gulch he hid his buried treasure. The story goes that laborers building the Phoenix Dam spent more time looking for Bill Williams's gold than working. When the lake was drained in the mid-1980s, workers attempted another fruitless treasure hunt. The legend persists that Bill's hidden treasure remains buried here to this day.

But you can easily find this treasure of a trail, snaking into the canyon basin, following the Bill Williams Creek into the seclusion of redwoods. Maidenhair and woodwardia ferns, trilliums, huckleberry, creeping mint, and yerba buena make up the understory.

The MMWD, strapped for money, almost sold Phoenix Lake for development in 1982. The Phoenix, reborn as its name implies, took on heroic proportions when it was tapped during the 1986–1989 drought (it is a backup water supply).

The single-track Ross Trail returns you to the parking lot in Natalie Greene Park.

MILES AND DIRECTIONS

0.0 START in the parking lot of Natalie Greene Park. Take the Phoenix Lake gravel road uphill toward the lake (Option: Take Ross Trail east of the lot to Bill Williams Road and the lake).

0.2 Phoenix Reservoir Dam is on the left, the park residence to the right. Continue straight on Phoenix Lake Road (north of the lake) to visit the log cabin.

0.5 Check out the log cabin. Turn around and head back to the dam.

0.8 Back at the park residence, turn right to cross Phoenix Reservoir Dam. Continue straight alongside the lake.

1.2 Trailhead to Harry Allen Trail. Turn left onto the trail. Harry S. Allen built the trail that bears his name as a shortcut from his summer house in Larkspur over the top of Kent Woodlands to Phoenix Lake. The founder of Allen Newspaper Clipping Company, he was at one time president of the Tamalpais Conservation Club (TCC).

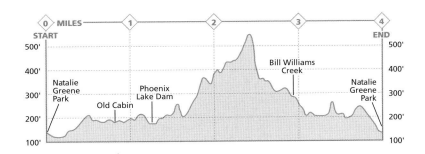

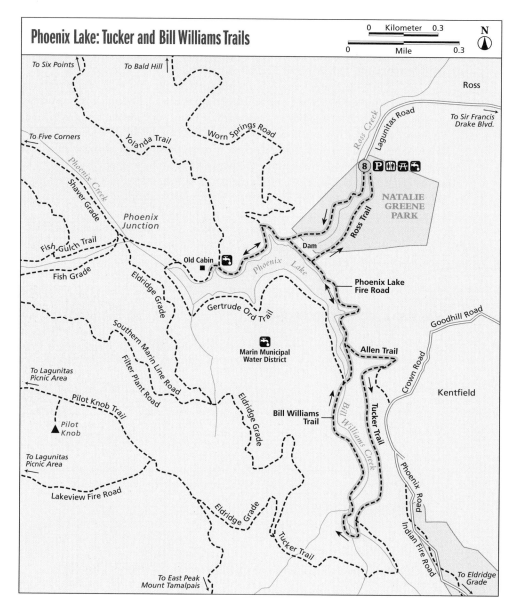

Phoenix Lake: Tucker and Bill Williams Trails

1.4   Trailhead and fork in the road. Bear right onto Tucker Trail to Eldridge Grade. The trail passes over seasonal springs and through a small grove of redwoods. Tucker Trail runs south into Williams Gulch.

2.1   Trailhead for Bill Williams Trail. Stay to your right on the trail. Stairs help as you head downhill, still on single-track dirt. Around a hairpin turn at the end of the canyon, a bridge built by local Boy Scout Troop 101 in 2001 crosses the

Stairs on trail
LEEANN WALLACE

creek. This leads to the canyon floor, following Bill Williams Ravine, one of three feeder streams to Phoenix Lake.

2.2 Stay right on Bill Williams Trail past a small 1886 dam. (***Note:*** A trailhead sign warns that the path to the left is not a trail.) Eventually a trailhead in the middle of the trail leads to Phoenix Lake. Take this trail, which becomes double-track dirt. (***Note:*** Trail can be muddy in winter.)

2.8 Junction with dirt and gravel Bill Williams Road. Continue by the lake until just before the dam.

3.3 Take the single-track Ross Trail on your right.

3.5 Arrive back at the parking lot.

Alternate routes: Circle the lake (2.8 miles) by continuing on Phoenix Lake Road past the cabin until it meets Phoenix Lake Trail. It ends at Bill Williams Road.

The Yolanda Trail takes you on a climb to Bald Hill (1,141 feet) for a 360-degree view of the surrounding bay area (4.25 miles).

9. STEEP RAVINE LOOP TO STINSON BEACH

WHY GO?

This loop is considered by many the best hike in the North Bay. It starts out mostly downhill through the dappled shade of mixed forest and over grassy slopes soaking in the sunlight to the Pacific Ocean. On the way back up, the Steep Ravine Trail is in a deep-crested canyon and crosses the cascading Webb Creek by bridge multiple times under a canopy of tall redwoods. Beside a 15-foot waterfall, you will need to clamber up a 10-foot ladder back to the starting point.

THE RUN DOWN

Start: Pantoll parking lot
Elevation gain: 1,500 feet
Distance: 7.2-mile loop
Difficulty: Moderate
Hiking time: About 4 hours
Seasons/schedule: 7 a.m. to sunset year-round
Fees and permits: Parking fee, cash only
Trail contact: Mount Tamalpais State Park Pantoll Station, 3801 Panoramic Hwy., Mill Valley 94941; (415) 388-2070; www.parks.ca.gov/?page_id=471; and Stinson Beach Lifeguard Tower; (415) 868-0942; www.nps.gov/goga/stbe.htm.
Dog-friendly: No dogs allowed

Trail surface: Mostly single- and double-track dirt trail with stairs and a 10-foot ladder to climb; short stint walking beside highway
Land status: State park and national recreation area
Nearest town: Stinson Beach/Mill Valley
Nat Geo TOPO! Map: San Rafael
Nat Geo Trails Illustrated Map: Mount Tamalpais, Point Reyes #266
Other trail users: Hikers only, except at Stinson Beach
Special considerations: Facilities at start and at Stinson Beach. Restaurants available at Stinson Beach. Consider leaving time to hang out on the beach.

FINDING THE TRAILHEAD

From US 101 exit at the Stinson Beach/CA 1 exit. Merge onto CA 1 (Shoreline Highway). Turn right onto the Panoramic Highway. Turn left into the parking lot at Pantoll Station. **GPS:** N37 53.47' / W122 36.58'

WHAT TO SEE

The Matt Davis Trail—named for its builder, who worked on it for over fifty years—leads you down through Douglas fir forest. Bridges take you over cascading creeks in the canyons. A blast of sunlight greets you in the grasslands that roll out, green in late

Dipsea Trail with Stinson Beach beyond

Steep Ravine ladder

winter and early spring, golden the rest of the year. The springtime hills host patchworks of yellow buttercups, orange poppies, and purple lupine. Raptors hover, hunting over the hillsides. You might see a bobcat run low to the ground for cover. Rabbits skitter by, especially at dusk and dawn. Open views to the northwest reveal Stinson Beach and the Bolinas mesa. To the southwest, Montara Mountain juts up beside the sea. Through every ravine is a reprieve in a shaded woodland of firs, oaks, and California bay trees, perfuming the path with peppery spice. Table Rock presents a pleasant vista through trees that drip with grandfather's beard. On a clear day, you can see the Farallon Islands 30 miles offshore.

The Bischof Steps bring you to Belvedere Avenue and downtown Stinson Beach, along the Shoreline Highway. A short walk past boutiques, galleries, a deli, restaurants, and the local library takes you to the crescent-shaped beach.

With light, white sand, level at the surf, Stinson Beach is good for picnicking, fishing, wading, swimming, and surfing (but always beware the rip current). Lifeguards on duty Memorial Day to Labor Day can guide you. You can rent boogie boards, wetsuits, surfboards, kayaks, paddleboards, and bicycles from shops near the beach. With 3.5 miles of sand, Stinson is also a good running beach. There are several restaurants and cafes and several shops to browse.

Divided into three sections, the main part of the beach, by the parking lot, is run by the Golden Gate National Recreation Area (GGNRA). North of the parking lot, the county of Marin owns the land, and dogs are allowed. Farther north, the Seadrift subdivision, an upscale community of mostly weekend homes (some vacation rentals), owns the beach but allows public use. South of the Panoramic Highway, nestled in a cove, is clothing-optional Red Rock Beach. Don't be alarmed if you hear the quick bleep of a siren while visiting. The Stinson Beach Siren is tested regularly.

Back on the Dipsea Trail, you ascend into oak woodland and descend gently into an open marshy meadow past an old military site, Hill 640. Up some stairs, the trail climbs moderately, parallel to the California shoreline, until it connects to Steep Ravine Trail.

Dipsea is the oldest trail on Mount Tamalpais, dating back to dairy farm days. In 1905 it became the route of the famous 7.4-mile Dipsea footrace, the second oldest in the United States, from downtown Mill Valley to Stinson Beach. Each June 1,500 runners race down this trail. For more information visit http://dipsea.org.

In Steep Ravine a lush, moist, cool canyon follows Webb Creek through redwoods and bay trees. You will climb 1,000 feet in 2 miles. Picturesque wood bridges crisscross the flowing stream. A popular 10-foot ladder takes you to the path above a rock face beside a plummeting waterfall. Near the top is the site of an old mining claim. Prospectors dug for gold and silver here in 1863.

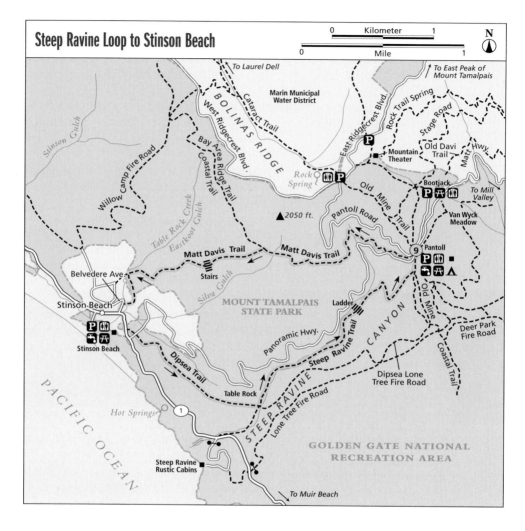

Steep Ravine Loop to Stinson Beach

To Laurel Dell

Marin Municipal Water District

To East Peak of Mount Tamalpais

BOLINAS RIDGE

Cataract Trail

West Ridgecrest Blvd.

East Ridgecrest Blvd.

Rock Trail Spring

Stage Road

Old Davi Trail

Matt Hwy.

Stinson Gulch

Willow Camp Fire Road

Bay Area Ridge Trail

Coastal Trail

Rock Spring

Old Mine Trail

Mountain Theater

Bootjack

To Mill Valley

Van Wyck Meadow

▲2050 ft.

Pantoll Road

Table Rock Creek

Eastkoot Gulch

Matt Davis Trail

Matt Davis Trail

Stairs

Pantoll

Deer Park Fire Road

Belvedere Ave.

Silva Gulch

MOUNT TAMALPAIS STATE PARK

Ladder

Old Mine

CANYON

Stinson Beach

Panoramic Hwy.

Steep Ravine Trail

Coastal Trail

Stinson Beach

Dipsea Trail

Table Rock

Dipsea Lone Tree Fire Road

PACIFIC OCEAN

Hot Springs

Lone Tree Fire Road

STEEP RAVINE

GOLDEN GATE NATIONAL RECREATION AREA

Steep Ravine Rustic Cabins

To Muir Beach

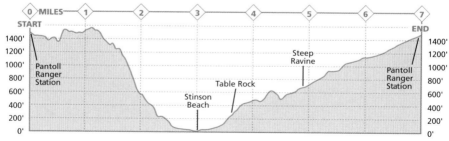

MILES AND DIRECTIONS

0.0 START in the Pantoll parking lot. Cross the Panoramic Highway via a wooden staircase across the parking lot from the restrooms and continue up the steps to the signed Matt Davis Trail.

0.4 Cross upper Webb Creek, continuing on Matt Davis Trail.

1.2 The trail enters grasslands open to sunlight and views. To the southwest is Montara Mountain.

1.7 At the junction for Coastal Trail, continue on Matt Davis Trail to Stinson Beach. There are stairs around the switchbacks.

3.5 Table Rock (marked by sign). Continue on Matt Davis Trail. Bischof Steps lead down 1,500 feet from Bolinas Ridge.

3.9 Stay on Matt Davis Trail (ignoring trails to your left). Table Rock Creek trickles down the Easkoot Gulch by the trail.

4.1 The trail ends on Belvedere Avenue. Turn left and pass the community center to Shoreline Highway.

4.3 Turn right (north) and walk beside CA 1 into downtown Stinson Beach.

4.5 Past most of the shops and restaurants on the coast side is the main entrance to Stinson Beach. Return to CA 1, heading south the way you came. Pass Belvedere Avenue. Look for Arenal Avenue, which goes west off CA 1.

4.8 Just after Arenal Avenue, on the left (east) side of the highway, is the trailhead for Dipsea Trail. Take Dipsea Trail.

5.0 The trail crosses Panoramic Highway (and two other residential roads after that).

5.8 Junction with Steep Ravine Trail; turn left (northeast) onto Steep Ravine Trail.

6.4 Climb up the 10-foot ladder beside the waterfall (there is no alternate route).

7.2 Come out onto park service road at Pantoll. Walk up the road about 30 feet and the parking lot is on your left.

Alternate routes: For families or just a fun treat, consider taking the Steep Ravine Trail to the Dipsea Trail into Stinson Beach and spend the day on the beach and in town. Then catch the West Marin Stagecoach: South Route 61 back to Pantoll. Check departure times at www.marintransit.org/routes/61.

10. **MT. TAMALPAIS: EAST PEAK LOOP**

WHY GO?

Mount Tam, the "Sleeping Maiden," is a Bay Area treasure. This hike features the diverse habitat of the 6,300-acre park, starting with incredible views. Varied woodland leads to grass-covered meadows and hillsides of gnarled manzanita and coyote brush as well as statuesque outcroppings of green serpentine and white chert stones. These trails also walk you through Mount Tam history, from the East Peak Visitor Center, down Railroad Grade, where the gravity cars used to run, to West Point Inn, and past a traditional Greek-style amphitheater.

THE RUN DOWN

Start: East Peak parking lot
Elevation gain: 700 feet
Distance: 7-mile loop
Difficulty: Moderate, with a strenuous section on International Trail
Hiking time: About 4 hours
Seasons/schedule: 7 a.m. to sunset year-round
Fees and permits: None
Trail contact: Mount Tam State Park, 801 Panoramic Hwy., Mill Valley 94941; (415) 388-2070; www.parks.ca.gov/?page_id=471; and Marin Municipal Water District, 220 Nellen Ave., Corte Madera 94925; (415) 945-1180; www.marinwater.org

Dog-friendly: Dogs on leash (and on leash on paved roads only in state park areas)
Trail surface: Some paved road, dirt fire road, single-track dirt trail (1 short steep, rocky section)
Land status: State park and municipal water district
Nearest town: Mill Valley
Nat Geo TOPO! Map: San Rafael
Nat Geo Trails Illustrated Map: Mount Tamalpais, Point Reyes #266
Other trail users: Mountain bikers and equestrians on fire roads
Special considerations: Campgrounds, picnic areas, and facilities are available at several locations along the way.

FINDING THE TRAILHEAD

From US 101 take the Stinson Beach/CA 1 exit. Merge onto CA 1 (Shoreline Highway). At the split, turn right on Panoramic Highway (signed for Muir Woods and Mount Tamalpais). At the next intersection, continue up the hill toward Mount Tamalpais. At Pantoll Station turn right (uphill) on Pantoll Road toward East Peak. Turn right on East Ridgecrest Boulevard and go 3 miles to the East Peak parking lot. **GPS:** N37 55.38' / W122 34.50'

View from Old Railroad Grade

WHAT TO SEE

Nevermore, however weary, should one faint by the way who gains the blessings of one mountain day.

—John Muir

At 2,571 feet, East Peak is the highest accessible point on Mount Tam. On a clear day you can see the Farallon Islands 25 miles out to sea, the Marin County hills, San Francisco and the bay, the hills and cities of the East Bay, and Mount Diablo. On rare occasions, you can even glimpse the snow-covered Sierra Nevada, 150 miles away.

Weekdays and crisp winter days—some of the best on Tam—keep away the majority of the half million people who drive to the top of the mountain each year, which used to be populated by elk, caribou, and even grizzly bears.

The local Miwok Indians who lived in the mountain's foothills rarely climbed to the peak, the place of "the poison people," or magic practitioners. The nickname of the mountain's ridgeline, the "Sleeping Maiden," comes from a Miwok legend about a young Miwok girl who was saved from a rival tribe by the shuddering mountain. Afterward, her reclining profile could be seen in the mountain's contour.

Lupine by the trail

That contour drew hikers and outdoor enthusiasts as early as the 1800s. In the post–gold rush era, visitors rode partway up in stagecoaches. In 1896 Sidney Cushing and other local businessmen bought rights to build a tourist railroad up to the East Peak. Displays at Gravity Car Barn (visitor center) tell the story.

In 1925 developers began to subdivide lots for sale. The Tamalpais Conservation Club (TCC), a community group established in 1912 to be the "Guardian of the Mountain," intervened, raising $30,000 in 1928 to purchase the land and donate it to the state. In 1931 the park officially opened.

Of all the buildings once in operation on the mountain, only the Mountain Theater and West Point Inn are left. This hike visits both. Built in 1904, West Point Inn was a restaurant and stopover point for passengers taking the stage to Bolinas and Willow Camp (later renamed Stinson Beach). The inn was called West Point because this is the westernmost point of the Old Railroad Grade. Member-maintained, West Point Inn is still in operation with rooms and cabins for rent and fund-raising pancake breakfasts.

The Civilian Conservation Corps (CCC) constructed the Mountain Theater (the Cushing Memorial Theater) out of local stone in the 1930s. It seats 3,750 people, who come to see the Mountain Play (a musical) each summer and have since 1913, before the stone theater was created.

Other features of this hike include manzanita on Old Railroad Grade and banks of "blue goo," the thick clay holding hillsides together on Mount Tam. In the wet season it turns into a gelatinous mass. On the Rock Spring Trail, you pass numerous streams

HOW MOUNT TAM GOT ITS NAME

Mount Tamalpais has many legends surrounding its name. In 1770 two explorers named the mountain La Sierra de Nuestro Padre de San Francisco. In the 1820s the mountain was simply called Table Mountain. The name Tamalpais first appeared in 1845, its origin a source of controversy. Spanish soldiers referred to the land as mal-pais (bad-lands). Others say Tamalpais is a Miwok Indian term—tamal, meaning "bay," pais meaning "mountain." Another legend claims that the Spaniards mistook the Miwok for Tamals and added pais to the name of the wrongly assumed tribe name, calling the mountain Tamalpais (Tamal country). Another story declares the name originated from an Aztec word for a cornmeal dumpling (tamal). Bay Area residents now know it best as Mount Tam.

and small waterfalls. After a small clearing, watch for a large boulder on your right with a dedication to Austin Ramon Pohli and Garnet Holme, founders of the Mountain Theater. Pohli died twenty days after the debut performance. His ashes are scattered on the mountain. Holme fell on Mount Tam, and his ashes are embedded in this rock. The Benstein Trail takes you through a Douglas fir forest out into the wide Potrero Meadow. The Lakeview Trail gives you just that, with partial views of the watershed lakes through branches.

MILES AND DIRECTIONS

0.0 START in the East Peak parking lot. Walk down the parking area exit road to Old Railroad Grade, a gated fire road.

0.1 Turn left on Old Railroad Grade, passing the entrance gate (sign reads To West Point and Mill Valley). (**Note:** This is a popular trail for mountain bikers.)

1.6 West Point Inn. Pass the cabins on your left and proceed to the main lodge. Across the driveway, to the west and slightly north of the inn, is the trailhead for single-track Rock Spring Trail.

2.3 Enter Mountain Theater. Continue along the upper tier of seats straight onto a paved road that slopes down to Ridgecrest Boulevard.

2.4 Cross Ridgecrest Boulevard and turn right, walking about 40 feet. Turn left onto single-track dirt Simmons Trail.

2.5 Turn right on Cataract Trail.

2.6 Turn right on Benstein Trail. A series of hairpin turns lead uphill.

4.6 Benstein Trail comes out on Laura Dell Fire Road. Turn left and go about 20 yards to where Benstein Trail continues to the left. Turn left back onto Benstein at the trailhead.

5.1 Benstein Trail dead-ends on Laurel Dell Fire Road. Cross the fire road and continue straight on a single-track dirt trail through a small grove of trees to Potrero Camp and Laurel Dell, so named for the once-dominant bay laurel trees (Be careful not to go down Kent Trail.)

5.2 At Potrero Camp turn right onto a single-track trail marked To Rifle Camp. Located here was one of five ranches established on Mount Tam after the gold rush.

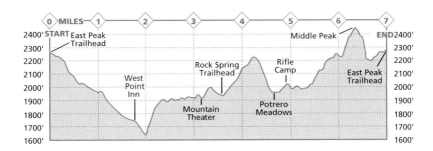

Mt. Tamalpais: East Peak Loop

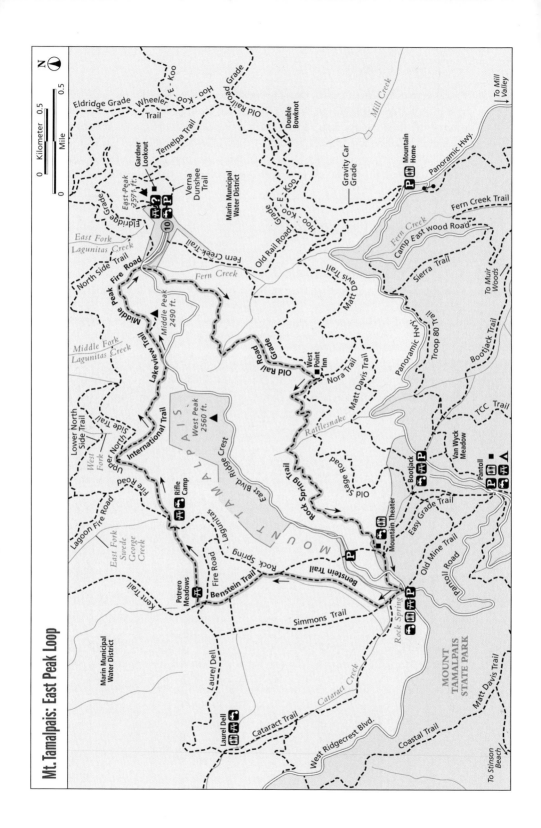

5.5 At Rifle Camp go right to the trailhead for Northside Trail. Follow Northside about half a mile.

6.0 Turn right on International Trail.

6.5 Trail ends at Ridgecrest Boulevard. Do not cross the street. Turn left and walk on the paved road 36 yards to Lakeview trailhead. Turn left on Lakeview Trail (to East Peak).

6.7 Turn left on Middle Peak Fire Road.

6.9 The fire road meets Ridgecrest Boulevard. Cross the road and turn left onto a paved road marked for hikers and bicyclists only up to the East Peak parking lot.

7.0 Arrive back at the parking lot.

Alternate routes: Families might enjoy the Verna Dunshee Trail, a 20-minute, 0.75-mile paved loop trail around the peak, named for the avid hiker and protector of open space.

Go to http://friendsofmttam.org for several suggested shorter loops ranging from 2.2 to 5 miles in distance.

THE CROOKEDEST RAILROAD IN THE WORLD

To reach the peak, a 30-ton engine traversed a double bowknot, where the tracks parallel themselves five times, the shortest radius of the curves at the turns being 75 feet. Locals and tourists alike in the early twentieth century riding the Mill Valley and Mount Tamalpais Scenic Railway delighted in jaw-dropping vistas at the summit, dinner at the Tavern of Tamalpais, and two-stepping in the Dance Pavilion on East Peak. The $1.90 round-trip ticket from San Francisco to the summit attracted some 50,000 people each year. At day's end the daring would climb aboard the gravity car. The "gravity man" would "turn on the gravity," and down they would coast, around 281 turns on the mountain's 7 percent grade, to the Mill Valley depot or Muir Woods. The line became known as "the crookedest railroad in the world." Sir Arthur Conan Doyle (creator of Sherlock Holmes) was among the passengers. "In all my wanderings, I have never had a more glorious experience," he said. Silent film actor/director Erich von Stroheim worked at the Tamalpais Tavern starting in 1912 and met his first wife there.

In 1929 a great fire burned across the south face of the mountain, destroying 1,000 acres, primarily along the rail route. Already usurped in popularity and practicality by the automobile, the train was not resurrected, and soon thereafter the railway was torn up and sold.

Few remnants of the historic buildings remain. The dance pavilion is now a parking lot. The tavern is the site of two geodesic domes that serve as radio towers.

11. MARIN HEADLANDS: MIWOK TRAIL TO POINT BONITA

WHY GO?

The Marin Headlands feature 15 square miles of beaches, marsh, lagoon, grass-covered valleys, and coastal hills with magnificent views. There is a large population of wild animals including bobcats, mountain lions, hunting raptors, and birds that frequent the Pacific Flyway. You'll see about 150 years of military history, with batteries, bunkers, cannons, and missile launching sites all along the hike, adding an eerie contrast to the natural beauty. The walk takes you to the cliff-top suspension bridge to Point Bonita Lighthouse for a dramatic view.

THE RUN DOWN

Start: Marin Headlands Visitor Center
Elevation gain: 900 feet
Distance: 8.4 mile loop
Difficulty: Moderate, with a few strenuous hills
Hiking time: About 4 hours
Seasons/schedule: Sunrise to sunset year-round
Fees and permits: None
Trail contact: Marin Headlands Visitor Information Center, 948, Fort Barry, Sausalito 94965; (415) 331-1540; and Golden Gate National Recreation Area; (415) 561-4700; www.nps.gov/goga/marin-headlands.htm
Dog-friendly: Dogs on leash
Trail surface: Double-track and single-track dirt trail, stretch of beach and sandy trail, paved trail, short stints walking beside the road
Land status: National recreation area
Nearest town: Sausalito
Nat Geo TOPO! Map: Point Bonita
Nat Geo Trails Illustrated Map: Mount Tamalpais, Point Reyes #266
Other trail users: Mountain bikers and equestrians; hikers only on Wolf Ridge, Rodeo Beach, and Point Bonita Trails
Special considerations: The tunnel halfway to the lighthouse is open only during visiting hours: Saturday, Sunday, and Monday from 12:30 p.m. to 3:30 p.m., but a walk on the suspension bridge and view of Point Bonita is still great on any day.

FINDING THE TRAILHEAD

From US 101 north of the Golden Gate Bridge, take the Alexander Avenue exit, following signs to Marin Headlands. Make sure not to get back onto the freeway, but take Conzelman Road west away from the bay. At the traffic circle take the first exit onto McCullough Road. Turn left onto Bunker Road, left onto Field Road, and then right at Bodsworth Road into the parking lot for Marin Headlands Visitor Information Center. (The center is open daily from 9:30 a.m. to 4:30 p.m.)
GPS: N37 49.51' / W122 31.29'

WHAT TO SEE

The experience of this hike actually starts on the drive in. The view of San Francisco and the Golden Gate and Bay Bridges from Hawk Hill (Battery 129) at the top of Conzelman Road is postcard perfect. After that point Conzelman becomes a one-way street winding down to the headlands above death-defying cliffs. People afraid of heights should check the alternate route using Bunker Road to make sure the one-way tunnel is open.

Where the hike starts, you have already stepped back in time, surrounded by white-washed wooden buildings with red roofs. The visitor center was the old Fort Barry chapel; the youth hostel up the hill (two buildings) was the army hospital, dating back to 1907.

The Marin Headlands served as a military base until the late 1960s, designed, along with the Presidio, to protect the San Francisco Bay from invasion from the Civil War through the Cold War. Sadly, each of the five installations constructed among the rolling hills was obsolete upon or before completion. Happily, none of them ever fired a gun.

The lagoon you pass—like Rodeo Beach—may have been named for the Rodier family, who settled nearby in the mid-1800s. Ducks, gulls, herons, and egrets are almost always present, resting in the reeds.

The Miwok Trail, starting at historic military warehouse building T1111, takes you above the Gerbode Valley into windswept hills. Alongside the trail are patches of tight-knit scrub, colorful rock outcrops, and marshes. In late winter and spring, the valley and hills are covered with nearly fifty species of wildflowers. A pamphlet describing them is available at the visitor center. As the trail ascends into the hills, you are entertained

Tunnel to Point Bonita Lighthouse

Drive in to Marin Headlands
NICK FULLERTON (FLICKR.COM/PEOPLE/18203311@N08/)

by hunting raptors. The headlands are home to the Golden Gate Raptor Observatory's hawk-watch site. Depending on the season, use your binoculars to spot ospreys, red-shouldered hawks, rough-legged hawks, ferruginous hawks, golden eagles, American kestrels, merlins, and peregrine falcons.

From Wolf Ridge Trail you can look down at a farmhouse, barn, windbreak, and pond in the Tennessee Valley, a reminder of the area's ranching days. Up at the top of Wolf Ridge Trail is Hill 88, a former radar installation for guiding Nike missiles. Wander through the abandoned Cold War buildings and enjoy 360-degree views of Marin towns and foothills, the metropolis east and west of the bay, beautiful coastland, and the Pacific Ocean.

Down the Coastal Trail you pass World War II–era bunkers and batteries to wander in and explore. The massive slabs of cement are slowly being taken over by nature. You can see where long-range cannons pointed out to the sea.

Rodeo Beach is popular with weekend sunbathers and surfers. Because of its strong currents and deadly undertows, it is not recommended for swimming.

A highlight of the hike is Point Bonita Lighthouse. On the hike in you may see the remains of a shipwreck, the bobbing black heads of sea lions in the water, and harbor seals lounging on rock islands. The lighthouse, built in 1855, was moved to its current location in 1877. It sits at the headlands' outermost tip. With the cliff slowly melting into the sea, someday the lighthouse will sit on an isolated sea stack. You also pass the Nike Missile Site, with missiles on the premises. Even unarmed, they look spooky.

MILES AND DIRECTIONS

0.0 START at the visitor center. A dirt fire road leads downhill to Bunker Road.

0.1 Turn left to walk beside Bunker Road to the old warehouse.

0.2 On the right side of the warehouse is the clearly marked trailhead for Miwok Trail, which starts out fire road wide (1.6 miles to Wolf Ridge Trail).

0.6 Stay on Miwok Trail to the left as it passes the trailhead for Bobcat Trail.

1.7 Trailhead for Wolf Ridge Trail. Turn left onto the single-track, hikers-only trail. (**Note:** Stay on the trail to avoid poison oak.) To the northwest is one of the few remaining old ranch buildings in the Tennessee Valley. The valley and the cove were named for the 1853 wreck of the SS Tennessee.

2.7 At the junction with paved Coastal Trail, turn left to the top of Hill 88.

2.9 Top of Hill 88. The buildings for the Nike Missile IFC (Fire Control) are still here, but are in a state of disrepair. Even at only 833 feet, the coastal view is amazing: north past Tennessee Point to the Point Reyes Peninsula, south past Point Bonitas to Ocean Beach, west to the Farallon Islands. Head back down on Coastal Trail.

3.1 Continue down paved Coastal Trail toward Rodeo Beach (2.3 miles). Notice remains of gun batteries. Below and ahead is Rodeo Beach and old military buildings.

3.9 Turn left to stay on Coastal Trail; trail narrows. Stairs on the trail help with the gradual descent.

4.1 Back to the paved Coastal Trail. Turn right. Listen for the foghorn of Point Bonita Lighthouse. Detour on right to Battery Townsley (World War II defense station). Then continue on Coastal Trail.

5.1 At a curve in the road—near an inviting grassy hillside—there is a double-track dirt trail right of the road to Rodeo Beach. Take this trail to Rodeo Beach. When it splits, bear left toward the beach on the path with the wooden railing.

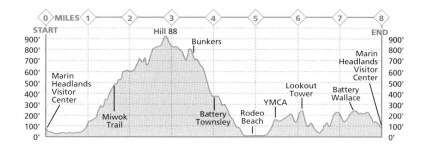

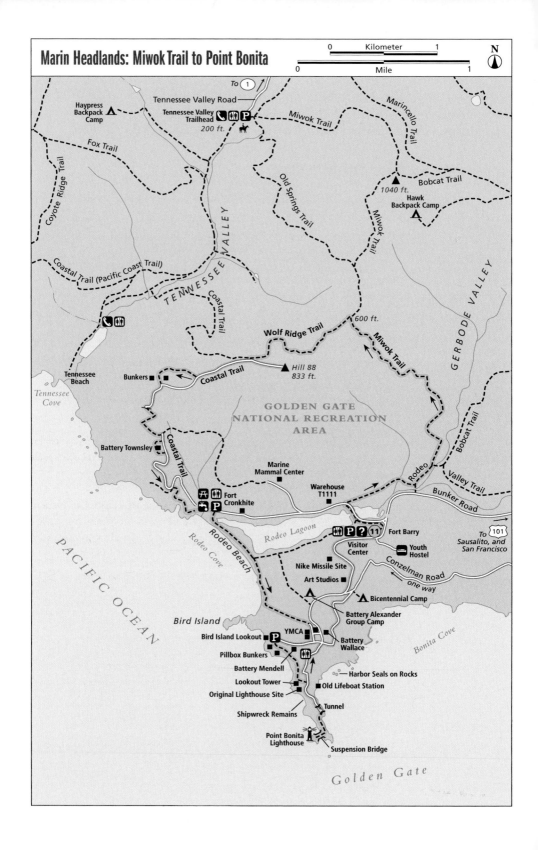

Marin Headlands: Miwok Trail to Point Bonita

0   Kilometer   1

0   Mile   1

N

To 1

Tennessee Valley Road

Haypress Backpack Camp

Tennessee Valley Trailhead
200 ft.

Miwok Trail

Marincello Trail

Fox Trail

Old Springs Trail

Coyote Ridge Trail

1040 ft.

Bobcat Trail

Hawk Backpack Camp

Miwok Trail

TENNESSEE VALLEY

Coastal Trail (Pacific Coast Trail)

Coastal Trail

GERBODE VALLEY

600 ft.

Wolf Ridge Trail

Miwok Trail

Tennessee Beach

Bunkers

Coastal Trail

Hill 88
833 ft.

GOLDEN GATE
NATIONAL RECREATION
AREA

Tennessee Cove

Battery Townsley

Coastal Trail

Bobcat Trail

Marine Mammal Center

Warehouse T1111

Rodeo

Valley Trail

Fort Cronkhite

Bunker Road

Rodeo Lagoon

Fort Barry

To 101
Sausalito, and
San Francisco

PACIFIC OCEAN

Rodeo Cove

Rodeo Beach

Visitor Center

11

Youth Hostel

Nike Missile Site

Conzelman Road
one way

Art Studios

Bicentennial Camp

Bird Island

Battery Alexander Group Camp

YMCA

Bonita Cove

Bird Island Lookout

Battery Wallace

Pillbox Bunkers

Harbor Seals on Rocks

Battery Mendell

Lookout Tower

Old Lifeboat Station

Original Lighthouse Site

Tunnel

Shipwreck Remains

Point Bonita
Lighthouse

Suspension Bridge

Golden Gate

5.3   The trail again meets paved Mitchell Road. Turn right and walk the remaining short distance to the beach.

5.4   Arrive at Rodeo Beach. Walk along the beach, heading south, toward the bluffs on the other side. The sea stack beyond the point is Bird Island. Beyond it, to the west, is a shallow sandbar called the Potato Patch. (**Note:** Surf is dangerous here.)

5.7   Head up the bluff on the steep, single-track sand trail nearest the water. The unmarked path goes toward Point Bonita Lighthouse.

5.9   Turn right to tour Battery Alexander.

6.0   Turn right onto Field Road.

6.3   At the Bonita Lighthouse parking lot, take a slight left onto the paved trail to Point Bonitas. Along the way, it turns to dirt, and a bridge takes you onto the bluff. You also pass Battery Mendell.

6.8   Come to the Point Bonita Lighthouse bridge. Look down and to the right to an isolated beach and the rusty remains of a wrecked ship. Watch to the left for an old pier and remains of a US Coast Guard Life Saving Station, established in 1899. Turn around to return to the Point Bonita parking lot.

7.3   From the parking area, take Field Road right.

7.6   Detour to Battery Wallace (1942) on your right and Battery Alexander to your left.

7.8   To the left is Nike Missile Site SF-88. Continue walking beside Field Road.

8.4   Arrive back at the visitor center and parking lot.

Alternate routes: Young families may enjoy a history loop along the beach to the lighthouse to a couple of the batteries, missile site, visitor center, and back to the beach for a picnic.

There are three valleys in the Marin Headlands: Rodeo Valley (featured here), Tennessee Valley, and Gerbode Valley. You can find lovely 5-mile loops in the other two valleys that feature the coastal landscape. Try the out-and-back hike from the Tennessee Valley trailhead along the Coastal Trail to Pirate's Cove (4.75 miles). Check trail maps for routes through Gerbode Valley.

12. MARIN MUNICIPAL WATER DISTRICT: KENT TRAIL ALONG ALPINE LAKE

WHY GO?

This is an exhilarating hike along the conifer shores of Alpine Lake, up through a dark redwood forest, emerging onto a manzanita-covered ridge with good views. Along the way, you can pick huckleberries in the early fall and admire the many water-loving flowers among the ferns and mosses along the banks.

THE RUN DOWN

Start: Parking area below Bon Tempe Dam in Marin Municipal Water District
Elevation gain: 700 feet
Distance: 5.2-mile loop/lollipop
Difficulty: Moderate
Hiking time: About 3 hours
Seasons/schedule: Sunrise to sunset year-round
Fees and permits: Vehicle entrance fee
Trail contact: Sky Oaks Watershed Headquarters, Fairfax-Bolinas Rd., Fairfax 94930; (415) 945-1181

Dog-friendly: Dogs on leash
Trail surface: Gravel and dirt road, single-track dirt trail, double-track fire road
Land status: Municipal water district
Nearest town: Fairfax
Nat Geo TOPO! Map: San Rafael
Nat Geo Trails Illustrated Map: Mount Tamalpais, Point Reyes #266
Other trail users: Equestrians on all; mountain bikers on Rocky Ridge Fire Road

FINDING THE TRAILHEAD

From Fairfax heading east, turn right on Broadway, then left onto Bolinas Road and left onto Sky Oaks Road. Turn right onto Bon Tempe Road to the Bon Tempe Lake trailhead. **GPS:** N37 57.33' / W122 36.35'

WHAT TO SEE

Leaders of the 90-year-old Marin Municipal Water District (MMWD) would tell you that managing the 21,600-acre watershed comes first, recreation is second. But both seem a passion and a source of pride.

Around the watershed's five lakes and through the numerous forests, the MMWD maintains 138 miles of trails. The beginning of Kent Trail, skirting Alpine Lake, is magical with the lake shimmering through mature Douglas firs and skinny, peeling madrones

Bon Tempe Lake from the dam

stretching into patches of sun like a Sierra scene. Inlets near the trail expose hundreds of minnows squirming about the shore, feeding on algae.

Las Lagunitas and Bon Tempe Lakes are stocked with rainbow trout that then migrate to Alpine Lake. Bass, bluegill, crappie, and catfish are also here. Anglers pick key spots along the shore; the Bon Tempe Dam seems to be a favorite. Catch and release is encouraged.

Along Kent Trail in spring, elegant white and lavender iris show off their blooms. Hound's tongue, pink shooting stars, and delicate white milkmaids decorate the forest floor. Farther along there are patches of grassland with orange poppies and yellow buttercups. Deer like to graze on the wild oats and Spanish grass during morning and late afternoon hours. Jackrabbits are also numerous, but are more often heard as a startling rustle in the scrub than seen. Butterflies flutter at the base of oaks in summer.

Turning inland from the lake, the sunlight dims as you enter a grove of redwoods. The sound of your footfall changes on the needle-blanketed ground. Sword and maidenhair ferns fawn onto the moist earth in this canopied grove. But in a short time the trees thin, the light brightens, and the trail warms in the sun.

On the sun-drenched Stocking Trail, the scenery takes a dramatic change, opening up into manzanita barrens, hillsides full of red snarled branches and green-penny leaves. The uphill trek to Rocky Ridge Fire Road rewards you with views.

Alpine Dam STEPHENG3

In drought years expect the lake levels to go down, like they did during the dry years of 1976–77, when MMWD gained recognition for its innovative conservation program that resulted in a 67 percent reduction in community water usage; or in 1986–89, when Marin County experienced the driest thirty-two months in 110 years, and Lake Lagunitas, usually kept in reserve, had to be tapped as a water supply. The oldest water district in the state, MMWD supplies almost 11 billion gallons of water a day to 190,000 homes and businesses in southern and central Marin County.

The Mount Tamalpais area makes an ideal watershed. Storms from the coast climb up the steep ridge. The rapid lifting of clouds causes warming. They wring out over the range, and the rainwater "runoff" drains into Lagunitas, Ross, Redwood, and Old Mill

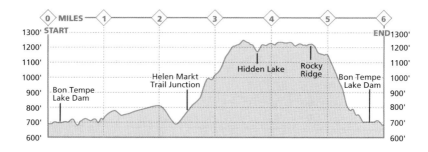

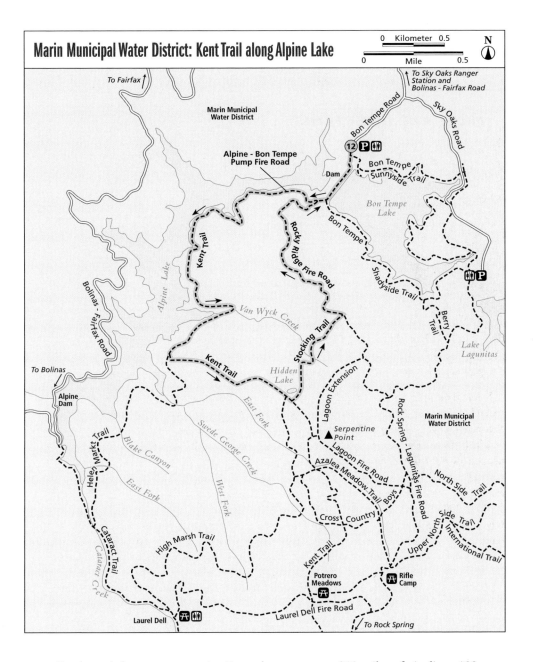

Marin Municipal Water District: Kent Trail along Alpine Lake

0   Kilometer   0.5

0   Mile   0.5

N

To Fairfax

To Sky Oaks Ranger
Station and
Bolinas - Fairfax Road

Marin Municipal
Water District

Bon Tempe Road

Sky Oaks Road

12 P

Alpine - Bon Tempe
Pump Fire Road

Bon Tempe
Sunnyside Trail

Dam

Bon Tempe
Lake

Kent Trail

Rocky Ridge Fire Road

Bon Tempe

P

Alpine Lake

Shadyside Trail

Bolinas - Fairfax Road

Van Wyck Creek

Stocking Trail

Berry Trail

Lake
Lagunitas

To Bolinas

Kent Trail

Hidden
Lake

Alpine
Dam

Helen Markt Trail

Blake Canyon

East Fork

Swede George Creek

East Fork

West Fork

Lagoon Extension

Serpentine
Point

Lagoon Fire Road

Azalea Meadow Trail

Rock Spring - Lagunitas Fire Road

Marin Municipal
Water District

North Side Trail

Cross Country

Boys

Upper North Side Trail

International Trail

Cataract Trail

Cataract Creek

High Marsh Trail

Kent Trail

Potrero
Meadows

Rifle
Camp

Laurel Dell

Laurel Dell Fire Road

To Rock Spring

Creeks and the seven reservoirs. From these are some 911 miles of pipelines, 128 storage tanks, nearly one hundred pump stations, and four treatment plants. Erosion control, whether through controlled burns, combating nonnative plant species, or limited road development, is very important. The quality of the water is directly related to the quality of the watershed, which is a good thing for hikers.

Restrooms and maps are available at the Sky Oaks Ranger Station when it's open; drinking water is available there anytime (close to the source too).

MILES AND DIRECTIONS

0.0 START at the parking lot below Bon Tempe Dam, then head uphill to the spillway. Cross the 94-foot-high dam overlooking Bon Tempe Lake on your left.

0.3 Continue right beside Alpine Lake onto the Alpine-Bon Tempe Pump Fire Road toward Kent Trail.

0.8 At the pump house Kent Trail officially begins, a single-track path following the curves of Alpine Lake.

1.8 Kent Trail continues through a conifer forest. Following the shoreline the trail winds around the lake. Just ahead the trail enters Van Wyck Canyon, with two small waterfalls and a bridge. The trail then enters a silted canyon with a narrow streambed.

2.3 Continue on Kent Trail at the junction with Helen Markt Trail. You soon start heading away from the lake. After skirting Foul Pool on the right, the trail follows the east fork of Swede George Creek into a redwood grove.

3.1 Junction with Stocking Trail. Stay left (straight) onto Stocking Trail to Hidden Lake. The trail soon heads downhill about 200 yards, passing Hidden Lake, then follows the ridge; to the left is Van Wyck Creek.

3.5 Cross a bridge and continue on Stocking Trail away from the creek. This leads to a heavily wooded area, then a manzanita barren and open prairies.

3.7 Stocking Trail dead-ends at Rocky Ridge Fire Road. Turn left (north). About 200 feet ahead is a great view of the bay: Angel Island, Marin foothills and neighborhoods, and Richmond refineries across the bay. The road then heads downhill. (**Note:** Watch for loose rock.) This is all double-track, allowing side-by-side hiking.

4.9 Back at Bon Tempe Lake. Cross the spillway and head back to the parking lot.

5.2 Arrive back at the parking lot below the dam.

Alternate routes: Families might enjoy the 3.9-mile hike around Bon Tempe Lake (Bring your fishing poles!)

For an 8.9-mile loop to Cataract Falls (see Bonus Hikes: Cataract Trail), turn from Kent Trail onto Helen Markt Trail and take it to Cataract Trail. It intersects at the top of the falls. Follow the water down (on Cataract Trail) to see more of the cascade, then double back. Take High Marsh Trail to Stocking Trail (back to featured hike) to Rocky Ridge and back to the start.

13. MOUNT BURDELL OPEN SPACE PRESERVE

WHY GO?

Starting in Novato's backyard, this hike ascends the mountain, past the quarry sites that provided cobblestones for the streets of San Francisco. It takes you over great expanses of grassland, sprinkled with wildflowers and butterflies in spring. It dips under the dappled shade of bay and oak trees, along gurgling seasonal creeks, then back through open hillsides before you reach the ridge of this extinct volcano. A low stone wall invites you to sit for a while before the descent, though it is hardly wilderness, with a repeater station and satellite nearby. But the views are rewarding.

THE RUN DOWN

Start: Open space preserve gate near the end of San Andreas Drive
Elevation gain: 1,200 feet
Distance: 5-mile loop
Difficulty: Moderate to strenuous due to elevation change
Hiking time: About 2.5 hours
Seasons/schedule: Best in late winter and spring; 24 hours year-round
Fees and permits: None
Trail contact: Marin County Parks Open Space District, 3501 Civic Center Dr., Ste. 260, San Rafael 94903; field office (415) 499-6405; ranger (415) 473-2816; www.marin

countyparks.org/depts/pk/divisions/open-space
Dog-friendly: Dogs on leash
Trail surface: Mostly wide, rocky in places; dirt trail and gravel fire road at the end
Land status: Open space preserve
Nearest town: Novato
Nat Geo TOPO! Map: San Rafael
Nat Geo Trails Illustrated Map: Mount Tamalpais, Point Reyes #266
Other trail users: Mountain bikers and equestrians on fire roads
Special considerations: There are no facilities in this open space preserve.

FINDING THE TRAILHEAD

From US 101 North past San Rafael, take the Atherton/San Marin exit in Novato. At the light turn left on San Marin Drive, which takes you through a neighborhood. Turn right on San Andreas Drive. Near the end, look for the Mount Burdell Open Space Preserve gate on the right side of the road. Park on San Andreas Drive. **GPS:** N37 56.57' / W122 34.25'

WHAT TO SEE

Around 12 million years ago, long after the ocean had receded and the coastline here (15 miles farther out then) had sprouted life and animals settled into the new habitat, molten

Mount Burdell Open Space Preserve
MATTHEW MCLEAN

rocks worked their way through the jumbled oceanic rocks. They erupted to create a rise of dark lava over the pale yellow Franciscan sandstone and greenish serpentine. This disturbance became Mount Burdell. Landslides over the years continued to shape the mountain, until bunch grass, native scrub, and oak and bay trees took their place, growing in and over the rocky mixture.

Long ago its name was Mount Olompali (Miwok for "southern village" or "southern people"), the hunting grounds and acorn-gathering site for the Miwok Indians, who had a village at its base for 6,000 years.

Sir Francis Drake reported in his 1579 journals that the people were friendly and contented, blessed with an abundant food supply and an excellent climate. In 1776 an exploring party from the Presidio in San Francisco arrived at the village of Olompali. The villagers welcomed them warmly. According to the story, the explorers repaid their hosts by showing them how to make adobe bricks and to use them to create a building. The natives built two adobe houses, modernizing their village. (Historians doubting this story say the Native Americans may have built them under the tutelage of the priests at Mission San Rafael Archangel as late as 1830 or 1840.) And then Olompali was taken away from the Miwoks.

The Spanish, Mexican, and later American governments gave the land to settlers, encouraging them to ranch and farm the area. On sections of the trail, it still feels like old ranch land, as you pass through meadows and canyons and up the side of the mountain. The patches of bay trees and oak savannah, typical of the Bay Area, were once part of the 8,877-acre Olompali Rancho, a wedding gift to Dr. Galen Burdell and his wife, Mary Black, from her father.

Now the park is bordered by houses and horse stables. The mountain that you climb has been returned to the western meadowlarks and savanna sparrows, red-shouldered hawks and American kestrels, gray squirrels, black-tailed deer, and mountain lions. But

Thistle on Mount Burdell
FRANK SCHULENBURG

the steep-cut hills and deep depressions in the earth that you see from the trails are reminders of the busy quarries that in 1888 produced the cobblestones to pave the streets of San Francisco. The southeast spur was quarried for asphalt as late as 1954.

Mount Burdell is now part of the Marin County Open Space District, which, since 1972, has preserved nearly 14,000 acres of land in thirty preserves. Mount Burdell was acquired in parcels starting in 1978, with the last addition in 1994, totaling 1,558 acres, most of it on the south-facing slopes above the city of Novato. Parcels were bought from a private owner, development companies, and Exxon Corporation.

Burdell is now an entirely new place, from the Spanish grasses that turn golden every summer, to the old roads and exposed patches of ancient rock in the quarry sites. Oak trees now feed the many birds and mammals that make the mountain home. Views on the ridge reveal the pattern of suburban streets and a busy Highway 101 corridor, but between each neighborhood there are other hillsides, preserved and treasured by the communities. Mount Tamalpais rises high and quiet to the southwest, and the rivers of the delta snake through the valley to the northwest. And there is new growth in the renewal of the Bowl Meadow (Hidden Pond).

MILES AND DIRECTIONS

0.0 GO through the open space gate and turn right onto a double-track flat dirt trail, San Andreas Fire Road (San Andreas Fire Road also goes straight). After about 350 feet turn right (north) onto San Marin Fire Road.

0.2 Bear left onto Big Tank Fire Road.

0.4 Turn right onto signed, hikers-only Michako Trail. Pass over a seasonal creek that has the potential of mud after rain. Pass through a cattle gate.

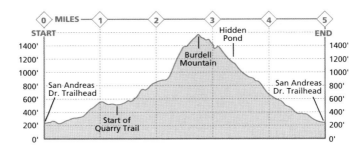

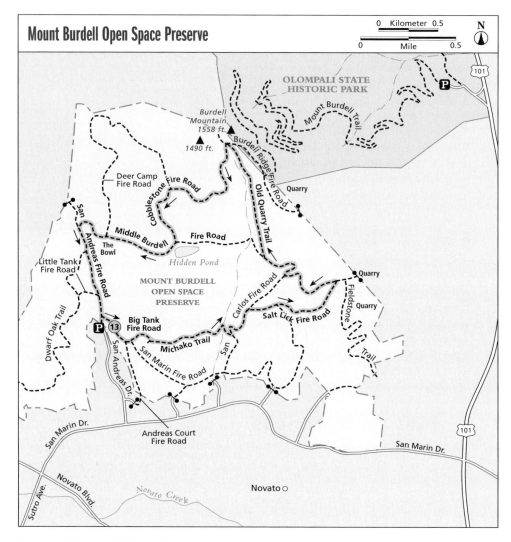

Mount Burdell Open Space Preserve

0 Kilometer 0.5

0 Mile 0.5

N

OLOMPALI STATE
HISTORIC PARK

Burdell
Mountain
1558 ft.

1490 ft.

Burdell Ridge Fire Road

Mount Burdell Trail

Deer Camp
Fire Road

Cobblestone Fire Road

Old Quarry Trail

Quarry

San Andreas Fire Road

Middle Burdell

Fire Road

The
Bowl

Little Tank
Fire Road

Hidden Pond

MOUNT BURDELL
OPEN SPACE
PRESERVE

Quarry

Carlos Fire Road

Salt Lick Fire Road

Quarry

Fieldstone

Dwarf Oak Trail

Big Tank
Fire Road

13

Michako Trail

San

Trail

San Andreas Dr.

San Marin Fire Road

Andreas Court
Fire Road

San Marin Dr.

San Marin Dr.

Novato Blvd.

Sutro Ave.

Novato Creek

Novato

101

0.8   Michako Trail bears right at the water trough.

0.9   Turn left onto San Carlos Fire Road. It loops around a curve. Stay on San Carlos past Salt Lick Fire Road.

1.3   Turn left on Old Quarry Trail. Cross through a gate. It starts out flat, curves under a few trees, with hillside views, and starts to ascend.

1.5   Take a short jog left onto Middle Burdell Fire Road and then turn right on Old Quarry Trail where it resumes. For a while this trail is steep and rocky.

2.2   Old Quarry Trail ends at a junction with Cobblestone Fire Road and paved and gravel Burdell Mountain Ridge Fire Road, which is also part of the Bay Area Ridge Trail. Go straight, crossing over the Burdell Mountain Ridge Fire

Road up the hill. A stone wall is ahead, built by Chinese laborers in the 1870s. At the fence enjoy views to the north. Head back down to the trailhead on the fire road. (A detour turning right, or southeast, on Burdell Mountain Ridge Fire Road will get you to the old cobblestone quarry.)

2.3 Take the double-track dirt Cobblestone Fire Road that heads at a 45-degree angle right of Old Quarry Trail. It is also part of the Bay Area Ridge Trail. Watch your footing on loose rocks on the trail. The trail moves into partial shade and becomes smooth and moderately sloped.

2.9 At the junction with Deer Camp Fire Road, continue straight on Cobblestone Fire Road away from the summit.

3.3 Turn right onto Middle Burdell Fire Road. To your left is Hidden Pond and beyond it The Bowl, a lovely meadow in fall and summer that is under restoration.

3.8 Stay left on Middle Burdell Fire Road. Deer Camp Fire Road goes right.

4.2 Turn left onto San Andreas Fire Road, also part of the Bay Area Ridge Trail, a gravel road.

4.8 Stay on San Andreas Fire Road past the Dwarf Oak trailhead and Little Tank Fire Road trailhead.

5.0 Arrive back at the gate on San Andreas Drive.

Alternate routes: Families can enjoy a loop on the relatively flat San Andreas and Big Tank Fire Roads and Michako Trail. Or hike Olompali State Park instead to see the oldest surviving house north of the San Francisco Bay, built in 1776 of adobe bricks by the chief of the Olompolli, as well as other historic buildings and a re-created Miwok village. Enjoy a fairly easy 3-mile loop trail.

With two cars you can start in Burdell and hike over the mountain, ending in Olompali.

SUDDEN OAK DEATH

Sudden oak death (SOD) is a pathogen discovered in 1995 that has since killed millions of tan oak, coast live oak, Shreve's oak, and black oak trees and devastated forests in California and Oregon. The fungus has also infected rhododendrons, native huckleberry, Pacific madrone, California bay trees, and coast redwoods. No one knows the origin or exactly how it came to California, but scientists isolated the pathogen *Phytophthora ramorum* in European nurseries and as early as 1993 on ornamental rhododendrons in Germany and the Netherlands.

Infected trees start seeping a dark brown, viscous sap from lower portions of the main stem. Dead, discolored patches appear beneath the bark. Small insects, such as oak bark beetles, tunnel into the weakened tree. Leaves turn pale green, brown, wilt, and fall. The tree dies. This can happen quickly or can take months or even a year or two from the time of the initial infection.

The California Oak Mortality Task Force is a nonprofit organization that diagnoses and manages the disease, bringing together many agencies. Individuals can help prevent the spread of infection by staying on trails, avoiding muddy areas, not gathering or transporting leaves or wood, and washing muddy boots before hiking again. In the car, avoid driving or parking vehicles in areas where they may become contaminated with soil or mud.

For more information go to www.suddenoakdeath.org or call (415) 499-3041.

14. RING MOUNTAIN OPEN SPACE PRESERVE

WHY GO?

A ridgetop between the towns of Tiburon and Corte Madera, Ring Mountain is enjoyable to hike and explore, although *mountain* is a misnomer. Still, the hike includes a moderate 600-foot climb that invigorates. On the way up, enjoy expanses of native grasslands, a compact bay, oak, and buckeye woodland, sculptural rock outcrops, trickling seasonal springs, and colorful wildflowers. Miwok Indians left signs of their inhabitation from 2,000 years ago, and environmentalists left traces of the strong spirit in which they fought to protect these precious 377 acres for hikers and nature lovers.

THE RUN DOWN

Start: On Paradise Drive in Corte Madera, just past Westward Drive
Elevation gain: 600 feet
Distance: 2.3-mile loop/lollipop
Difficulty: Moderate
Hiking time: About 1.5 hours
Seasons/schedule: Best in spring; sunrise to sunset year-round
Fees and permits: None
Trail contact: Marin County Parks Open Space District, 3501 Civic Center Dr., Ste. 260, San Rafael 94903; field office (415) 499-6405; ranger (415) 473-2816; www.marin

countyparks.org/depts/pk/divisions/open-space
Dog-friendly: Dogs on leash (sensitive wildlife)
Trail surface: Mostly sunny dirt trail with some rocky and rutted areas
Land status: County open space preserve
Nearest town: Corte Madera
Nat Geo TOPO! Map: San Quentin, CA
Nat Geo Trails Illustrated Map: Mount Tamalpais, Point Reyes #266
Other trail users: Mountain bikers and equestrians on fire roads

FINDING THE TRAILHEAD

From US 101 South take the Paradise Drive/Tamalpais Drive exit and turn left off the freeway. Make the first right on San Clemente Drive, which becomes Paradise Drive. Park on Paradise Drive just past Westward Drive, and walk along the street toward the Marin Country Day School. Look for the Nature Preserve sign and gate. **GPS:** N37 55.15′ /W122 29.39′

WHAT TO SEE

At the start of the hike, the single-track Loop Trail crosses a bridge in Triangle Marsh, full of sticky gumplant, salt grass, salty pickle weed, and cordgrass. In the rainy season

Richardson Bay, Sausalito, as seen from Ring Mountain
FRANK SCHULENBERG

the muddy fill is like solidified Jell-O underfoot. In the fall the ground is dry, the leaves on certain scrub turn golden and orange behind clumps of shiny toyon berries, and the grasses, thin and suntanned, sway in the slightest breeze.

Enter the Ring Mountain Open Space Preserve (named for George E. Ring, who served as a Marin County supervisor from 1895 to 1903), a native flora and fauna refuge designed to "preserve plants, animals and natural communities that represent the diversity of life on earth." Ring Mountain was once threatened by development. And it has also bounced back from a 2012 fire that burned 14 acres.

Of greatest pride is the Tiburon mariposa lily (*Calochortus tiburonesis*). Its long, shiny bronze leaves and yellow-green flowers can be seen nowhere but Ring Mountain. In 1973 Dr. Robert West, a physician and amateur photographer and botanist, identified the plant as a new species.

Other rare plants include Marin dwarf flax, Tiburon buckwheat, Tiburon paintbrush, and Oakland star tulip.

The springs and watercourses in the rocks along the trail provide for many resident animals and insects. The most unique is the rare and endangered blind harvestman spider, a type of daddy longlegs. While most of its kind are cave dwellers, this species resides under rocks on exposed hillsides, a true anomaly.

Though the spider may be blind, the three mice that commonly dwell here are not. Meadow mice move through tunnels in the valley to reach their seeds. Harvest mice, nocturnal omnivores, make birdlike nests in the marshes. Deer mice, a rather cuddly cinnamon brown with white underbellies, hide in burrows in the forest and feed at night on berries and insects.

Humans used to live here too. Miwok Indians ground acorns in bedrock mortars along one of the seasonal streams. They left a midden site and made petroglyphs, or rock carvings, in thirty sites on the mountain, the only ones recorded in Marin County. The meaning of these prehistoric rock symbols, some dating back 2,000 years, is unknown. Some archaeologists believe they are fertility symbols. Years of vandalism have destroyed the integrity of the petroglyphs, which should be treated with great care. Some are protected by fences.

Until 1965 cattle grazed the land here. In the 1970s it became a favorite run for motorcyclists. In the 1980s' grassroots effort, Phyllis Ellman (for whom a trail is named) saved Ring Mountain. In 1995 the California Nature Conservancy transferred ownership of the nature preserve to the Marin County Open Space District, who have a successful stewardship program to care for the land.

Even on this short circuit, there's a lot to see. Climbing up you see the ominous San Quentin Prison and ferries and freighters skidding through the water. The serpentine soil that you walk on is a truly unique mixture that includes a rare mineral called lawsonite. Looking closely you may see minuscule garnets and watermelon tourmaline sparkling in the dirt.

Through clumps of hobbit trees and up the hills with grass rippling, you reach Turtle Rock. Only 602 feet above sea level, it still offers expansive views of bayside towns and the San Francisco skyline. To the west are the Marin Headlands, the towers of the Golden Gate Bridge, and shapely Mount Tamalpais. The loop back is equally entertaining with flora, fauna, and more views before crossing back on the bridge over the marsh.

Ring Mountain petroglyph in closed area
FRANK SCHULENBERG

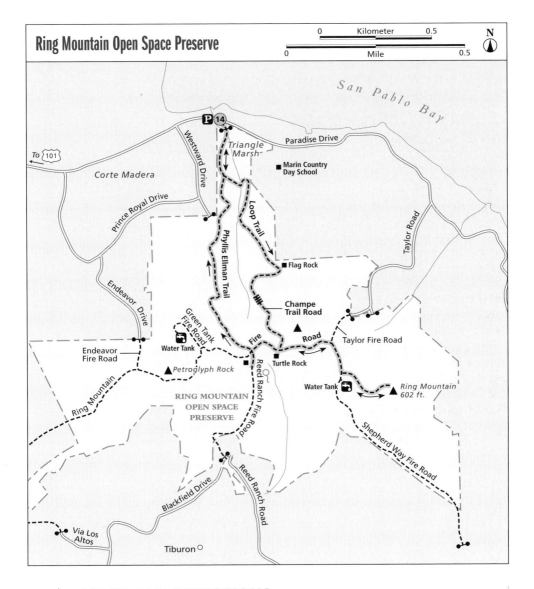

MILES AND DIRECTIONS

0.0 START at Paradise Drive in Corte Madera, just past Westward Drive. Look for a Nature Preserve sign and gate. Go through the gate. The trail crosses a small bridge to an information display. (**Note:** Pick up a nature guide if available.)

0.2 Just past the information display, the trail splits. Take the trail to the left through a stand of blackberry bushes and onto Loop Trail. There are sixteen

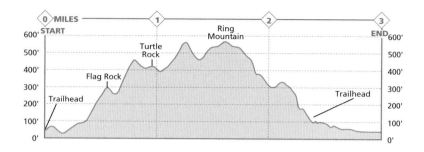

numbered signposts on the self-guided nature trail. Turn right at marker #2 for the nature walk. The trail heads up moderately past some boulders.

0.3   At marker #4 there are several unofficial crossing trails. Continue right on the main trail. It parallels a stand of oak and bay trees on the right.

0.4   At marker #5 turn left. Pass through grassland.

0.5   Rock maze left of marker #6. The biggest rock is named Flag Rock. Years ago Marin Country Day School children used to play "Capture the Flag" near it.

0.7   At marker #7, look left up the hill to see the "guarding man" rocks set in a clump of juniper trees. Cross two bridges; follow the trail that goes straight up about 20 feet, then take the trail right, across the mountain and slightly downhill (parallel to the bay). The trail flattens out, curves, and heads toward the bay. Railroad ties protect the trail edges. Stay to the left going uphill. At marker #8 there's a little shady grove. You can see the next marker ahead. On the railroad ties "Trail" and an arrow are carved into the wood to assure you that you are on the right trail. Looking back down toward the street, you can see part of Marin Country Day School.

0.8   At a trail post, with more railroad ties to mark your way, turn right into the grove of bay trees. Though not signposted, this is Champe Trail, named for the Nature Conservancy intern who laid out this part of the trail. The main trail takes you through the woods. Bear left to marker #10, where you can view Mount Tamalpais. The trail again splits, but you can see the next marker. The single-track trail opens up at marker #11.

0.9   Cross over the gravel and dirt ridge road to Turtle Rock. Walk east on the fire road along the hilltop.

1.1   The road becomes paved. Turn around and head back to Turtle Rock.

1.3   Back at Turtle Rock, head west on Ring Mountain Fire Road.

1.5   Trailhead for Phyllis Ellman Trail. Turn left. At marker #13, to the left, is where the Tiburon mariposa lily grows. Stay on the path.

2.3   Arrive back at the gate and Paradise Drive.

Alternate routes: To extend your hike another 2 miles, continue on the Ring Mountain Fire Road into the Tiburon Open Space Preserve, then retrace your steps back down Ring Mountain.

TWO TRAILS TO CONNECT IT ALL: THE SAN FRANCISCO BAY TRAIL

This amazing circuit is a planned 500-mile walking and cycling path that hugs the entire San Francisco Bay, running through all nine Bay Area counties and forty-seven cities, and across seven toll bridges. Currently, over 350 miles of trail are in place, connecting many open spaces and parks. Nearly 225 miles of the existing Bay Trail are paved, and 127 miles are natural surface trails of varying widths. The trail is widely used in San Francisco, Sausalito, Oakland, Berkeley, and San Mateo. In the North Bay—Novato, Petaluma, Napa, and Benicia—the segments of trail tend to be quieter. The trail started with a senate-passed bill in 1987. For maps and more information, see http://baytrail.org/get-on-the-trail/walking/.

Bay Area Ridge Trail

Bay Area Ridge Trail, which will be over 550 miles when completed, now offers 375 miles of connector trails for hikers, runners, cyclists, and equestrians. It stretches as far north as the Ridge Trail in Napa and Sonoma Mountain Ridge, and as far south as Harvey Bear Trail by Coyote Lake in Gilroy, west to Stern Grove and Lake Merced, and east to the Carquinez Strait shoreline. The Bay Area Ridge Trail started as an idea over thirty years ago by park visionary William Penn Mott Jr., who served as director of the National Park Service as well as East Bay Regional Park and California State Parks. The first Ridge Trail segment was dedicated in May 1989, and with a grassroots effort and coordination between public agencies it has grown from there. You can find maps and more information at http://ridgetrail.org.

Bonus Hikes: Mount Tamalpais and Its Foothills

C. CHINA CAMP STATE PARK: SHORELINE-BAYVIEW LOOP TRAIL

WHY GO?

China Camp offers 15 miles of trails, most of which are open to hikers, bikers, and equestrians. Young families might enjoy the 0.75-mile Turtle Back Hill Nature Trail (hikers only). The Shoreline-Bayview Loop Trail offers views, vistas, and seasonal wildflowers. It is very popular for mountain biking and trail running. Though China Camp has a rich Coastal Miwok and natural history, its name comes from the post–gold rush and railroad building period when it was a coastal fishing village with nearly 500 Chinese residents. By 1880 it produced nearly 3 million pounds of shrimp each year, But after the Chinese Exclusion Act of 1882, the population rapidly declined. Visit the museum and Quan Brothers' Snack Shack to learn more.

THE RUN DOWN

Start: Shoreline trailhead near the park entrance kiosk. GPS: N38 0.31' / W122 29.42'
Elevation gain: 760 feet
Distance: 8.5-mile loop
Difficulty: Moderate due to elevation gain
Hiking time: About 4.5 hours
Seasons/schedule: 8 a.m. to sunset year-round
Fees and permits: Parking fee
Trail contact: China Camp State Park, 101 Peacock Gap Trail, San Rafael 94901; (415) 456-0766; www.parks.ca.gov/?page_id=466
Dog-friendly: No dogs allowed
Trail surface: Single- and double-track dirt trail
Land status: State park
Nearest town: San Rafael
Nat Geo TOPO! Map: Petaluma Point
Nat Geo Trails Illustrated Map: Mount Tamalpais, Point Reyes #266
Other trail users: Mountain bikers and equestrians

D. CATARACT TRAIL

WHY GO?

One trail and a dozen waterfalls—that's the ratio on the Cataract Trail. Above Alpine Lake in the Mount Tamalpais watershed, the trail follows Cataract Creek steeply uphill. The first waterfall is less than 100 yards up. And they get bigger and louder as you climb, especially in late winter and spring.

Consider including the Laurel Dell picnic area on your hike, from where you can connect to many trails on Mount Tamalpais. For a pleasant loop take Laurel Dell Fire Road to the Potrero picnic area. Cross the bridge and make a left on Kent Trail. This connects to the Helen Markt Trail around the edge of Alpine Lake. You can take it back to the Cataract Trail Bridge. Or you can turn around at the top and go back down the hill, admiring the falls from the top down for an out and back of 2 miles. Either way be sure to take a look at Alpine Dam before you go.

THE RUN DOWN

Start: Cataract trailhead on Fairfax-Bolinas Road. GPS: N37 56.12' / W122 38.17'
Elevation gain: 720 feet
Distance: 2.6 miles out and back (with many options for longer hikes)
Difficulty: Moderate due to quick elevation gain
Hiking time: About 2 hours
Seasons/schedule: Best in late winter and early spring; sunrise to sunset year-round
Fees and permits: None

Trail contact: Marin Municipal Water District, 220 Nellen Ave., Corte Madera 94925; (415) 945-1180; www.marinwater.org
Dog-friendly: Dogs on leash (not allowed in surrounding state park land)
Trail surface: Dirt trail and stairs
Land status: Municipal water district
Nearest town: Fairfax
Nat Geo TOPO! Map: Bolinas, CA
Nat Geo Trails Illustrated Map: Mount Tamalpais, Point Reyes #266
Other trail users: Hikers only

SAN FRANCISCO AND THE BAY

San Francisco is an incredible city, one of the most visited in the world, with top-notch restaurants, museums, theaters, professional sports teams, music venues, and unique stores. But what many people don't know is that it also boasts the largest urban park system in the world, extending far north and south of the city. A short distance from this great metropolis, you could spend every weekend exploring some new trail or outdoor adventure. The coastal range and valleys support all kinds of plant and wildlife, in water and on land. And there's even great hiking right in the city.

A hike in Golden Gate Park goes through botanical gardens and memorial groves, past lakes, a rose garden, grazing bison, and Dutch windmills. At Lands End, 4 miles of Ocean Beach and Fort Funston offer good running or strolling, and from the historic Cliff House, a trail follows the bluff under Monterey cypress and eucalyptus trees with views of the Golden Gate. This path leads to China Beach and Baker Beach. The Coast Trail can take you all the way to Fort Point and across the bridge to Sausalito if you want. It also takes you to the Presidio, the oldest continuously operated military post in the nation, open to the public since 1994. Lovers' Lane, a forest of trees and military history, is there to explore. Crissy Field, once an airstrip, has lawns for picnicking near restored wetlands.

A ferry ride on the bay starts a memorable day of hiking on Angel Island. Past the infamous Alcatraz Island, its prison buildings still intact, the ferry docks at Ayala Cove. Hiking or camping up on Mount Livermore, the island is yours for a precious moment. Trails take you through history from the Civil War to an immigration station to a World War II army hospital.

To check out native plants more closely, consider the pleasant loop through chaparral to the peak of San Bruno Mountain. Fog may hamper the view—especially in summer—but that's the nature of the city by the bay.

Crissy Field Beach, San Francisco
BROCKEN INAGLORY

15. ANGEL ISLAND STATE PARK: MT. LIVERMORE

WHY GO?

Only reachable by ferry, this Angel Island hike includes a walk through US history and a good look at the present. You can take in the long Miwok history of the island before a fairly strenuous climb up Mount Livermore, awarding you with 360-degree views encompassing landmarks all around the San Francisco Bay. The loop back visits one of the few Civil War posts for the Union on the West Coast before returning to the ferry terminal with facilities and a cafe.

THE RUN DOWN

Start: Ayala Cove on Angel Island
Elevation gain: 788 feet
Distance: 6.2-mile loop
Difficulty: Easy, with strenuous climb up and down Mount Livermore
Hiking time: About 3 hours
Seasons/schedule: 8 a.m. to sunset year-round
Fees and permits: Ferry fare round-trip from San Francisco. (Note: Fees are different from Tiburon.)
Trail contact: Angel Island State Park, 1416 9th St., Sacramento 95814; (415) 435-5390; www.parks.ca.gov/?page_id=468
Dog-friendly: No dogs allowed

Trail surface: Well-maintained single-track path uphill, less maintained dirt path downhill, double-track dirt road, paved road
Land status: State park
Nearest town: Tiburon
Nat Geo TOPO! Map: San Francisco North, CA
Nat Geo Trails Illustrated Map: Mount Tamalpais, Point Reyes #266
Other trail users: Roads accessible by mountain bikers
Special considerations: Bring snacks or a picnic lunch and carry water. Binoculars are a plus on Mount Livermore.

FINDING THE TRAILHEAD

Catch a ferry from Tiburon or San Francisco at Pier 41 to Angel Island. Proceed to Ayala Cove on Angel Island. The trailhead is to your right as you face inland from the ferry dock.

For the Blue and Gold ferry from Pier 41 in San Francisco, check the current schedule and prices, and book online at www.blueandgoldfleet.com.

For the Angel Island-Tiburon Ferry from Tiburon, call (415) 435–2131 or go to http://angelislandferry.com. **GPS:** N37 52.8'/ W122 26.7'

The view from Camp Reynolds

WHAT TO SEE

When you disembark from the Blue and Gold ferry at Ayala Cove on Angel Island, you are already steeped in history. For nearly 2,000 years, when the salmon were spawning through Raccoon Strait, the Miwok rowed across the bay from their Marin homeland in narrow canoes made of tule to camp, hunt, fish, and gather acorns.

In August 1775 Juan Manuel de Ayala, whose mission was to complete the first accurate survey of the area for future Spanish conquest, christened this little island Isla de Los Angeles. Over the years the island served as a Spanish cattle ranch, a quarry during the war between Mexico and the United States, a Civil War installation, a quarantine station during the Spanish-American War, a detention camp during the Philippine Insurrection, a US Army discharge depot and processing center, a World War I immigration station, a World War II POW camp, and a Nike missile site.

In 1892 the quarantine station was opened at Ayala Cove (known as Hospital Cove). The forty buildings at the cove included a 400-bed detention barracks, a disinfection plant, and laboratories. The buildings are gone now, except for the bachelor officers' quarters (now the park museum) and the surgeons' homes (used as park offices).

Serpentine climbing leads up the steep North Ridge Trail, where you pass native island trees and shrubs: oak, bay, and madrone, sagebrush, chamise, manzanita, toyon, elderberry, and coyote brush. Deer and raccoons live on the island, but you don't see them much anymore. In the 1970s the deer overpopulated the island. They were so tame you could pet them, and they hovered over picnickers on Ayala Beach. After efforts to export the deer became too expensive, many were killed to protect the ecology of the island.

Mount Livermore (781 feet) is named for Marin County conservationist Caroline Livermore, who led the campaign to create Angel Island State Park in 1958. On a clear day, you have fabulous views of San Francisco, the Golden Gate

Artifacts in the immigration station

Bridge, and the Marin Headlands. Look east to the Bay Bridge and Treasure Island, and upon East Bay hills, the campanile of the University of California–Berkeley, and the castle-like Mormon Temple.

Heading down the unmarked Battery Trail, you pass spectacular campsites. Suddenly you see a massive block of cement. This is Battery Wallace. In 1886 a report critical of Pacific Coast harbor defenses led to the development of gun batteries facing the Golden Gate. You can't miss another massive slab, Battery Ledyard, on the Perimeter Road. Five years after they were built, these artillery units became obsolete and were decommissioned.

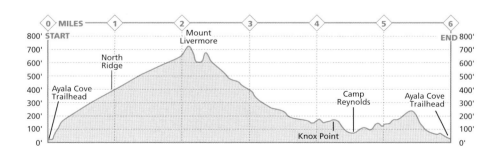

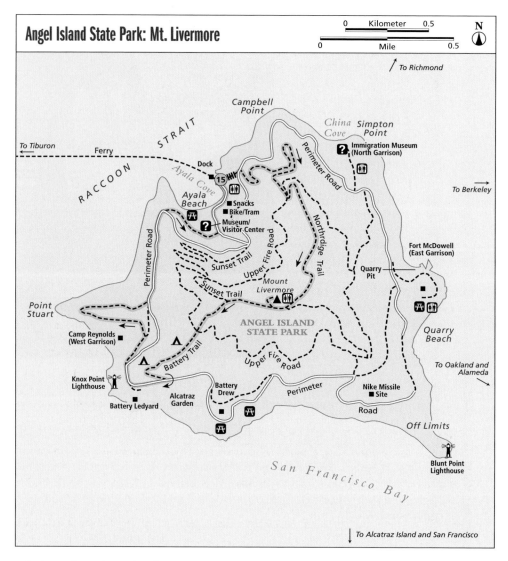

Angel Island State Park: Mt. Livermore

In just a few minutes' walk on Perimeter Road, you come to Angel Island's Civil War site, Camp Reynolds. Fearing Confederate sympathizers might slip into the bay and attack Union resources, the federal government established Camp Reynolds in 1863, among other installations. Rebel troops never did invade; accounts of soldiers stationed here reveal that their biggest challenge was fighting boredom.

After a pleasant loop to Point Stuart, it's about 25 minutes back to the Ayala Cove ferry terminal. On the ride back you can plan your next visit to tour the other side of Angel Island, with Fort McDowell and the immigration station.

MILES AND DIRECTIONS

0.0 START at the ferry dock in Ayala Cove. The North Ridge trailhead is clearly marked and starts with wooden steps.

0.1 Cross over Perimeter Road. North Ridge Trail continues up across the road to the right (northeast).

1.2 Cross over the dirt Fire Road. North Ridge Trail continues on the other side of the road.

2.4 Reach Sunset Trail. Follow the trail north to the top of Mount Livermore.

2.7 Arrive on top of Mount Livermore. Return to Sunset Trail.

3.0 Turn right (west) on Sunset Trail.

3.3 Reach a well-defined but unmarked trail to the left (southwest). Turn left onto unsigned Battery Trail. (**Note:** Watch for poison oak.)

3.5 Pass over the Fire Road, continuing on Battery Trail.

3.8 Battery Wallace is on the right (north).

3.9 Reach Perimeter Road. Turn right (north) to head toward Camp Reynolds.

4.1 Pass Battery Ledyard on the left (west).

4.3 Take the path that heads down to the left of Perimeter Road to the chapel.

4.5 Reach Camp Reynolds (West Garrison). At the top of the slope are the officers' quarters, gardens, and bake house. Walk the grassy parade yard down toward the bay to see the cannon fired. Facing the officers' quarters, go left on the small road that curves west toward Point Stuart.

4.7 Pass restrooms on the left.

4.9 Reach Point Stuart. Continue as the road turns to a hiker-only footpath going east toward Perimeter Road.

5.3 Back on Perimeter Road, turn left (north).

5.7 Take the footpath on the left (north) to Ayala Cove. The sign reads "To the Ferry Dock."

6.0 Arrive back at the visitor center, picnic area, and Ayala Beach.

6.2 Arrive back at the ferry dock.

Alternate routes: Perimeter Trail is a paved 5.5-mile loop around the island that visits all the sites. Go counterclockwise to see most in chronological order. There are a couple of steep hills. Doing this on bikes with side hikes to all the historic sites is a great family adventure.

A 3-mile out-and-back hike takes you from Ayala Cove to the US Immigration Station and back on the North Ridge and Perimeter Trails.

16. GOLDEN GATE NATIONAL RECREATION AREA: SAN FRANCISCO'S LANDS END

WHY GO?

A popular family and tourist trail, this wide and pleasant dirt path follows the cliffs above the bay. It occasionally heads inland through scrub and eucalyptus trees, then works its way back to stunning views of the Golden Gate Bridge. Enjoy great views at Eagle's Point Overlook, and end your hike with a fun tour of the Sutra Baths ruins and the famous Cliff House.

THE RUN DOWN

Start: Trailhead at the Lands End Lookout Visitor Center parking lot
Elevation gain: 500 feet
Distance: 3.4 miles out and back
Difficulty: Easy
Hiking time: About 3 hours
Seasons/schedule: 24 hours a day year-round; visitor center 9 a.m. to 5 p.m.
Fees and permits: None
Trail contact: Lands End Lookout, 680 Point Lobos Ave., San Francisco 94123; (415) 426-5240; and Golden Gate National Recreation Area,

Bldg. 201, Fort Mason, San Francisco 94123-0022; (415) 561-4700; www .nps.gov/goga/planyourvisit/ landsend.htm
Dog-friendly: Dogs on leash
Trail surface: Paved path, double-track and single-track dirt trail, lots of stairs
Land status: National recreation area
Nearest town: San Francisco
Nat Geo TOPO! Map: Point Bonita, CA
Other trail users: Mountain bikers

FINDING THE TRAILHEAD

In San Francisco make your way to Geary Boulevard heading west. Geary turns into Point Lobos Avenue and ends at Lands End Lookout Visitor Center and parking lot, where you'll find the trailhead. **GPS:** N37 46.47' / W122 30.42'

WHAT TO SEE

The Coastal Trail at Lands End is immensely popular but should not be missed. The walk along the northwest end of San Francisco and edge of the continent offers breath-taking views of the Marin Headlands and Point Bonita Lighthouse, the copper-stained Golden Gate Bridge, old shipwrecks at low tide, and small rocky beaches.

A few worthwhile detours along the way offer historical and eye-pleasing features. Take in the views at the Mile Rock Overlook. Take the stairs down to Mile Rock Beach

Golden Gate Bridge from overlook at Lands End
CADEN DIVELBISS

and enjoy a contemplative walk in the Lands End Point labyrinth built on a turn-of-the-century gun battery.

Lands End was originally dunes and rocky hills covered with low-lying coastal scrub and almost no trees. The Monterey cypress by the trail were planted in 1933. Starting in the 1880s a stream train ran on rails along today's Coastal Trail, taking guests to Sutro Baths. Landslides in 1925 took out the tracks, ending the railroad's run.

Guiding sailboats into the Golden Gate used to be a treacherous undertaking. Painted Rock was one of several navigational aids used to avoid wrecks until trees obscured its view in the 1900s. In 1904, Mile Rocks Lighthouse was built to help ships navigate safely past a pair of large stones sticking out of the water about a half mile north of Point Lobos in San Francisco (named Mile Rocks). Both were extremely hard to see in fog. In 1901,

Labyrinth on Mile Rock Beach
CADEN DIVELBISS

when the *Rio de Janeiro* was wrecked near Fort Point and 140 lives were lost, the dangerous construction of the lighthouse began, with deep-water sailors working out in the water at low tide. They managed to erect a three-tiered steel tower and a lantern room. Keepers had to commute by boat during low tide and climb a ladder to the lighthouse to do their isolated job. They wore earplugs for the loud fog signal. In powerful waves and high winds, a keeper could literally be blown from one of the tower's catwalks. Despite these hazards, some keepers enjoyed the assignment. Keeper Lyman Woodruff served on

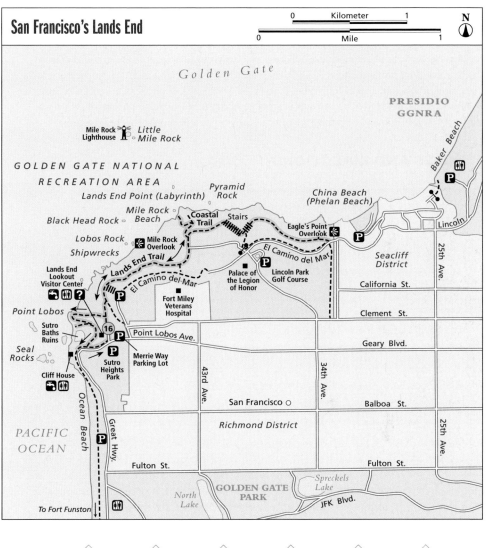

San Francisco's Lands End

Golden Gate

PRESIDIO
GGNRA

Mile Rock Lighthouse
Little Mile Rock

GOLDEN GATE NATIONAL
RECREATION AREA

Lands End Point (Labyrinth)
Pyramid Rock

China Beach
(Phelan Beach)

Black Head Rock
Mile Rock Beach
Coastal Trail
Stairs
Eagle's Point Overlook

Lobos Rock
Mile Rock Overlook
Shipwrecks
Lands End Trail
El Camino del Mar
Seacliff District

Lands End Lookout Visitor Center
El Camino del Mar
Palace of the Legion of Honor
Lincoln Park Golf Course
California St.

Point Lobos
Fort Miley Veterans Hospital
Clement St.

Sutro Baths Ruins
16
Point Lobos Ave.
Geary Blvd.

Seal Rocks
Merrie Way Parking Lot

Cliff House
Sutro Heights Park

San Francisco
Balboa St.

PACIFIC OCEAN
Ocean Beach
Great Hwy.
Richmond District
43rd Ave.
34th Ave.
25th Ave.

Fulton St.
Fulton St.

Spreckels Lake
GOLDEN GATE PARK
North Lake
JFK Blvd.

To Fort Funston

Lincoln
Baker Beach
25th Ave.

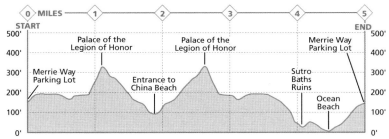

MILES | START | END
Palace of the Legion of Honor
Palace of the Legion of Honor
Merrie Way Parking Lot
Merrie Way Parking Lot
Entrance to China Beach
Sutro Baths Ruins
Ocean Beach

Mile Rocks for eighteen years. In the 1960s, despite protests from the general public, the tower of Mile Rocks was dismantled in the name of progress. The US Coast Guard deemed the station best suited to automation.

Stairs on the Upper Sutro Bath Trail take you down to the ruins of the grand old Sutro Baths, erected by philanthropist Adolph Sutro in 1886. Six baths, a large amphitheater, and three restaurants once sprawled across 3 acres. In 1966 land developers bought the Sutro Baths site to build high-rise apartments and began demolition. A fire destroyed what was left. In 1980 the remains became part of the Golden Gate National Recreation Area.

MILES AND DIRECTIONS

0.0 START at the Lands End Lookout Visitor Center, then take Merrie Way to Lands End Trail/Coastal Trail.

0.4 Stop at Mile Rock Overlook. At low tide look for shipwrecks.

0.8 Detour downstairs to Mile Rock Beach and Lands End Point labyrinth. Look for the remains of Mile Rock Lighthouse offshore.

1.1 Return to Lands End/Coastal Trail and continue northeast.

1.3 Take the stairs on the trail up toward Eagle's Point.

1.8 Enjoy the views at Eagle's Point. Turn around and return the way you came.

2.8 Back to Mile Rock Overlook.

3.0 Bear right (west) down the stairs to the Sutro Baths ruins.

3.2 Explore the Sutro Bath ruins, then head back up to Lands End/Coastal Trail.

3.3 At the junction, go straight and then up more stairs.

3.3 Back to Merrie Way and the parking lot.

3.4 Arrive back at the visitor center.

Alternate routes: If you wish to make the route a loop, walk back on the sidewalk on El Camino del Mar. You pass the Lincoln Park Golf Course, which hosts the oldest and largest ongoing tournament event in US golf history; the site of an old Chinese cemetery; a Memorial for Peace; a Holocaust memorial; and the California Palace of the Legion of Honor, hosting an impressive collection of mostly European art, including an early cast of *The Thinker* by Rodin. On the El Camino del Mar Trail you pass Fort Miley and can take short detours to the now defunct Battery Chester and Lands End Octagon House. It was built in 1927 as the Point Lobos Marine Exchange Lookout Station to aid ships coming into the harbor (before the trees were planted).

Continue your walk through the lovely Seacliff neighborhood beyond Eagle's Point Overlook to China Beach and even Baker Beach beyond that.

Continue past the visitor center to the Cliff House. On the back balcony is the Camera Obscura, based on a fifteenth-century design by Leonardo da Vinci. Walk Ocean Beach and on your way back, cross Point Lobos Avenue to stroll through Sutro Heights Park. These were once the gardens and grounds surrounding Sutro's mansion.

17. SWEENEY RIDGE: SAN FRANCISCO BAY DISCOVERY SITE

WHY GO?

This open space area on scrub-covered moors is a small oasis in an urban desert, which includes the San Francisco International Airport and the busy I-280/US 101 corridors. This is where Captain Gaspar de Portolá stood and saw the San Francisco Bay for the first time in 1769. Protected as Golden Gate National Recreation Area in 1984, the ridge (at about 1,250 feet) offers 360-degree views up to 30 miles on clear days. The north ridge is also home to an abandoned Nike missile site.

THE RUN DOWN

Start: Gate at the end of Sneath Lane
Elevation gain: 550 feet
Distance: 5.8 miles out and back
Difficulty: Moderate due to elevation gain
Hiking time: About 3 hours
Seasons/schedule: 8 a.m. to sunset year-round
Fees and permits: None
Trail contact: Golden Gate National Recreation Area, Bldg. 201, Fort Mason, San Francisco 94123-0022; Pacifica Visitor Center; (650) 355-4122; www.nps.gov/goga/sweeney.htm
Dog-friendly: Dogs on leash

Trail surface: Paved path, double-track and single-track dirt trail
Land status: National recreation area
Nearest town: San Bruno and Pacifica
Nat Geo TOPO! Map: San Francisco South, CA; Montara Mountain, CA
Nat Geo Trails Illustrated Map: Skyline Boulevard #815
Other trail users: Equestrians and mountain bikers
Special considerations: There are no facilities. Wear layers. You can download a brochure about the Discovery Site at www.nps.gov/goga/learn/historyculture/san-francisco-bay-discovery-site.htm.

FINDING THE TRAILHEAD

From the San Francisco Bay Bridge, take US 101 South to I-280 South. Take the Pacifica/CA 1 exit. Get off at Skyline Boulevard South (CA 35). Go about 4 miles, past Skyline College entrance, and turn right onto Sneath Lane. Take it to the end through a residential area. The parking area is on the right past the entrance gate. **GPS:** N37 37.10' / W122 27.15'

WHAT TO SEE

In 1769 a Spanish expedition led by Don Gaspar de Portolá was ordered to find a land route from colonial Mexico to Monterey Bay, a "fine harbor, sheltered from winds."

San Francisco Bay Discovery Site marker
PANEGYRICS OF GRANOVETTER (FLICKR.COM/
PEOPLE/SARAH_C_MURRAY/)

Leaving from the tip of Baja California in July of that year with sixty-four men and 200 horses, Portolá was guided only by vague descriptions of the place as seen from the sea and a mariner's navigation handbook of the California coastline. When Portolá and his men saw the mouth of the Salinas River, they were greeted by stinging winds and rough seas. Concluding this could not possibly be the place, they continued north.

Food and supplies were running short when they reached the peaceful San Pedro Valley. One of Portolá's scouts, Jose Francisco Ortega, climbed a nearby ridge. To his surprise, there to the east was, in his own words, "an enormous area of the sea or estuary, which shot inland as far as the eye could see." He became the first European reported to see the San Francisco Bay. On November 4, 1769, Captain Portolá and the entire party followed Ortega up to the ridge to see for themselves. Portolá named the body of water San Francisco Bay and claimed it as part of New Spain.

You can stand in the spot where Ortega took in this vista for the first time. A monument on the site is dedicated to Carl McCarthy, who was among those who ensured public ownership of this open space. From here you can see several peaks: Mount Diablo, Mount Hamilton (the highest peak in the region), Montara Mountain, Point San Pedro, Mount Tamalpais, and San Bruno Mountain.

A paved path and hearty cardiovascular climb take you up the hill to the ridge, with pretty San Andreas Lake to your left (east). The active San Andreas Fault runs beneath it and Crystal Springs Reservoir to the southeast.

A short stint north brings you to the decaying structures of the US Army Nike Missile Radar Station, which was in operation here starting in 1957, rendered obsolete by the Anti-Ballistic Missile Treaty signed in 1972, and deactivated in 1974. It remains a stark reminder of the Cold War.

The loop going south offers a peaceful stroll on narrow paths—muddy after rains—showing off the vegetation and wildlife on the ridge in quiet detail. Hopefully someday you will be able to continue your hike south past the reservoir on the Bay Area Ridge Trail. The Friends of Sweeney Ridge group and the Pacific Trust were successful in making Sweeney Ridge part of the GGNRA.

If you end up hiking in the fog, you won't see much beyond white-tailed rabbits and wildflowers. Sometimes it gets so thick you can barely see 20 feet ahead. It is isolating and disorienting, so stay on the trails. The yellow line down Sneath Lane is a fog line painted to keep bikers and hikers from going off the edge. When you actually see it in fog, you totally understand its necessity.

The view from Sweeney Ridge with coastal scrub
MIGUEL VIEIRA (FLICKR.COM/PHOTOS/MIGUELVIEIRA/)

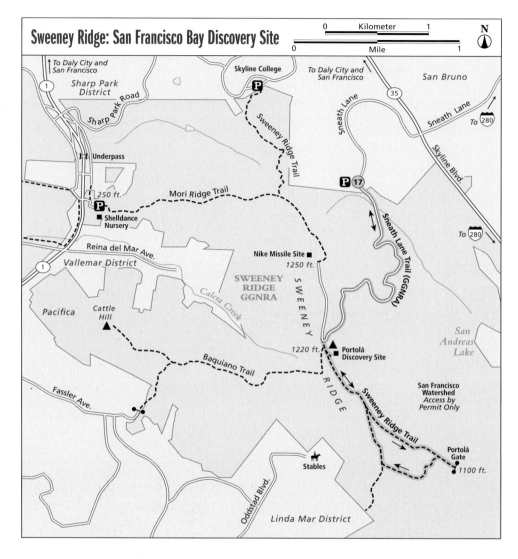

Sweeney Ridge: San Francisco Bay Discovery Site

Kilometer 0 1

Mile 0 1

N

To Daly City and San Francisco

Sharp Park District

Sharp Park Road

Skyline College

P

Sweeney Ridge Trail

To Daly City and San Francisco

San Bruno

Sneath Lane

35

Sneath Lane

To 280

Skyline Blvd.

Underpass

250 ft.

P

Mori Ridge Trail

P 17

Sneath Lane Trail (GGNRA)

To 280

Shelldance Nursery

Reina del Mar Ave.

Vallemar District

Nike Missile Site

1250 ft.

SWEENEY RIDGE GGNRA

Calera Creek

S W E E N E Y

San Andreas Lake

Pacifica

Cattle Hill

Baquiano Trail

1220 ft.

Portolá Discovery Site

San Francisco Watershed Access by Permit Only

Fassler Ave.

R I D G E

Sweeney Ridge Trail

Oddstad Blvd.

Stables

Portolá Gate

1100 ft.

Linda Mar District

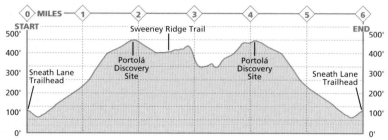

0 MILES 1 2 3 4 5 6

START

Sweeney Ridge Trail

END

500' 500'

400' 400'

Portolá Discovery Site

Portolá Discovery Site

300' Sneath Lane Trailhead

Sneath Lane Trailhead 300'

200' 200'

100' 100'

0' 0'

MILES AND DIRECTIONS

0.0 START at the gate at the main entrance to Sweeney Ridge. Get on the double-track, paved Sneath Lane. To the south is San Andreas Lake.

1.0 Fog line begins on the pavement, and the road gets steeper. A stand of eucalyptus grows near the top of the trail to the south.

1.7 At the top of the ridge, you get ocean views to the west on clear days. The double-track dirt trail is Sweeney Ridge Trail. Turning south (left facing the ocean), walk a short way to the Portolá monument on the left side of the trail. Return to the main trail and continue south on Sweeney Ridge Trail. Pass the Baquiano trailhead.

2.3 Come to a Bay Area Ridge Trail sign. Stay on Sweeney Ridge Trail past this single-track dirt trail, which goes to the horse stables at the end of Linda Mar Valley; you will return on this trail on the southwestern loop.

2.8 Just before the locked gate, turn right on single-track Sweeney Meadow Trail (may be unmarked). The trail rises and falls in scrub.

3.2 At the junction take the fork to the right, part of the Sweeney Horse Trail, which heads back to Sweeney Ridge Trail (left to horse stables).

3.6 Back on Sweeney Ridge Trail, turn left.

4.1 Turn right on Sneath Lane back down the hill.

5.8 Arrive back at the trailhead and parking lot.

Alternate routes: After heading south, extend your hike to 7.4 miles by going north past the junction with Sneath Lane on the Sweeney Ridge Trail toward Skyline College to see the abandoned Nike missile radar site (a graffiti–ed small building in disrepair with an interpretive sign), which is less than a mile from here.

Fog on Sweeney Ridge

18. SAN BRUNO MOUNTAIN STATE PARK: SUMMIT LOOP TRAIL

WHY GO?

San Bruno Mountain doesn't look like much at first glance, with cars on the Guadalupe Parkway speeding past. But though the sounds of urban white noise are unavoidable on the lower trails, this can be a highly enjoyable hike with incredible detail and stunning vistas. The mountain's ridgeline runs in an east–west configuration, with considerable slope and elevations ranging from 250 feet to 1,314 feet at the summit. A protected zone in Golden Gate National Recreation Area since 1983, the state park's 2,416 acres also serve as a model plan for conserving natural habitats in an ever-spreading metropolis.

THE RUN DOWN

Start: Picnic area parking lot near park entrance
Elevation gain: 690 feet
Distance: 3.8-mile loop/lollipop
Difficulty: Moderate due to elevation gain
Hiking time: About 2 hours
Seasons/schedule: 8 a.m. to sunset year-round
Fees and permits: Parking fee, cash only
Trail contact: San Bruno Mountain State and County Park, 555 Guadalupe Canyon Pkwy., Brisbane, CA, 94005; (650) 589-5708; http://

parks.smcgov.org/san-bruno -mountain-state-county-park
Dog-friendly: No dogs allowed
Trail surface: Paved path, single-track dirt trail, crossing paved service roads
Land status: State and county park
Nearest town: Daly City
Nat Geo TOPO! Map: San Francisco South, CA
Other trail users: Equestrians
Special considerations: Full facilities and a picnic area are at the trailhead. Dress in layers. Wear sunscreen.

FINDING THE TRAILHEAD

On US 101 take the Bayshore Boulevard/Brisbane exit. Drive south on Bayshore Boulevard to Guadalupe Canyon Parkway. Turn west on Guadalupe Canyon Parkway and drive uphill about 2 miles to the park entrance on the right side of the road.

On I-280 take the Mission Street exit. Head left (north) on Junipero Serra Boulevard. Turn right onto San Pedro Boulevard. San Pedro turns into East Market Street, and East Market Street turns into Guadalupe Canyon Parkway, which takes you eastward up the canyon. The park entrance is on your left toward the top of the hill.
GPS: N37 41.49' / W122 26.2'

WHAT TO SEE

When you look around San Bruno Mountain, you are seeing a slice of an ancient Bay Area, long before European settlement. In the Cretaceous period, 130 million years ago, this was all underwater. The earth's crust buckled in the region, creating fault blocks. One of the fault blocks was elevated, becoming San Bruno Mountain. For perhaps a thousand years, until the 1800s, Costanoan Indian tribes camped here seasonally, gathering seeds and plants for food, collecting materials for basketry, and hunting small game in the scrub. Tule elk and antelope fed on the grasses. Every few years the Indians set fire to the mountain in controlled burns to encourage new growth of grasses and to keep the scrub under control. A lot of the scrub you see today has replaced grasslands in the last twenty or so years.

Captain Bruno Heceta explored the western shore of the San Francisco Bay in 1775 for Spain. He named the largest landmass on that side of the peninsula Mount San Bruno, after his patron saint. By 1869 civilization surrounded the mountain, but no people lived on it. This was a saving factor for the native coyote brush, yarrow, and snowberries.

In the 1870s railroad baron and banker Charles Crocker acquired the property. After his death the Crocker Land Company leased or sold parcels of land for light industrial uses and mineral resources recovery. During the Cold War in the 1950s, the summit became home to a Nike missile early warning radar site. Ruins mark the location.

In the 1960s the urban tide threatened the mountain. Housing developers and industrialists started slugging it out with conservation groups, individual citizens, and

On the Bog Trail in San Bruno Mountain State Park
TIM ADAMS (FLICKR.COM/PHOTOS/36217981@N02)

View from San Bruno Mountain
DEEK SPEREDELOZZI, ADDICTED TO DIRT:
CONFESSIONS OF A BACK-COUNTRY JUNKIE
(WWW.DEEKADELIC.COM)

government agencies for the land. It wasn't until 1982 that the fight was settled with the creation of the San Bruno Mountain Habitat Conservation Plan.

Some areas around the mountain are designated for housing, but according to the conservation plan, construction and grading must occur at a time and in a way that protects endangered butterfly habitats, including those of the rare Mission blue butterfly, the San Bruno elfin butterfly, the Callippe silverspot butterfly, and the Bay checkerspot. Also, fourteen endangered plants survive here, including San Bruno Mountain manzanita,

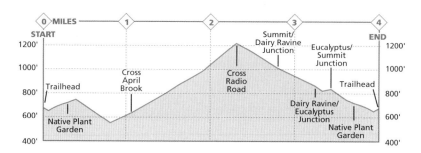

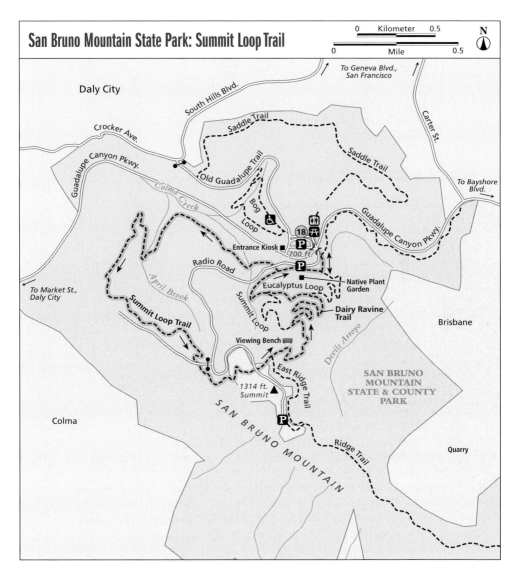

San Bruno Mountain State Park: Summit Loop Trail

Daly City

Crocker Ave.

South Hills Blvd.

Saddle Trail

Saddle Trail

Guadalupe Canyon Pkwy.

Carter St.

To Geneva Blvd., San Francisco

To Bayshore Blvd.

Old Guadalupe Trail

Colma Creek

Bog Loop

Entrance Kiosk

700 ft.

Native Plant Garden

Radio Road

April Brook

Eucalyptus Loop

Summit Loop

Dairy Ravine Trail

To Market St., Daly City

Summit Loop Trail

Guadalupe Canyon Pkwy.

Viewing Bench

East Ridge Trail

Devils Arroyo

Brisbane

1314 ft. Summit

Colma

SAN BRUNO MOUNTAIN STATE & COUNTY PARK

SAN BRUNO MOUNTAIN

Ridge Trail

Quarry

coast rock cress, Pacifica manzanita, and Franciscan wallflower. Along with the more sensitive species, the common raven and red-winged hawk, deer, and bush rabbits are pretty happy to have a home too.

A grassroots group called San Bruno Mountain Watch are stewards of the mountain, offer docent-led hikes, and work to remove invasive nonnative plants and maintain critical butterfly habitat. They sell native plants grown in a nearby nursery (www.mountain watch.org).

While listening to the song sparrows and meadowlarks along your hike, you can differentiate the coffeeberry, with its round little fruits in shades of maroon, from red elderberries, some growing into trees, with bunches of bright red berries. Enjoy the wonderful wildflower display in spring that includes wild coastal iris, orange California poppies, clumps of blue, cream, and lavender lupines, and pink checkerbloom. From February to April, start looking for those very special moths and butterflies.

At the top of the mountain, the magnificent vistas distract you from the unsightly antennae, satellite dishes, and service vehicles.

MILES AND DIRECTIONS

0.0 START at the picnic area parking lot near the park entrance. Facing the restrooms, turn right on the paved path and right (south) again at its end, following signs to Summit Loop Trail. Pass under the Guadalupe Canyon Parkway overpass to the main trailhead.

0.2 Reach the native plant demonstration garden and trailhead. Facing the sign, turn right (west) to start Summit Loop Trail. Continue on Summit Loop to the right (northwest) at the junction. Cross Radio Road (a service road for vehicles to the summit), staying on the single-track Summit Loop Trail. Pass coffeeberry and red elderberry in a diverse riparian creek side plant community. A wooden bridge crosses over April Brook.

0.5 The trail heads away from the street and begins a moderate climb on the northeast side of the mountain.

2.1 Cross over Radio Road again, continuing on the dirt Summit Loop Trail. To the southwest you can see Montara and San Pedro Mountains; to the northwest, Ocean Beach. Beyond is Rodeo Beach and Tennessee Point in the Marin Headlands and Mount Tamalpais. Nearby are San Bruno, Daly City, Colma, and South San Francisco.

2.4 Pass a green building and cross the service road once more to continue on Summit Loop Trail. At the junction with East Ridge Trail, continue straight (east) on Summit Loop Trail.

2.5 Take the short trail to your right for a great viewing point. Continue on Summit Loop Trail.

2.8 At the junction with the Dairy Ravine Trail, turn right (east) on Dairy Ravine.

3.2 At the intersection with Eucalyptus Trail, take the leg to the left (west), to pass through the eucalyptus grove.

3.5 Reach the Summit Loop trailhead. Stay right (east), heading back to the native plant garden.

3.6 Return to the garden and the upper parking lot. Go back the way you came on the sidewalk and paved trail under the Guadalupe Canyon Parkway.

3.8 Arrive back at the parking lot and picnic area.

Alternate routes: For a family hike, try the 0.8-mile Bog Trail (starting from the picnic area).

Bonus Hikes: San Francisco and the Bay

E. GOLDEN GATE PARK

WHY GO?

Golden Gate Park is green, lush, varied, and utterly man-made. In fact, it is one of the largest man-made parks in the world. The park runs from the Haight-Ashbury area to Ocean Beach, past the Sunset District. Near Kezar Stadium is the National AIDS Memorial Grove. Just west of the California Academy of Sciences are the Shakespeare Gardens, with flora chosen from lines in the bard's plays. Nearby are well-tended rose gardens. Across Martin Luther King Jr. Drive from the Shakespeare Gardens is the Strybing Arboretum. Some paved and some dirt trails take you through native plant life from around the world. You can stroll around Stow Lake while people paddle across on rented boats, and even cross a bridge onto Strawberry Island. West of Cross-Over Drive are numerous small lakes. At Spreckels, you can watch model yacht sailing, and at Lloyd Lake walk through the "Portals of the Past." Elk Glen Lake and North Lake have trails leading to them too. Ocean Beach makes a great destination point on a walk or run through the park. In the spring visit the Queen Wilhelmina Tulip Garden, famous for its 10,000 tulips and two windmills.

THE RUN DOWN

Start: National AIDS Memorial Grove on Bowling Green Drive, Golden Gate Park. GPS: N37 46.11' / W122 27.37'. (Can also start from many other places in the park.)
Elevation gain: 280 feet
Distance: Anything from 0.5-mile to 10-mile loops are possible
Difficulty: Easy
Hiking time: From 1 hour to all day
Seasons/schedule: 24 hours a day year-round
Fees and permits: None; fee to visit San Francisco Botanical Garden. (Note: Some street parking within Golden Gate Park has time limits.)

Trail contact: City of San Francisco Parks and Recreation; (415) 666-7200. Each attraction in the park has its own contact information; see https://goldengatepark.com.
Dog-friendly: Dogs on leash
Trail surface: Packed dirt trail, pavement, grass
Land status: City park
Nearest town: San Francisco
Nat Geo TOPO! Map: San Francisco North, CA
Other trail users: Bikers and Segways on paved paths

F. THE PRESIDIO: LOVERS' LANE AND THE ECOLOGY TRAIL

WHY GO?

There are so many wonderful ways to roam through the Presidio. From the memorable Presidio Visitor Center, go through the parade ground, passing the Walt Disney Museum to see a couple of the oldest cannons in North America (from the Spanish Empire) in Pershing Square and then the old Presidio chapel and the Presidio bowling alley. Lovers' Lane is a straight shot to the Presidio Gate. This was the path taken by soldiers to their lovers in the Mission District in the late 1800s.

At the end of Lovers' Lane is artist Andy Goldworthy's Wood Line, a must-see. It connects you to the Mountain Lake Trail. The park has trail maps that feature several of the artist's sculptures.

The Upper Ecology Trail takes you through woodlands of eucalyptus, cypress, and pines planted by soldiers in 1883, as well as hillsides and gardens of restored native plants. It's hard to believe this used to be simply dunes and bunch grass. El Polin, restored in 2011 on the Lower Ecology Trail, is said to be a spring of fertility. The vegetation it supports attracts many birds to the area.

Consider taking in the vista at Inspiration Point before you return to Funston Avenue and Officer's Row, dating back to the 1860s. You may also want to try the Batteries to Bluffs Trail for military history and great views of the Golden Gate Bridge.

THE RUN DOWN

Start: William Penn Mott Jr. Presidio Visitor Center, 210 Lincoln Blvd. (open 10 a.m. to 5 p.m. year-round). GPS: N37 48.7' /W122 27.25'
Elevation gain: 450 feet
Distance: From 1 mile to 4-plus miles
Difficulty: Easy
Hiking time: Varies
Seasons/schedule: Sunrise to sunset year-round
Fees and permits: Parking fee (or park outside the Presidio and walk in)
Trail contact: National Park Service, William Penn Mott Jr. Presidio Visitor Center, 210 Lincoln Blvd., San Francisco 94123; (415) 561-4323; www.nps.gov/prsf/index.htm
Dog-friendly: Dogs on leash
Trail surface: Wide gravel and dirt trail, some stairs, paved path and sidewalk
Land status: National recreation area
Nearest town: San Francisco
Nat Geo TOPO! Map: San Francisco North, CA
Other trail users: Bikers
Special considerations: Leave time to visit the Walt Disney Museum, go bowling, visit Crissy Fields or Fort Point, or walk across the Golden Gate Bridge.

SAN MATEO COUNTY COASTLINE

California boasts one of the most accessible coastlines in the world, and San Mateo County has a lot of it to explore. You can walk through dunes, along coastal bluffs full of lemon-yellow lupine, and on trails under windblown cypress trees.

In Pacifica, San Pedro Valley County Park offers rolling coastal hills and wildflowers, a seasonal waterfall, and mellow picnicking in an area that was once the winter camp for the Coast Miwok Indians. Above it, Montara Mountain invites a climb. Walking on a wide path of Montara granite through manzanita and Monterey pines, you enjoy almost continuous ocean views. The James V. Fitzgerald Marine Reserve at Moss Beach has the longest intertidal reef in California. Hundreds of marine animals hang out in the pools, and you can see them all. Combined with a walk on the bluffs, where rum was smuggled during Prohibition, it forms a great loop hike. Along the Coast Trail through Half Moon Beach, hikers can access more than five separate beaches and swim on hot summer days.

The little town of Pescadero, besides its artichoke and strawberry fields, has several great hikes nearby. Pescadero Marsh is host to migrating seabirds in the Pacific Flyway. Egrets, geese, ducks, and loons rest in the lagoon among the rushes and feast on fish and insects, readying to continue their journey. Across from the wetlands, harbor seals lounge on rocks by Pescadero Beach. Just inland, Butano State Park, the coast's best-kept secret, has creeks and alder trees, redwoods and oaks, wildflowers in spring, and mushrooms in winter. A little farther down the coast at Año Nuevo, visitors gawk at the hundreds of snorting elephant seals gathered to give birth, mate, and molt on the beach. In March and September, gray whales cruise by the coast on their semiannual migration. It is quite a sight to see one breach.

And for after hiking, all the way down the coast there are little coastal towns with friendly bed-and-breakfasts and great fresh fish restaurants with Pacific views. Can't beat that.

Sunset on Pescadero Beach

19. PESCADERO MARSH TRAIL

WHY GO?

In Pescadero Marsh's 360 acres of protected wetland, the trails are short but rich with life, including some 250 species of birds. You meander along a hill above North Pond and then follow marshes, creeks, lagoons, and levees. Look for a nesting site for herons, egrets, and cormorants in an old eucalyptus grove, and the "singing tree," a eucalyptus sprawled over the water that makes lovely sounds if you hold your ear up to one of its twisted branches. Interpretive signs entertain and educate along the way. The hike concludes with a walk on the dunes of Pescadero State Beach.

THE RUN DOWN

Start: Parking lot for Pescadero State Beach, across CA 1 from the marsh
Elevation gain: 200 feet
Distance: Up to 3-mile loop/lollipop
Difficulty: Easy
Hiking time: About 1.5 hours
Seasons/schedule: 8 a.m. to sunset year-round
Fees and permits: Parking fee
Trail contact: Pescadero State Beach (and Pescadero Marsh Natural Preserve), 95 Kelly Ave., Half Moon Bay 94019; (650) 726-8819; www .parks.ca.gov/?page_id=522; www .coastsidestateparks.org/pescadero-marsh-natural-preserve

Dog-friendly: No dogs allowed
Trail surface: Sand, single-track dirt trail, bridges
Land status: Natural preserve
Nearest town: Pescadero
Nat Geo TOPO! Map: San Gregorio, CA
Nat Geo Trails Illustrated Map: Skyline Boulevard #815
Other trail users: Hikers only
Special considerations: Beware of poison oak. Bring water and binoculars. Check the website for any trail closures due to winter flooding or overgrowth of flora. Be careful crossing CA 1 at the start of the hike.

FINDING THE TRAILHEAD

On CA 1, 14 miles south of Half Moon Bay, look for the sign for Pescadero State Beach. Turn west into the northernmost parking lot. **GPS:** N37 16.25' /W122 24.32'

WHAT TO SEE

Historically, wetlands like this were often viewed as wastelands. According to the old adage, being sold a piece of old swampland meant you were robbed. Agriculturally minded humans looked upon marshes like this, with their dry coarse plants, muddy unmanageable earth, and strong smell of methane, as nothing but acres of wasting decay. But consider that

The Sequoia Audubon Trail

it was in mud and slime like this that life was born. And those microscopic one-celled organisms, our evolutionary ancestors, are still here, coexisting with complex creatures that have evolved over hundreds of millions of years. This is a very special ecosystem.

Ninety percent of California's wetlands are around the San Francisco Bay and estuary, but over 90 percent of the salt marshes around the bay have been filled in. Organizations like the Trust for Public Land purchase and preserve as much prime habitat along the Pacific Flyway as they can. It's a battle. Yet the wetlands provide even more than vital nesting and feeding areas for wildlife. They act as giant sponges that help regulate winter flood-waters, refill underwater aquifers, filter pollutants from runoff, and improve water quality.

Along with the 250 species of birds here (www.inaturalist.org/places/pescadero -marsh-natural-preserve), more than fifty species of mammals, thirteen kinds of rep-tiles and amphibians, and 300 varieties of plant life call this home. Look for blue her-ons, snowy egrets, and white-faced ibis, among other birds. Many of them can survive nowhere else but in wetland areas, which are only 10 percent of what they were before Europeans settled here (from 4 million acres down to some 450,000 acres in California).

In and around the marsh are several endangered animals, including the red-legged frog, salt marsh harvest mouse, and San Francisco garter snake. The western aquatic garter snake and the elusive western pond turtle keep the many migrating and local waterfowl company. There are interpretive signs along the trail to help you identify features. You'll undoubtedly see animals around the eucalyptus grove on the Sequoia Audubon Trail. The plants on this watery ground grow quickly, sometimes cutting off the end of this

Pescadero Beach

trail. But there are additional trails to explore, accessed from different trailheads (see "Alternate routes" on page 112).

Pescadero Marsh includes not just marsh but sand dunes, tidal flats, and rolling hills. The freshwater streams—Pescadero Creek and Butano Creek—meet in the lagoon and flow into the sea.

In geologic terms the brackish marsh is a baby (the word *brackish* refers to a blend of fresh and salt waters). Fifteen thousand years ago, neither it nor the beach was here. The ocean was 300 feet lower, the coastline 15 miles farther west. Glacial melting later caused the sea level to rise, flooding the depression at Pescadero Valley and forming a marsh about 6,500 years ago.

Crossing under the highway bridge, you walk on the nearly 40-foot-high Pescadero sand dunes, formed from 5,000 to 3,000 years ago by drifting sand. Plants here have grown tough, impervious to the strong sun and salty air. Low to the ground, they avoid the harsh winds and keep the hillsides together.

On the beach, surf scoters crush bottom-dwelling shellfish with their thick beaks. Sanderlings scurry after the waves, searching the wet sand for small bits of food. The endangered snowy plover also nests on this beach, laying its eggs in low depressions in

WHAT IS A WETLAND?

A wetland is an area saturated or covered by water for at least part of the year. There are five major types: marine, estuarine, lacustrine, riverine, and palustrine. Marine and estuarine wetlands are connected to the ocean and include coastal wetlands, such as tidal marshes. Lacustrine wetlands are found around lakes. Riverine wetlands are associated with rivers and streams. Palustrine wetlands include marshes, swamps, and bogs and may be isolated or connected to wet areas.

the sand. Just offshore, parallel to the bridge, a crowd of lazy harbor seals often lie against the contours of the rocks, basking in the sun.

Consider visiting the delightful town of Pescadero after your hike.

MILES AND DIRECTIONS

0.0 START from the northernmost parking lot for Pescadero State Beach. Cross the highway (carefully) to single-track dirt North Pond Trail, which ascends up the ridge.

0.1 Pass an interpretive sign with pictures of some of the animals in the area; continue on.

0.6 Come to an observation platform.

0.7 Cross the North Pond bridge to connect with Sequoia Audubon Trail. Follow Sequoia Audubon between CA 1 and the creek.

0.8 At the junction continue east on Sequoia Audubon Trail, away from the ocean (you will take the western trail on the way back to the Pescadero dunes and beach).

1.0 Continue on Sequoia Audubon Trail east, following the creek.

1.2 Pass a eucalyptus grove along the trail.

1.5 Take the short loop that ends Sequoia Audubon Trail and return the way you came. This is the lollipop portion of the loop.

2.1 Turn left on trail, an unmarked section of the Sequoia Audubon Trail, pass a seasonal pond, and then turn right to walk through the scrub along the bluff.

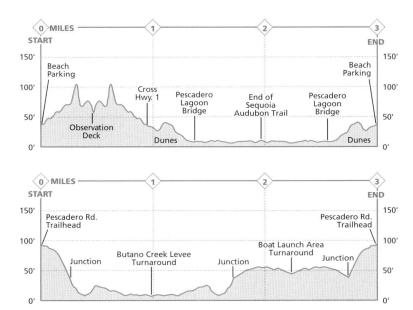

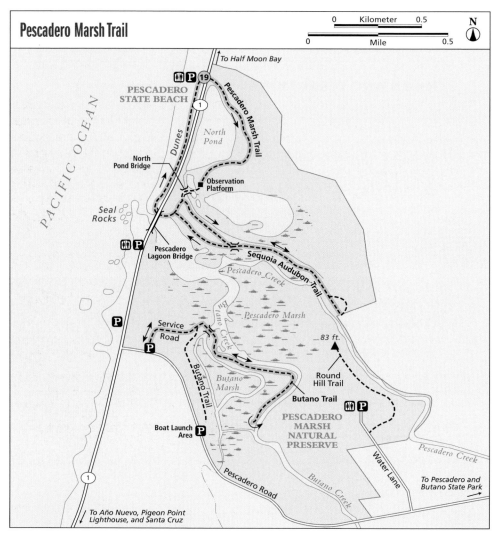

Pescadero Marsh Trail

0 Kilometer 0.5

0 Mile 0.5

N

To Half Moon Bay

PESCADERO STATE BEACH

Pescadero Marsh Trail

19

1

North Pond

Dunes

North Pond Bridge

Observation Platform

PACIFIC OCEAN

Seal Rocks

Pescadero Lagoon Bridge

Sequoia Audubon Trail

Pescadero Creek

Pescadero Marsh

Butano Creek

Service Road

83 ft.

Butano Marsh

Round Hill Trail

Butano Trail

PESCADERO MARSH NATURAL PRESERVE

Boat Launch Area

Pescadero Creek

Water Lane

1

Pescadero Road

Butano Creek

To Pescadero and Butano State Park

To Año Nuevo, Pigeon Point Lighthouse, and Santa Cruz

2.3 Turn left and follow the sandy path to the beach and pass under the highway. Walk along the dunes and beach.

3.0 Arrive back at the parking lot.

Alternate routes: If you want to see more of the wetlands, you can take the Butano Trail on the levees through the marsh (although part of it will be completely blocked with wildflowers in summer). The trailhead is off Pescadero Creek Road, just east of the junction with the highway.

The Round Hill Trail follows Pescadero Creek as it flows into the marsh. The trailhead is on Water Lane, north of Pescadero Creek Road and 1.6 miles east of CA 1.

20. BUTANO STATE PARK

WHY GO?

In the secluded wilderness of 3,560-acre Butano State Park, you have the opportunity to walk miles under pillared groves of coastal redwoods. As a matter of fact, most of this hike is under the shade of trees that insulate you from the outside world. Stop on numerous wooden bridges to admire cascading and gurgling creeks. Take in views from the contrasting high ridges among dry manzanita and knobcone pines. There you see an unforgettable picture of the densely wooded Santa Cruz Mountains before the sweeping Pacific Ocean. The camping here is great, the crowds minimal.

THE RUN DOWN

Start: Six Bridges trailhead
Elevation gain: 650 feet
Distance: 8.3-mile loop
Difficulty: Moderate
Hiking time: About 4.5 hours
Seasons/schedule: Sunrise to sunset year-round
Fees and permits: Parking fee
Trail contact: Butano State Park, 1500 Cloverdale Rd., Pescadero 94060; (650) 879-2040; www.parks.ca.gov/?page_id=536
Dog-friendly: No dogs allowed on trails

Trail surface: Single- and double-track dirt trail, many wooden bridges crossing creeks
Land status: State park
Nearest town: Pescadero
Nat Geo TOPO! Map: Franklin Point, CA
Nat Geo Trails Illustrated Map: Skyline Boulevard #815; Big Basin, Santa Cruz #816
Other trail users: Equestrians and mountain bikers on Butano Fire Road only

FINDING THE TRAILHEAD

 On CA 1 (Cabrillo Highway) turn east (inland) on Pescadero Creek Road. In 2.5 miles turn right (south) on Cloverdale Road. Watch for a sign for Butano and take a left into the main entrance. Past the kiosk, go to the next parking area you see on your right, where there are picnic tables, barbecues, and restrooms. Look for the Six Bridges trailhead. **GPS:** N37 12.12' / W122 20.15'

WHAT TO SEE

Butano, according to Native American lore, means "drinking cup" or "a gathering place for friendly visits." The park lends itself to just that, fantastic for day hikes or overnight camping.

Butano's second-generation redwoods and mature Douglas fir trees survived because of the canyons that made them hard to remove. The mother redwoods, some 500 or even

Wildflowers in Butano

1,000 years old, were not so lucky. They provided good revenue for families during the post–gold rush growth spurt of Northern California.

The natives we know as the Butanoans—their tribal names were lost when Spain colonized the area—lived in the valley but rarely ventured into the forest of giants. They had spiritual and practical reasons to avoid it. They felt a "presence" among the trees, concluding that the redwoods hosted powerful spirits and were not to be disturbed. (Some hikers say those spirits are alive and well.) The canopy's shadow does not allow for the growth of many edible and usable plants, so they had little motivation to go into the woods.

There are a few signs of past human inhabitants visible on this hike. An abandoned landing field sits on top of the Butano Fire Road. The county used it for fire suppression. In the 1860s the Jackson family occupied the north side of the canyon, known as Jackson Flats. Descendants of the European settlers continued to live in the canyon until the State of California purchased the land and dedicated the park in 1961.

Forged by nature and the presence of man, Butano contains a diverse range of habitats, each with its own community of plant life and wildlife. This loop hike gives you a taste of all the different environments and is a great introduction to the park.

Starting on Six Bridges Trail from the picnic area, you'll crisscross a feeder creek lined with chalky-barked alder trees. Beneath are stinging nettles, dogwood, willow, and lots of different berry bushes providing shelter for insects, reptiles, and small mammals.

Around the ranger station is open grassland, dominated by coyote brush and bush lupine, with its purple flowers in spring. Blue-eyed grass and yellow coastal suncups grow among them. This is where you are most likely to spot the larger mammals in the park: black-tailed deer, bobcats, coyotes, and rabbits. This area and the chaparral on the upper slopes are the most popular hunting grounds for peregrine falcons. (During summer and off-season weekends, the nature center offers insights about what you see along the trail.)

The Jackson Flats Trail takes you into redwood groves. Some of the trees damaged by fire over the last 150 years have caves in their wide bases, providing homes for bats. Huckleberries top the wide stumps of fallen trees. You share the trail with slow-moving banana slugs (in late spring you'll see hundreds) and California newts. Blooming from February to April is the park's star attraction, the purple calypso orchid. The Little Butano Creek Trail shows off the redwoods the best, with ferns and clover around the pretty cascading creek.

Redwoods in Butano

The top of Jackson Flats and Butano Fire Road are bathed in sunlight; the path is sandstone. The chaparral consists of long-needled knobcone pines, scrub oaks, and manzanita. Indian paintbrush provides dabs of red-orange in the springtime landscape.

On Goat Hill you go through a section of tan bark oak woodland. Stay on the path to avoid poison oak. Enjoy the sight of bright orange chanterelles—thick fluted gourmet mushrooms—and honeysuckle among the berry bushes where chickadees and warblers whistle spring tunes.

MILES AND DIRECTIONS

0.0 START at the Six Bridges trailhead in the picnic area, about 20 yards east of restrooms. A single-track dirt trail leads back to the park entrance, crossing over one of the six bridges on the trail. (*Note:* Be careful of poison oak.) The trail splits; take the fork to the right.

0.1 Come to the bat habitat. Turn left for a quick detour to see it. Return to Six Bridges Trail.

0.2 Turn left, continuing on Six Bridges Trail. Cross the first two bridges.

0.3 At the trailhead for Año Nuevo Trail, turn right and cross the creek to stay on Six Bridges Trail.

0.4 Cross the road to the nature center and Jackson Flats Trail, a narrow, single-track trail that serpentines moderately uphill.

1.2 At the trailhead for Mill Ox Trail, stay on Jackson Flats Trail.

1.4 Pass a marsh on your left. (*Note:* Watch out for newts in this area, especially in February and March.)

2.7 At the trailhead for Canyon Trail, stay on Jackson Flats Trail, bearing left. There's one steep grade toward the top.

3.0 Reach the top of the ridge. Views open up to the Pacific Ocean beyond the densely wooded Santa Cruz foothills.

3.2 Trailhead for Butano Fire Roa, a double-track, multiuse fire road. Turn left onto Butano Fire Road.

3.7 Pass the ruins of an old cabin on your right. Land to the north along Big Butano Creek is still privately owned.

4.7 Trailhead for Mill Ox Trail. Turn left onto the single-track dirt trail going downhill. (*Note:* Trail is steep in some sections.) The route follows an old logging skid trail.

4.9 Cross over Jackson Flats Trail, staying on Mill Ox Trail.

5.2 Come to Little Butano Creek and a picnic table. Take the bridge across the creek to the paved main park road. Stay on the same side of the street, turn left, and walk about 150 yards to the trailhead for Little Butano Creek Trail to the left. Turn left onto the hikers-only, single-track dirt trail. The creek is on the left. Cross the bridge again; the trail widens to double-track. Cross over several more bridges, following the creek.

6.0 A social trail to the left follows a feeder creek with a 5-foot cascade during the wet season just off the main trail. Continue on Little Butano Creek Trail. The trail soon starts to climb to the pump house, above the creek to the left.

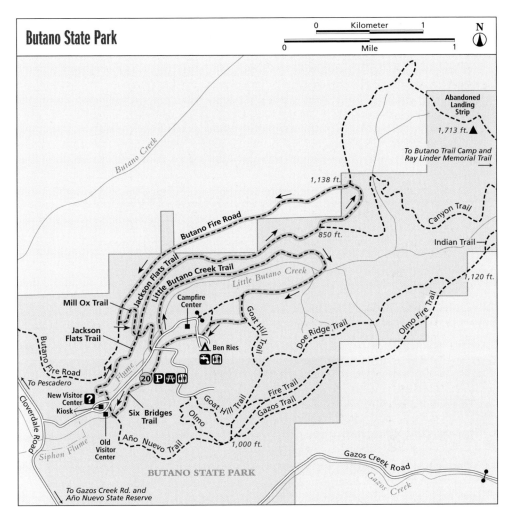

Butano State Park

0 Kilometer 1

0 Mile 1

N

Abandoned Landing Strip

1,713 ft. ▲

To Butano Trail Camp and Ray Linder Memorial Trail →

Butano Creek

1,138 ft.

Butano Fire Road

Canyon Trail

850 ft.

Indian Trail →

Jackson Flats Trail

Little Butano Creek Trail

Little Butano Creek

1,120 ft.

Mill Ox Trail

Campfire Center

Goat Hill Trail

Doe Ridge Trail

Olmo Fire Trail

Jackson Flats Trail

Ben Ries

Butano Fire Road

To Pescadero

Flume

20 P A

Fire Trail

New Visitor Center

Kiosk ?

Six Bridges Trail

Goat Hill Trail

Gazos Trail

Olmo

Cloverdale Road

Siphon Flume

Old Visitor Center

Año Nuevo Trail

1,000 ft.

Gazos Creek Road

BUTANO STATE PARK

Gazos Creek

To Gazos Creek Rd. and Año Nuevo State Reserve

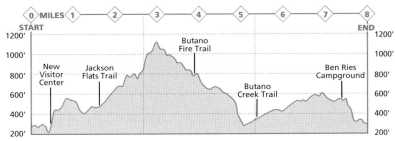

0 MILES 1 2 3 4 5 6 7 8

START END

1200' 1200'

1000' 1000'

800' 800'

600' 600'

400' 400'

200' 200'

New Visitor Center

Jackson Flats Trail

Butano Fire Trail

Butano Creek Trail

Ben Ries Campground

6.7 Little Butano Creek Trail merges into dirt Pump House Road, which intersects with the main park road (gravel and dirt here). Go uphill on Pump House Road.

7.0 Turn left onto single-track Goat Hill Trail.

7.2 Turn right onto the trail to Ben Reis Campground.

7.4 When the trail splits, continue left to the campground. Pass the walk-in campsites and take the stairs up to the campground loop road. Turn left, past campsites 16, 15, and counting down. Continue downhill on the paved campground road.

7.6 Pass a sign for the campground host, then watch for a sign to the Campfire Center. Turn left onto the trail.

7.7 Arrive at the Campfire Center. Before reaching the campfire stage, look for the Six Bridges trailhead. Take Six Bridges Trail through a mixed woodland. Watch for another seasonal pond. After one bridge, cross a gravel and dirt fire road and continue on now single-track Six Bridges Trail on the other side. The creek separates you from the paved main park road on the right. Pass by the employee residence, continuing on Six Bridges Trail to where the trail splits; go right.

8.3 Arrive back at the picnic area and parking lot.

Alternate routes: A fun family hike is on Little Butano Creek Trail, which leads 1.5 miles into the heart of the park's redwoods.

Inside a fire-damaged live redwood on the Little Butano Creek Trail

21. **AÑO NUEVO STATE PARK**

WHY GO?

For a truly unique experience, take this easy hike (self-guided or with a docent) through scrub-lined coastal bluffs, dunes, and flower-speckled grasslands to watch giant, molting elephant seals bask on beaches, visible from viewpoints along the trail. You'll see migrating birds and other sea mammals invading a nineteenth-century lighthouse. The human history is rich here too, with a shipwreck, midden sites of the Quiroste Indians who lived peacefully here for thousands of years, an 1862 dairy farm, and more.

THE RUN DOWN

Start: Parking lot of Año Nuevo State Park
Elevation gain: Negligible
Distance: 3-mile loop/lollipop
Difficulty: Easy
Hiking time: About 2.5 hours
Seasons/schedule: Best in April through November for viewing elephant seals; 8:30 a.m. to sunset year-round
Fees and permits: Parking fee; visitor permits free
Trail contact: Año Nuevo State Park Año Nuevo State Park, 1 New Years Creek Rd., Pescadero 94060; (650) 879-2025 or (650) 879-0227 (recorded park info); www.parks.ca.gov/?page_id=523
Dog-friendly: No dogs allowed

Trail surface: Loose sand and some rocks
Land status: State reserve
Nearest town: Pescadero
Nat Geo TOPO! Map: Point Ano Nuevo, CA
Nat Geo Trails Illustrated Map: Big Basin, Santa Cruz #816
Other trail users: Hikers only
Special considerations: Elephant seals can be observed here year-round either on a docent-led tour or through a self-guided hike. If self-guided, you must obtain your free visitor permit from the entrance station between 8:30 a.m. and 3:30 p.m. The wildlife viewing area is closed December 1 through December 14.

FINDING THE TRAILHEAD

From the San Francisco Bay Bridge, take US 101 South to I-280 South to scenic CA 1 South. Año Nuevo State Reserve is located on CA 1 between Santa Cruz and Half Moon Bay, about 1.5 hours south of San Francisco. Reserve signs are located on the highway in both directions. (Some people miss the brown signs. Be alert about 27 miles south of Half Moon Bay and 20 miles north of Santa Cruz.) Turn right into the parking lot of Año Nuevo State Park where you will find restrooms and drinking water. Signs direct you to the visitor center where you begin your hike.
GPS: N37 7.11' /W122 18.27'

Cove Beach and an elephant seal

WHAT TO SEE

Ah, the sound of the surf crashing against rocks, the squawk of seagulls, the wind whistling in the dunes . . . burps, gurgles, farts, and growls. No, it's not an out-of-hand beach party. These are the sounds of the Point of the New Year: Año Nuevo, the most popular beach on the West Coast—for northern elephant seals. Here the blubbery animals take a break from cruising the Pacific to breed, give birth, and molt.

How much fun can you have watching apathetic 2.5-ton creatures fighting, lusting, sleeping, losing skin, and flipping sand over themselves? A lot. It's a rare thing to be able to observe animals in their natural habitat without disturbing them. Elephant seals were almost entirely wiped out by hunting and disease, but slowly their population has been growing, thanks to this preserve.

Inside the wildlife protection area, you may also see harbor seals, California sea otters, and Steller sea lions, as well as many species of birds.

The Point of the New Year was seen and named by Father Antonio de la Ascension, chaplain for the Spanish maritime explorer Don Sebastian Viscaino, on January 3, 1603. Before the Spaniards arrived, the native Quroste people, a group of coastal Ohlone Indians, lived and fished on this shore for 12,000 years. On the beaches you can still see remnants of their ancient shell mounds that served as both compost heaps and burial grounds.

The elephant seals have chosen a dramatic setting: sandy, flower-covered bluffs with scurrying rabbits and songbirds, cresting dunes, beaches that sparkle with mica, and fields of coastal plants like sand lupine and arroyo willow. Look closely because this place will be different the next time you visit. The dunes are constantly changing.

On the other side of a channel, you can see Año Nuevo Island, where today the seals live communally with sea lions and seabirds in a lovely old Victorian house built in 1904 for a resident lighthouse keeper. Between 1880 and 1920, hundreds of wooden-hulled steam schooners sailed the West Coast in dangerous conditions to haul lumber, farm products, and passengers between growing coastal towns. The federal government bought the island in 1870 and built a five-story lighthouse to help put an end to shipwrecks in the area. But still, the schooner *Point Arena* wrecked at Pigeon Point in 1913. Some of the wreckage drifted to the beach at Año Nuevo and was uncovered by storm waves in 1983. You can see part of the bow near the Año Nuevo Point Trail.

In early December the male elephant seals arrive for mating. The 5,000-pound bulls battle it out to determine dominance. They throw back their heads and make deep sounds called "clap-threats" with their long noses (inflatable "proboscis"). Only 10 percent of the males actually get to mate, so they learn even as pups how to chest butt on the beach.

Fossils in the rocks on Cove Beach

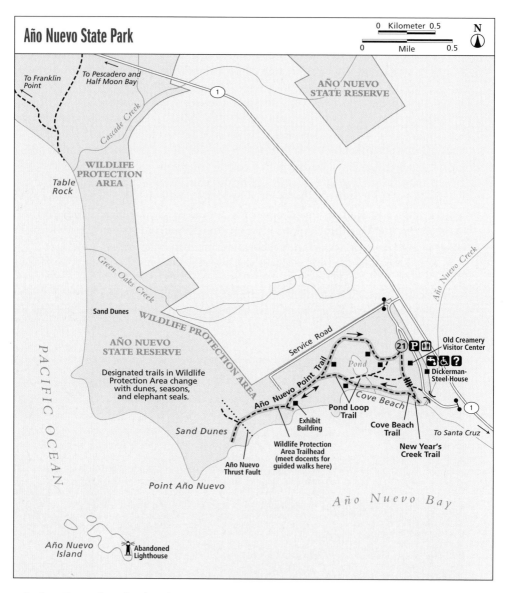

Año Nuevo State Park

In late December the females arrive to form "harems." Females, pregnant from the previous year, give birth to a single pup within three to five days of arriving. The mother vocalizes to the newborn pup, so it will know her voice and be able to identify its mother among the hundreds of seals on the beach. If they are separated, there is a chance they won't come back together, and the pup will starve.

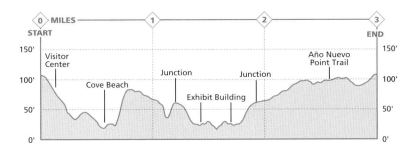

The molting season is April to May for females and juveniles, May to June for subadult males, and July to August for adult males. From September through November is the "juvenile haul-out," when the "teenage" seals dominate the beach.

MILES AND DIRECTIONS

0.0 START from the parking lot and follow signs to the visitor center. If taking the guided hike, rangers will tell you where to meet. Take the Año Nuevo Point Trail, which goes back toward the parking lot and bends left at the trailhead.

0.7 Junction with Pond Loop Trail. Turn right, staying on Año Nuevo Point Trail to an exhibit building.

1.0 Come to the exhibit building (with information on seals and sea lions). This is the entrance to the wildlife protection area. You must obtain a permit to enter the area. For the next 0.5 mile, hike dunes and beach among the elephant seals. (***Note:*** Stay 25 feet away from the animals.)

1.2 Reach Lawrence of Arabia Dune, the largest in Año Nuevo.

1.5 Cross Año Nuevo Thrust Fault, a branch of the San Gregorio Fault Zone. There's a view of Año Nuevo Island and the abandoned lighthouse cottage. Keep a lookout for the bow of the shipwrecked schooner Point Arena. There are several branches of trail here, only a few hundred feet long, providing different views of the seals' beach. Go back the way you came to exit.

2.0 Back at the exhibit building, retrace your steps on Año Nuevo Point Trail to a junction with Pond Loop Trail.

2.3 Turn right on Pond Loop Trail.

2.4 Turn right on Cove Beach Trail to Cove Beach. Continue on Cove Beach and cross over New Year's Creek.

2.7 Turn inland to New Year's Creek Trail.

3.0 Arrive back at the visitor center parking lot.

22. MCNEE RANCH AT MONTARA STATE BEACH

WHY GO?

McNee Ranch State Park (625 acres), adjacent to Montara State Beach, Gray Whale Cove State Beach, and Montara Mountain, offers a hillside climb with views and two short walks to caramel-colored beaches with wild, seething surfs. A stroll on the bluffs above the Cabrillo Highway, with glorious Pacific views, takes you to the historic McNee Ranch, in the shade of Monterey cypress and Monterey pine trees. Prepare to use those calves as you ascend both moderate and strenuous grades to the top of Montara Mountain (1,898 feet).

THE RUN DOWN

Start: Gray Whale Cove State Beach parking lot
Elevation gain: 1,650 feet
Distance: 8.1 miles out and back with a loop in the middle
Difficulty: Mostly moderate, strenuous on steep uphill sections
Hiking time: About 4.5 hours
Seasons/schedule: 8 a.m. to sunset year-round
Fees and permits: None
Trail contact: Montara State Beach; (650) 726-8819; www.parks.ca .gov/?page_id=532; and Golden Gate National Recreation Area, Bldg. 201, Fort Mason, San Francisco 94123-0022; (415) 561-4700; www.nps.gov/goga/rcdt.htm
Dog-friendly: Dogs on leash (allowed also on Montara Beach, but not Gray Whale Cove)
Trail surface: Sand and stairs to beach; single-track dirt trail through McNee Ranch, dirt fire road and broken pavement with some steep

portions. Trail floor becomes granite rock, then dirt and gravel at the top of Montara Mountain.
Land status: State park and state beach
Nearest town: Pacifica
Nat Geo TOPO! Map: Montara Mountain, CA
Nat Geo Trails Illustrated Map: Skyline Boulevard #815
Other trail users: Equestrians and mountain bikers
Special Consideration: Bring plenty of water as there are virtually no facilities. Leave time to hang out at Gray Whale Cove or Montara State Beaches after your hike. Gray Whale Cove State Beach's north side, separated from the main beach by a large pile of rocks, is clothing-optional. Be aware that the stables and farms in the area are working operations. Don't approach the animals without permission.

FINDING THE TRAILHEAD

The Gray Whale Cove parking lot is 3 miles south of the last stoplight in Pacifica (Linda del Mar) on CA 1 (8 miles north of Half Moon Bay). Parking is on the left-hand (east) side of the road. Signs read "McNee Ranch." There is more parking 0.5 mile down CA 1 at Montara State Beach. **GPS:** N37 33.47' / W122 30.46'

WHAT TO SEE

This hike starts with an optional venture down the wooden-railed steps to the small but dramatic Gray Whale Cove. Until 2001 Gray Whale was known as Devil's Slide Beach, named for the Devil's Slide area where rock slides onto CA 1 have taken out vehicles and blocked the road many times.

Why are slides so common here? The sparkling, camel-colored Montara Mountain granite, which makes up part of the floor and walls of the North Peak Trail, meets Paleocene sediments in the area, causing a crumbling effect. There's also the Pacific Ocean, wearing away the land's edge.

After enjoying the ocean view from the Gray Whale Cove Trail, a shaded road between rows of mature cypress and Monterey pines brings you to the flat valley of McNee Ranch. The bridge to the stables stretches over Martini Creek. Before the ranch days, Native Americans hunted and picked berries here, and in 1769 Don Gaspar de Portolá's scouting party camped here as they trekked north to discover the San Francisco Bay.

Claiming the area under an 1839 Mexican land grant, prominent San Franciscans Francisco Guerrero, one of the early mayors of San Francisco, and rancher Tiburcio Velasquez brought cattle to graze these hillsides. Their Rancho Corral de Tierra grant

Gray Whale Cove State Beach
TONY WEBSTER (FLICKR.COM/
PHOTOS/87296837@N00/25074275306)

View from Montara Mountain
MIGUEL VIEIRA (FLICKR.COM/PHOTOS/MIGUELVIEIRA/)

was the last privately held remnant of a Mexican-era land grant on the San Francisco peninsula. Saved by the Peninsula Open Space Trust (POST), the Golden Gate National Recreation Area (GGNRA) took it over in 2005. It contains four watersheds and one day could connect most of this coast by hiking trails. According to the GGNRA, the dramatic ascent of Montara Mountain from the sea to nearly 2,000 feet in just over 1 mile is not duplicated anywhere else in the park system, and in few other places on the California coast.

After California entered the Union in 1848, roads and railroads traversed McNee Ranch, opening up the coast to development; remnants, including the broken pavement on Old San Pedro Road, can be seen here. McNee Ranch became part of the empire of Duncan McNee, an early California land baron. During World War II the US Army moved onto the ranch, using it as a training ground. You can still see two of the bunkers.

The drought-tolerant natural grasses and chaparral on Montara Mountain act like superglue, holding the slopes together against erosion. The plant community changes subtly as you gain elevation. At the lower elevations, you find

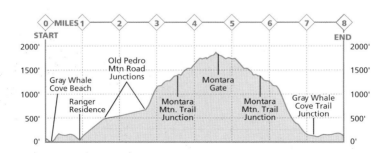

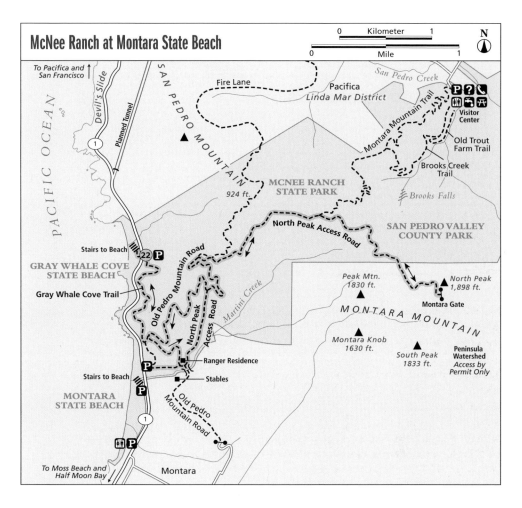

coastal scrub: coast sagebrush, seaside daisy, Pacific blackberry, and coast buckwheat. Next up is coastal chaparral, comprising of pink- and white-flowered manzanita (including the unique Montara manzanita), blue ceanothus, fuchsia, coffeeberry, and chinquapin. The marine chaparral at the highest elevation, consisting of manzanita, salal, and lupine, grows only in this location on the San Mateo coast. Native vegetation includes the endangered Hickman's cinquefoil, as well as San Francisco gumplant, Montara bush lupine, coast and San Francisco wallflowers, and coast rock cress.

The biodiversity on the mountain supports endangered wildlife such as the peregrine falcon, San Bruno elfin butterfly, San Francisco garter snake, and California red-legged frog.

In the late winter bring binoculars to spot gray whales in the Pacific on their migration north. Watch for Anna's and ruby-throated hummingbirds hovering to feed from sticky monkeyflowers in summer and berry blossoms anytime of year. Besides a healthy raptor population, large black ravens may be present, adding a Poe–like eeriness on foggy days. Look for tracks of coyotes, foxes, bobcats, deer, raccoons, and brush rabbits on the trail.

MILES AND DIRECTIONS

0.0 START in the parking lot across the street from Gray Whale Cove State Beach. Cross the street carefully to visit the cove. (***Note:*** Part of Gray Whale Cove Beach is clothing optional.) Turn right past a green shack and restrooms to a staircase that leads to the beach.

0.3 Arrive at Gray Whale Cove Beach. Come back up the stairs, retracing your steps. Cross the highway carefully.

0.6 Come to the trailhead at the south end of the parking lot for McNee Ranch, across from Gray Whale Cove State Beach. An interpretive sign with a park map marks the start of single-track Gray Whale Cove Trail. (***Note:*** Trail can get flooded after rain.)

1.2 Viewing bench on the bluff.

1.8 Turn left on the paved North Peak Access Road.

1.9 Pass the ranger residence and bridge to the stables. Go through a gate, starting uphill on double-track, dirt North Peak Access Road.

2.4 The trail splits; stay right on North Peak Access Road past unmarked Old Pedro Mountain Road to San Pedro Mountain. Trail becomes a maintained dirt fire road.

3.3 Stay right, continuing on North Peak Access Road to the top of Montara Mountain. The trail to the left is Montara Mountain Trail to San Pedro Valley County Park.

4.4 Arrive at the North Peak of Montara Mountain (1,898 feet). Beyond this point a gate blocks the fire road, which continues on permit-only San Francisco Water Department (SFPUC) Watershed. (***Note:*** For the last two decades, outdoor activists have attempted to open this, the Whiting Ridge Trail, sometimes called "Sweeney to the Sea Trail," to connect the entire mid-peninsula for hikers.) Note the repeater stations on the peak (used for relaying signals from cellular phones, radios, etc.). Return the same way down North Peak Access Road.

5.5 Pass Montara Mountain Trail again, staying on North Peak Access Road.

6.4 After about 0.1 mile of broken paved trail, turn right, due west, onto a single-track, dirt trail marked by two wooden posts on either side of the path. This is Old Pedro Mountain Road Trail. The path widens, then becomes single-track again. There are steep downhill sections. Follow the trail to Gray Whale Cove Trail.

7.2 Junction with Gray Whale Cove Trail. Turn right to head to the parking lot across from Gray Whale Cove State Beach.

8.1 Arrive back at the parking lot.

Alternate routes: Park at the Montara Mountain (Top of Mountain) trailhead parking lot and start at North Peak Access Road for a shorter hike to the peak.

23. JAMES V. FITZGERALD MARINE RESERVE: THE TIDE POOL LOOP

WHY GO?

The time of the low tide determines whether you walk along coastal bluffs first, with terrific Pacific views, or along sandy shores, with the longest intertidal reef in California to explore. These unforgettable tide pools are full of sea life, from urchins to octopi. On the bluff, you pass through a grove of old, tall cypress trees, shaped by the salty winds. Walks along Beach Way and Ocean Boulevard take you to the locals' favorite haunt (which is haunted itself), Moss Beach Distillery, along the cliffs to Ross Cove and the fishing harbor of Pillar Point.

THE RUN DOWN

Start: James V. Fitzgerald Marine Reserve Information Center and parking lot, corner of California and North Lake Streets
Elevation gain: 150 feet
Distance: 4.8-mile loop
Difficulty: Moderate due to return loop along beach through sand
Hiking time: About 2.5 hours
Seasons/schedule: Best at low tide; 8 a.m. to sunset year-round
Fees and permits: None
Trail contact: James V. Fitzgerald Marine Reserve, 200 Nevada Ave., Moss Beach 94038; (650) 728-3584; www.fitzgeraldreserve.org; http:// parks.smcgov.org/fitzgerald-marine -reserve

Dog-friendly: No dogs allowed on beach; dogs on leash on the bluff
Trail surface: Single-track dirt trail, paved road, paved trail, 2 miles on sandy and rocky beach
Land status: Marine reserve
Nearest town: Moss Beach
Nat Geo TOPO! Map: Montara Mountain, CA
Nat Geo Trails Illustrated Map: Skyline Boulevard #815
Other trail users: Hikers only on beach (no restrictions on bluffs)
Special considerations: It's important to check tide information before going. Go to www.fitzgerald reserve.org/newffmrsite/lowtides/ or call the park.

FINDING THE TRAILHEAD

 Take CA 1 (Cabrillo Highway) to Moss Beach. Turn west on California Street (follow signs for the marine reserve). Turn right at the end of California Street onto North Lake Avenue and immediately right into the parking lot on the corner. **GPS:** N37 31.27' / W122 30.58'

WHAT TO SEE

This stretch of coastline was officially protected as a reserve in 1969 and named James V. Fitzgerald Marine Reserve for a San Mateo County board member involved in the

Exploring the tide pools

process. With 30 acres of marine habitat, more than 400 species of animals, and 150 plant species revealed by the low tides, these tide pools are truly special. Docents teach families about the rocky shore ecosystem and offer guided tours to the public on the weekends.

Scientists studying the shallow marine shelf have discovered twenty-five plant and invertebrate species, as well as a few endemic ones living nowhere else but here. They include a worm, a type of seaweed, and a shrimp that lives in the gut of a sea anemone. Species are still being catalogued. At times some 300 harbor seals haul themselves out on the beaches. Always stay at least 300 feet away from the seals for your safety and theirs. The best time to see the tide pools is at minus tide, on the days following a full moon. If you come at high tide, only a short hike on the bluff and the walk on roads to Pillar Point is possible.

On the bluff you walk through a cypress grove planted as a windbreak by coastal farmers and ranchers around World War I. Cypress and eucalyptus trees were the most popular trees for this purpose on the Northern California coast, both fast growing and able to withstand extreme weather conditions.

The featured hike takes you on two residential streets, Beach Way and Ocean Boulevard, past seaside cottages, in order to include the entire stretch of beach. At the end of Beach Way is the Moss Beach Distillery. The lore of the Moss Beach Distillery gives you some insight into the colorful past of the San Mateo coast. During prohibition the coast was an ideal spot for rum running, bootleggers, and speakeasies that sold illegal booze to thirsty clients. One of the most successful speakeasies of the era was Frank's Place, built by Frank Torres in 1927 on the cliffs near Moss Beach. Frank's Place became a popular nightspot for silent film stars and politicians from the city. Under cover of darkness and fog, illegal whiskey was landed on the beach below the restaurant, dragged up the steep cliffs, and loaded into waiting vehicles for transport to San Francisco. The distillery is also famous for its resident ghost, the Blue Lady. The beautiful lady was reportedly killed while walking on the beach below the restaurant with her lover and still searches for him at the distillery.

Where Ocean Boulevard meets Bernal Avenue, the Jean Lauer Trail leads to Pillar Point and Ross Cove. Pillar Point, with its 175-foot crown, was once called Snake's Head for its unique shape. The Costanoans gathered shellfish at its base 5,800 years ago. Spaniards, Mexicans, and Americans grazed cattle on its hillsides from 1790 through the 1890s. Portuguese whalers used the high point as a lookout for humpback whales. Not until World War II did buildings appear on the point, when it became an observation post linked to the harbor defenses of San Francisco. Today Pillar Point is still an active US Air Force base, with soldiers stationed in the 120-foot tower, and its giant dish, 80 feet in diameter, still tracking military activity over long distances.

Just offshore from Pillar Point is Mavericks, famous for 100-foot waves that are the delight of professional surfers. During low tide you can walk around the base of the point for up to 3.5 miles of lovely beach walking and tide pools.

Looking north at Seal Beach from Jean Lauer Trail

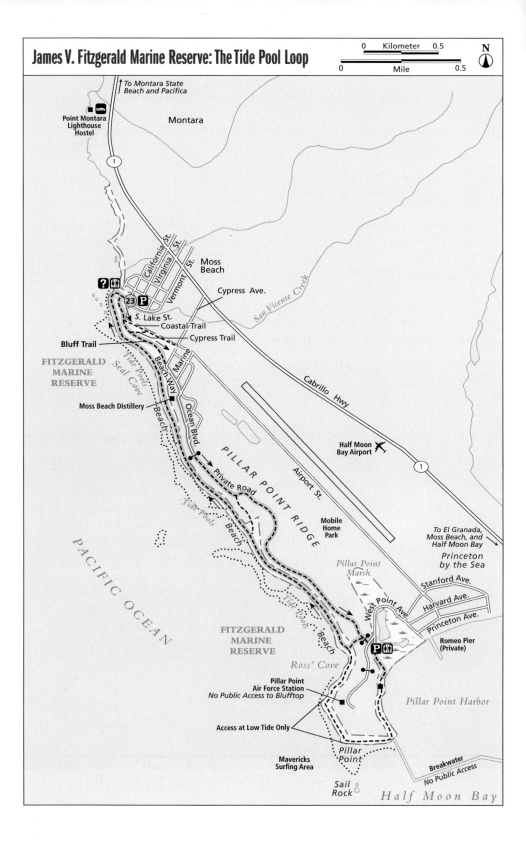

James V. Fitzgerald Marine Reserve: The Tide Pool Loop

0   Kilometer   0.5

0   Mile   0.5

N

To Montara State Beach and Pacifica

Point Montara Lighthouse Hostel

Montara

1

California St.

Virginia St.

Vermont St.

Moss Beach

Cypress Ave.

San Vicente Creek

?

23 P

S. Lake St.   Coastal Trail

Cypress Trail

Bluff Trail

FITZGERALD MARINE RESERVE

Tide Pools

Seal Cove

Beach Way

Marine

Moss Beach Distillery

Beach

Ocean Blvd.

Cabrillo Hwy

Airport St.

Half Moon Bay Airport

PILLAR POINT RIDGE

Private Road

Tide Pools

Beach

Mobile Home Park

Pillar Point Marsh

To El Granada, Moss Beach, and Half Moon Bay

Princeton by the Sea

Stanford Ave.

Harvard Ave.

Princeton Ave.

PACIFIC OCEAN

FITZGERALD MARINE RESERVE

Tide Pools

Beach

West Point Ave.

P

Romeo Pier (Private)

Ross' Cove

Pillar Point Air Force Station No Public Access to Blufftop

Pillar Point Harbor

Access at Low Tide Only

Mavericks Surfing Area

Pillar Point

Breakwater

No Public Access

Sail Rock

Half Moon Bay

MILES AND DIRECTIONS

0.0 START from the parking lot at the marine reserve information kiosk. Turn left (south) on Lake Street. Just past the parking lot, to the west, is a bridge that starts the Coastal Trail/Bluff Trail.

0.1 Turn left onto Coastal Trail through the Seal Cove Cypress Tree Tunnel.

0.2 Make a sharp right onto Cypress Trail to go through more of the cypress grove.

0.4 Cypress Trail meets Bluff Trail. Turn left (south) and follow the bluff.

0.7 Pass Seal Cove Trail to the beach and reach the corner of Beach and Cypress. Continue south, walking on the side of Beach Way past coastal houses and the stop sign at Marine Boulevard. Follow signs to Moss Beach Distillery.

0.8 Arrive at Moss Beach Distillery. The cement pillar in the water is a sighting for range artillery from Pillar Point, one of eighty including landmarks and lighthouses. Continue south, past the parking lots, onto Ocean Boulevard.

1.2 Ocean Boulevard dead-ends at a field and the Jean Lauer Trail. Ahead is Pillar Point with views of Montara Mountain and Half Moon Bay beyond.

1.4 Turn right (south) onto a narrower branch of Jean Lauer Trail (it also continues straight inland).

1.6 Jean Lauer Trail becomes a double-track trail. Shortly after, again take a smaller branch of the trail to the right, toward the bluff and following it.

2.0 Again the trail splits. Stay on the branch by the bluff for ocean views. It narrows considerably in between scrub. West Point Road is to the east.

2.6 Just before the trail meets West Point Road, turn right onto a trail toward the ocean and follow it down the bank to the beach.

2.7 Come to Ross Cove (formerly Whalers' Cove) on the north side of the point, a favorite surfing spot. To the southwest beyond Bird Rocks is the famous Mavericks surfing spot (named for a surfer's dog). It's best viewed from the south side of Pillar Point, but still hard to see in general. Turn north up the beach toward the tide pools. You'll be following the beach the entire way. (**Note:** If not hiking at low tide, you will have to return via the bluffs for an out-and-back hike.)

3.8 Reach Frenchman's Reef. Continue along the beach.

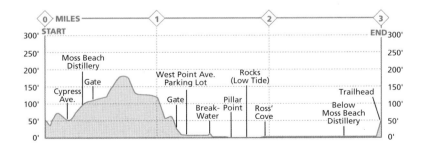

4.3 Reach Seal Cove. Keep a healthy distance from seal mammals if present.

4.7 Come to San Vicente Creek, which runs into the ocean. Carefully cross the creek and climb up a path to Lake Street, following it to the parking lot.

4.8 Arrive back at the parking lot.

Alternate routes: Families will enjoy the mile loop on the Bluff Trail through the Cypress tunnel and along the bluff with ocean views returning back to the main beach entrance at the end of Lake Street at Seal Cove for lots of tide pool exploration.

For a 4.2-mile loop, there is a path down to the beach off the Jean Lauer Trail at about 2.1 miles. (***Note:*** There is no easy beach access between the Moss Beach Distillery and this point on the Jean Lauer Trail.)

TAKING CARE OF TIDE POOLS

Twice a day, retreating tides leave seashore life clinging to the rocks. Intertidal plants and animals are well adapted to this changing world of surf and sand but have no defense against humans. Therefore, whenever you are tide pooling, observe the following guidelines:

- The best way to observe tide pools is to sit quietly until animals emerge from their hiding places and resume their activities. Watch out for the rising tide.

- You may touch marine life, but *do not* pick it up or place it in a container. If you do, it will die. Examine it in the place that you find it.

- Watch your step! Walk carefully around the tide pools for your own safety and to spare the marine life underfoot.

- Any rocks that get moved should be replaced with the seaweed side up. Life on the bottom of the rocks will die when exposed to sun and air. Avoid moving the rocks whenever possible.

- Shells and rocks are a natural part of the areas. Many serve as future homes for creatures such as hermit crabs. *Do not collect shells, vegetation, rocks, or marine life in the reserve.*

The Marine Mammal Center often uses the reserve as a place to reintroduce nursed harbor seals, sea lions, and other ocean creatures to the wilds of the Pacific, and this is usually the spot where they make the release. Call the Marine Mammal Center (415-289-7325) to find out scheduled releases; it's a great thing for kids to see.

24. **SAN PEDRO VALLEY COUNTY PARK**

WHY GO?

San Pedro Valley County Park has been a place to breathe easy for thousands of years starting with the Costanoans. Nestled between the northernmost Santa Cruz Mountains and the foothills of Pacifica, the valley is protected from harsh coastal winds and weather. Three freshwater creeks flow under the shade of willows, oaks, and dogwood with fish and riparian flora and fauna. Trails offer chaparral and views, meadows of deer and wildflowers, hillside grasslands, herbal eucalyptus groves, and a waterfall.

THE RUN DOWN

Start: Parking lots by the San Pedro Valley County Park Visitor Center
Elevation gain: 1,200 feet
Distance: 6.1-mile loop
Difficulty: Moderate
Hiking time: About 3 hours
Seasons/schedule: 8 a.m. to sunset year-round
Fees and permits: Parking fee
Trail contact: San Pedro Valley Park, 600 Oddstad Blvd., Pacifica 94044; (650) 355-8289; http://parks .smcgov.org/san-pedro-valley-park

Dog-friendly: No dogs allowed
Trail surface: Single- and double-track dirt trail, a couple of wooden bridges, some paved path
Land status: County park
Nearest town: Pacifica
Nat Geo TOPO! Map: Montara Mountain, CA
Nat Geo Trails Illustrated Map: Skyline Boulevard #815
Other trail users: Bikers on Weiler Ranch Road

FINDING THE TRAILHEAD

From CA 1 in Pacifica, turn east on Linda Mar Boulevard. Follow Linda Mar Boulevard until it ends at Oddstad Boulevard. Turn right on Oddstad Boulevard and proceed 1 block to the park entrance. Turn right up the hill into the park, pay at the kiosk, and park in either lot. **GPS:** N37 34.44' / W122 28.30'

WHAT TO SEE

It's easy to see why people have gathered in this valley for centuries. The south and middle forks of San Pedro Creek flow year-round and provide safe spawning areas for migratory steelhead trout. Brooks Creek during the rainy winter months puts on a show, with Brooks Falls splashing down 175 feet in three tiers. The Middle Valley is an artist's

Hiking in San Pedro Valley

palette with springtime wildflowers: California poppies, suncups, buttercups, wild mustard, and wild radish. At dusk, brush rabbits cautiously hop out of hiding to feed. Black-tailed does and fawns munch contentedly on flowers.

The Costanoan Indians had a seasonal camp here for possibly thousands of years. In 1769 Spanish explorer Gaspar de Portolá and his men arrived here sick and exhausted. Their expedition, which was supposed to end at Monterey, had missed the target, and they had walked on. They stumbled into this valley and set up camp. It was so peaceful and rejuvenating, they stayed for a while, and it was from this camp that Portolá's scout, Sergeant Jose Francisco Ortega, set out to explore the area and, climbing Sweeney Ridge, saw the San Francisco Bay for the first time.

Around the turn of the twentieth century, wealthy San Franciscans constructed palatial summer homes on the coast side. Not long ago, cattle still ruminated on the hillsides, and commercial farmers harvested crops of pumpkins and artichokes in the meadow. A fellow named John Gay operated a trout farm on the south fork of San Pedro Creek until 1962, when rainstorms washed out his operation.

In the early 1950s, developer Andres Oddstad bought up seven of the ranches in the San Pedro Valley and started construction on tract homes in Linda Mar. By 1957 nine hamlets along 6 miles of coastline incorporated as the city of Pacifica, Spanish

Iris trailside

for "peace." The new community found the natural meadows and hillsides a backyard paradise. With a citywide vote the citizens donated as much open space as possible to the National Park Service and the county. As a result Pacifica's population hasn't grown significantly in thirty years, and back at the end of Oddstad Boulevard are 1,150 acres of serene valley, hillsides, and cascading streams.

Of course nothing is perfect. Poison oak grows heartily along with everything else in the park. Fog can roll in, blocking views and chilling the bones. The park has great group picnic sites, but that means there are often crowds of people here on the weekends. Pooches have to stay home. Deer paths on the Valley View Loop require that a hiker pay attention to stick to the main trail.

These considerations are slight, however, compared with the hiking possibilities. The featured hike on Hazelnut and Valley View Trails takes in a little bit of everything on the hillsides on both sides of the valley for a satisfying loop.

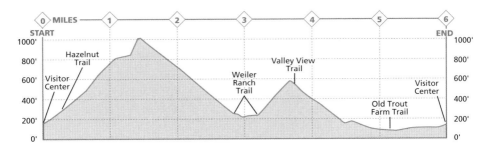

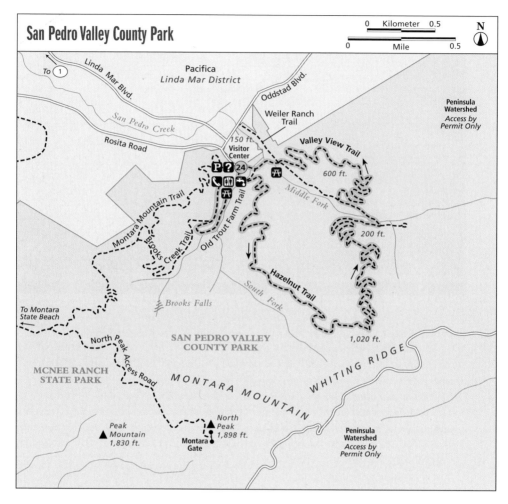

San Pedro Valley County Park

0   Kilometer   0.5

0   Mile   0.5

N

To ① Linda Mar Blvd.

Pacifica
Linda Mar District

Oddstad Blvd.

Peninsula
Watershed
Access by
Permit Only

San Pedro Creek

Weiler Ranch
Trail

Rosita Road

150 ft.
Visitor
Center

Valley View Trail

600 ft.

Montara Mountain Trail

Brooks Creek Trail

Old Trout Farm Trail

Middle Fork

200 ft.

Hazelnut Trail

To Montara
State Beach

Brooks Falls

South Fork

1,020 ft.

North Peak Access Road

SAN PEDRO VALLEY
COUNTY PARK

WHITING RIDGE

MCNEE RANCH
STATE PARK

MONTARA MOUNTAIN

Peak
Mountain
1,830 ft.

North
Peak
1,898 ft.

Montara
Gate

Peninsula
Watershed
Access by
Permit Only

MILES AND DIRECTIONS

0.0 START at the visitor center in San Pedro Valley County Park and walk toward the trailhead for Plaskon Nature Trail. Cross a bridge. After about 30 yards, turn right on signed Hazelnut Trail, which ascends a hill on switchbacks.

1.2 Higher up the trail you enter a drier sandstone area where rare Montara manzanita and giant golden chinquapin grow beside coyote brush, toyon, and coffeeberry. Continue on Hazelnut Trail, which eventually starts east on switchbacks down to the valley.

3.3 Turn right on Weiler Ranch Road.

3.6 Turn right on Valley View Trail. Valley View traverses south-facing slopes above the valley. Be careful of rocks on the trail, and watch for scat and footprints of coyotes and other critters. The trail rises, then descends.

Plasken Nature Trail

5.0 Valley View Trail ends. Turn right on Weiler Ranch Road, then left on a park service road, heading toward the visitor center. The road crosses over the Middle Fork of San Pedro Creek and passes by Walnut Grove Group Picnic Area. Continue on the service road to the north parking lot.

5.2 Continue on the sidewalk past the visitor center to the end of the south parking lot. Take Old Trout Farm Trail (signed) for 0.8 mile.

5.3 On Old Trout Farm Trail, pass by a picnic area on the left and, near the beginning of the trail, the remains of John Gay's trout farm, just a couple of tanks.

5.5 At a hairpin turn the trail looks up the ravine at Brooks Falls.

5.6 At the junction with Brooks Creek Trail, stay right on Brooks Falls Overlook Trail. (Option: For a different view of the falls, turn left and head another 0.3 mile to a bench.)

6.1 Arrive back at the parking lots and visitor center.

Alternate routes: The Montara Mountain Trail takes you to the top of Montara Mountain with its views of the Pacific Ocean. Take a lollipop loop back on the Brooks Creek Trail and Old Trout Farm Trail for a varied 4.5-mile hike.

If hiking with young children, the Plaskon Nature Trail and a tour of the visitor center make a nice outing. The Brooks Fall/Trout Farm Loop is a short 1.5 miles.

Bonus Hikes: San Mateo Coastline

G. MORI POINT

WHY GO?

The 105-acre park has raised boardwalks over a fragile habitat for endangered species, restored wetlands, and a pond. Trails were restored in 2012. Mori Point is famous as the site where Harold drives his Jaguar off a cliff in the cult movie *Harold and Maude* (1971). The Native American Aramai village of Timigtac was located here long ago, but the point is named for the Mori family who farmed here at the turn of the twentieth century, although they were better known for their primary business, the Mori Point Inn, a popular tavern, especially during Prohibition. Once in a 1923 raid, federal agents seized 24,000 cases of whiskey from the inn. It continued to operate as a hotel and dance hall until 1965. The Bootleggers Steps (186 stairs)—named for the liquor acquired and drank here during Prohibition—take you up to breathtaking views of the Pacific Ocean and Farallon Islands.

THE RUN DOWN

Start: Sharp Park State Beach. GPS: N37 37.47' / W122 29.38'
Elevation gain: 260 feet
Distance: 3-mile partial loop
Difficulty: Easy
Hiking time: About 2 hours
Seasons/schedule: Sunrise to sunset year-round
Fees and permits: None
Trail contact: Presidio Visitor Center, 210 Lincoln Blvd., San Francisco 94129; (415) 561-4323; www.nps.gov/prsf; and Pacifica Visitor Center, 225 Rockaway Beach Ave #1, Pacifica

94044; (650) 355-4122 www.pacifica chamber.com
Dog-friendly: Dogs on leash
Trail surface: Dirt trail and fire road
Land status: National recreation area
Nearest town: Pacifica
Nat Geo TOPO! Map: Montara Mountain, CA; San Francisco South, CA
Nat Geo Trails Illustrated Map: Skyline Boulevard #815
Other trail users: Bikers on levee and bike paths only
Special considerations: Pit toilet at trailhead; no water available

Alternate routes: You can extend your walk by continuing north along the seawall path to the Pacifica municipal pier.

H. CRYSTAL SPRINGS REGIONAL TRAIL

WHY GO?

The trail is currently 15.3 miles long on pristine Crystal Springs watershed land. Still being negotiated and built, when complete it will total 17.5 miles. There are three segments of the trail: The San Andreas segment extends from Cambridge Lane on the north to Hillcrest Boulevard on the south, where it connects to the Sawyer Camp segment. The historic Sawyer Camp segment connects to Crystal Springs Road in the south, and is probably the best-known length of trail in San Mateo County. As a result there are many trail users. The Crystal Springs segment starts at CA 92 on the north and runs along the westerly right-of-way of Cañada Road. Over 180 different species of birds have been identified. Most common are ducks, hawks, and various songbirds that make their home in the surrounding oaks and madrones. Along the Sawyer Camp Trail is the Jepson Laurel, a tree over 600 years old and the oldest and largest known laurel in California. About one-half mile south of the Cañada Road trailhead is the Pulgas Water Temple, a neoclassical structure with Corinthian capitals and fluted columns reflected in a tree-lined pool. It celebrates the achievement of bringing water from Hetch Hetchy to the Bay Area.

THE RUN DOWN

Start: Varies. Start of Sawyer Camp Trail: GPS: N37 31.51' / W122 21.52'
Elevation gain: Varies (mostly flat)
Distance: Varies
Difficulty: Easy
Hiking time: Varies
Seasons/schedule: Sunrise to sunset year-round
Fees and permits: None
Trail contact: County of San Mateo Parks Dept., 950 Skyline Blvd., Burlingame 94010; (650) 269-8140; http://parks.smcgov.org/crystal -springs-regional-trail

Dog-friendly: No dogs allowed
Trail surface: Paved, gravel, and double-track dirt trails
Land status: County park
Nearest town: Varies (all in San Mateo County)
Nat Geo TOPO! Map: San Mateo, CA
Nat Geo Trails Illustrated Map: Skyline Boulevard #815
Other trail users: Cyclists and equestrians

Crystal Springs reservoir from
Peninsula Watershed
MIGUEL VIEIRA (FLICKR.COM/
PHOTOS/MIGUELVIEIRA/)

THE NORTHERN
SANTA CRUZ MOUNTAINS

Hikers can take years to explore all the parkland and open space accessible from one road, Skyline Boulevard, or CA 35. Skyline follows the ridge of the northern Santa Cruz Mountains. Sloping down to valleys and coastline on either side are tens of thousands of acres and hundreds of miles of trails through thick forests, scrub, and grasslands. You can follow trails into the heart of Silicon Valley to the east and to the Pacific Ocean to the west.

The Midpeninsula Regional Open Space District alone has saved 63,000 acres in twenty-six preserves where sawmills once stood. Craig Britton Trail in Purisima Creek Redwoods Open Space Preserve provides a meditative stroll through giant redwoods. Portola Redwoods has its Old Tree Trail and out-of-the-way campgrounds. Castle Rock State Park, besides its groves of madrones and black oak trees, has amazing rock outcroppings. Rock climbers gather around Goat Rock to practice maneuvers.

Sawmills made their first appearance in these vast forests, dominated by coast redwoods, back in 1849. But the steep mountains and tight gullies that keep the redwoods protected from wind and sun also protected some of them from becoming timber. The mills only operated when prices were high enough to compensate for the cost of hauling the lumber out of here. Big Basin Redwoods State Park has the largest continuous stand of ancient coast redwoods south of San Francisco, some up to 2,000 years old. The waterfalls on Berry Creek Falls Trail are some of the most memorable in the Bay Area.

California's coastal mountain range formed when the North American Plate, supporting the continent, and the Pacific Plate, under the Pacific Ocean, collided and began rubbing past each other along the San Andreas Fault line, which follows Stevens Creek east of the Santa Cruz Mountains. The pressure caused the folding of the sea floor and formed an almost continuous series of ranges and valleys the length of California, separating the coast from the Great Central Valley and the deserts of the interior. The mountainous barrier here is what causes the weather pattern most important to the redwoods: fog. The line where thick forests end and primarily scrub and grasslands begin marks the fog line.

Where the fog comes in, you have green mixed forest up to the top of the ridge and slightly over the top where the fog spills, but then, suddenly, grasslands and scattered drought-resistant live oaks take over.

25. BIG BASIN REDWOODS STATE PARK: BERRY CREEK FALLS TRAIL LOOP

WHY GO?

This is a long but satisfying jaunt through the largest continuous stand of ancient coast redwoods south of San Francisco. Following the contours of the hillside, the Sunset Trail brings you through several deep canyons and cascading creeks. Berry Creek Falls Trail is the prize, with a series of waterfalls in a deep basin. The Golden Cascade and Silver Falls feature just that: manes of silver water against golden earth. Berry Creek Falls is a 60-foot vertical sheet of white water against dark rocks. The Skyline-to-the-Sea Trail takes you back through more lush canyons.

THE RUN DOWN

Start: Main parking lot across from Big Basin Redwoods State Park headquarters
Elevation gain: 2,000 feet
Distance: 11.6 miles
Difficulty: Moderate to strenuous due to distance
Hiking time: About 6 hours
Seasons/schedule: 6 a.m. to sunset year-round
Fees and permits: Parking fee
Trail contact: Big Basin Redwoods State Park, 21600 Big Basin Way, Boulder Creek 95006 (831) 338-8860; www.parks.ca.gov/?page_id=540
Dog-friendly: No dogs allowed

Trail surface: Single- and double-track dirt trail, some stairs and seasonal bridges, natural rock stairs with railing beside waterfall
Land status: State park
Nearest town: Boulder Creek
Nat Geo TOPO! Map: Big Basin, CA
Nat Geo Trails Illustrated Map: Skyline Boulevard #815; Big Basin, Santa Cruz #816
Other trail users: Hikers only
Special considerations: A nature guide purchased from the visitor center leads you to redwood fairy circles and burls, the Chimney Tree, and the largest redwoods in the park.

FINDING THE TRAILHEAD

Take CA 9 to Boulder Creek. In the town of Boulder Creek, turn west onto CA 236/Big Basin Way. Stay on this highway for 9 miles to Big Basin State Park. Proceed to park headquarters. **GPS:** N37 10.21' / W122 13.18'

WHAT TO SEE

These trees, because of their size and antiquity, are among the natural wonders of the world and should be saved for posterity.
   —Photographer Andrew P. Hill, savior of Big Basin, circa 1900

Beside the visitor center, a slice of an ancient redwood tree tells the first story of many on this hike. It sprouted in the year 544 during the Byzantine Empire and was already 1,392 years old when the park opened in 1902, the first state park in California. The early conservation effort that resulted in the park's creation came from photographer Andrew P. Hill, who started the Sempervirens Club to protect these redwoods (*sempervirens* means "ever living"). Today the club is still hard at work protecting forests for future generations.

The Ohlone Indians lived around Big Basin for nearly 10,000 years. They believed the redwoods to be spirit beings, part of a divine race that existed before humans, who taught people the proper way to live with nature. Even their houses, made out of planks split from fallen redwoods over pits, were understood to be living bodies.

Grizzlies, which the natives respected and feared, lived in the dense ravines. Other than mushrooms, there wasn't a lot the Ohlones needed in the shadowy woods, so they pretty much left them alone. Sometimes their controlled burns in the grasslands reached the forest, but the redwoods always withstood the flames.

West Berry Creek and Berry Creek Falls Trail
MIGUEL VIEIRA (FLICKR.COM/PHOTOS/MIGUELVIEIRA/)

Berry Creek Falls from Skyline-to-the-Sea Trail
MIGUEL VIEIRA (FLICKR.COM/PHOTOS/MIGUELVIEIRA/)

When Portolá's Spanish expedition came through in 1769, the men, sick with scurvy, camped at the mouth of Waddell Creek and gorged themselves on berries. With their miraculous recovery, they named the valley Cañada de la Salud, or Canyon of Health.

Logging of the redwoods happened at a frantic pace after the gold rush as cities rose in the Bay Area. Frustrated miners sought their fortune in lumber. Only a fraction of the ancient trees survived, but they are here in Big Basin, some 300 feet tall and 50 feet in circumference and as old as 2,500 years.

Single-track and double-track trails take you through cool canyons, following the contours of the hills. They meander by fern-lined creeks and immense tangled roots of fallen trees. This vast stand of giant redwoods, with their orangutan fur and citrus-scented needles, is overwhelming in scale. The mixed woodland also features very mature Douglas fir and tanbark oak trees, their trunks covered with soft, hairy moss. This landscape is uninterrupted for miles, except for the occasional orange monkeyflower, yellow banana slug, wild strawberry, or colorful mushroom beside the trail. Bridges take you over gurgling streams. Natural sulfur in a couple of the creeks causes some sharp smells. In the rainy season, marshes serve as breeding grounds for California newts.

After the Berry Creek crossing, this route climbs to the edge of the forest, where the startling afternoon sun blanches the scene for a tenth of a mile. Here you find knobcone pines, manzanita, and soft, dry sandstone. Most of the animals in the park live in chaparral like this, in the coastal valleys or oak groves. Foxes, coyotes, bobcats, opossums, and the rare mountain lion share this area with hunting raptors, brush rabbits, lizards, and western rattlesnakes.

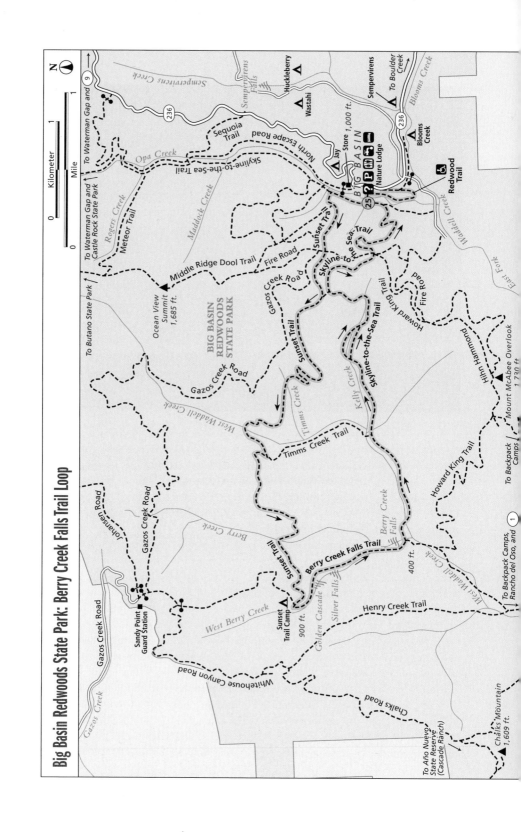

Big Basin Redwoods State Park: Berry Creek Falls Trail Loop

Back in woodland you reach the Berry Creek Falls Trail, which features almost continuous waterfalls. Golden Cascade, so named for the gold sandstone earth that forms the 20-foot slide beneath the falls, is followed by the two cascades of Silver Falls. A meditative walk beside Berry Creek brings you to 60-foot Berry Creek Falls, splashing bridal veil–fashion into the creek below.

The lush Skyline-to-the-Sea Trail, following Kelly and Timms Creeks, takes you back to the Redwood Trail Loop, a great finale to the day.

MILES AND DIRECTIONS

0.0 START at the parking lot outside park headquarters. Look for the trailhead for Redwood Nature Trail on the side of the parking lot opposite the park headquarters. Go straight.

0.1 Past the restrooms is the start of Skyline-to-the-Sea Trail, which connects to most other trails. Cross a bridge over Opal Creek to the trailhead. Turn right on Skyline-to-the-Sea-Trail to Sunset Trail. It becomes a single-track dirt trail following the creek.

0.3 Stay to the left on Skyline-to-the-Sea Trail toward Dool Trail.

0.4 Trailhead for Dool Trail. Turn left on Dool for 0.1 mile to Sunset Trail. Redwood Creek is on the right.

0.5 The trail splits. Turn left on Sunset Trail toward Middle Ridge Fire Road.

1.1 Up a small rise, pass over gravel-and-dirt Gazos Creek Road (which meets Middle Ridge Fire Road) and continue on Sunset Trail on the other side.

1.3 Come to the trailhead for a connector trail. Continue straight on Sunset Trail toward Timms Creek Trail. The trail goes through redwood groves and over hills. Cross several bridges, one of them over West Waddell Creek.

3.9 At the trailhead for Timms Creek Trail, make a sharp right turn uphill, continuing on Sunset Trail (sign reads "To the Sunset Trail Camp").

5.4 Cross Berry Creek. The trail begins to climb, then crosses a ridge.

5.5 At the turnoff to the Sunset backpacking camp, continue straight on Sunset Trail to Berry Creek Falls Trail.

5.6 Round a bend and you are now on Berry Creek Falls Trail. This is Golden Cascade. It is followed by the two cascades of Silver Falls, so that you have 0.1 mile of continuous waterfalls. Follow the trail down rock stairs right beside the falls. Watch your step; it can be slippery.

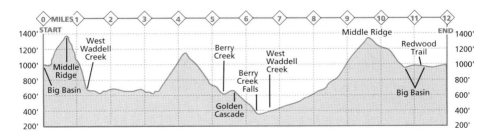

Redwoods in Big Basin

6.4 Arrive at Berry Creek Falls.

6.5 Come to a trailhead at a bridge. Turn left over the bridge toward Big Basin headquarters, now on Skyline-to-the-Sea Trail (uphill, with some flat areas and short descents all the way back to the start).

6.6 The trail passes over West Waddell Creek and follows the creek uphill. (**Note:** There are several old-growth trees on this trail.)

7.5 Continue straight on Skyline-to-the-Sea Trail as you pass the trailhead for Timms Creek Trail. Skyline-to-the-Sea Trail now follows Kelly Creek.

8.1 The trail splits; take either one. The lower trail passes over the creek and back; the upper trail goes along a ridge and passes through the burned-out base of a tree.

8.3 The two trails rejoin. Continue east on Skyline-to-the-Sea Trail.

9.2 At the trailhead turn right to stay on Skyline-to-the-Sea Trail. This is also a connector to Hihn Hammond Road.

9.6 Turn left and pass over Middle Ridge Fire Road, continuing on Skyline-to-the-Sea Trail, downhill.

10.7 Take the bridge here, continuing straight back toward park headquarters.

11.0 Past the restrooms, turn right between split-rail fencing to take Redwood Trail Loop, a great finale to the day. You pass great examples of a redwood circle (or fairy circle), redwood burls, the burned-out Chimney Tree, the Father of the Forest, and the Mother of the Forest. (***Note:*** On Redwood Trail, notice the memorial to Andrew Hill, who helped to preserve these redwoods as parkland.)

11.6 Arrive back at the parking lot.

Alternate routes: Young families will enjoy the Redwood Loop, a self-guided nature trail (0.6 mile).

The Sunset to Skyline Loop (2.9 miles) is a good short hike to take in some old-growth redwoods and creeks (Skyline-to-the-Sea Trail to the Sunset-Skyline connector trail to Sunset Trail).

LOGGER LEGENDS AND BIG BASIN PLACE NAMES

Waddell and West Waddell Creek—William White Waddell (b. Kentucky, 1818) arrived in Santa Cruz County in 1851 and built sawmills. One, along with a tramway and a wharf, was along the creek that now bears his name. They burned down. Waddell died in 1875 from complications to injuries resulting from a bear attack that ripped one of his arms off. Every Halloween there's a special night hike in Big Basin, "The Missing Arm of William Waddell."

Berry Creek—The Berry Creek flowing southward into Waddell Creek was named for an old lumberman, Tilford George Berry, probably an employee of old Waddell. Tilford, from Indiana, built a cabin at the base of the lower Berry Creek Falls in the mid-1860s. He mysteriously disappeared during the next decade, and finally, in 1890 his bones were found in the chaparral above Boulder Creek.

Dool Trail—William H. "Billy" Dool served as warden of Big Basin from 1911 until 1932. A Canadian, naturalized in Santa Cruz County in 1888, he was also a butcher, with a shop on what is now Central Avenue near Big Basin Way.

Hihn Hammond Road—Originally built in 1917 by the Hihn Hammond Lumber Company, it is a retired logging road.

Timms Creek—George Timms was a squatter and a timber claimant who had a cabin in an opening in the woods near the present Gazos Creek Road. Like many of the mountain men around here, Timms was a hard drinker and occasionally had delirium tremens (the DTs). Around 1884 he disappeared, leaving the basin's greatest mystery behind him. Three different stories pointed to murder, but none had sufficient factual evidence to make an accusation.

Kelly Creek—This short creek is named for Dr. Thomas Kelly, a surgeon in the Civil War who took up a timber claim in the area in the 1870s. The Kelly Cabin became a well-known rendezvous for hunters. He died in his bed in 1906 at the age of 70.

26. CASTLE ROCK STATE PARK: SARATOGA GAP/RIDGE TRAIL/CASTLE ROCK TRAIL

WHY GO?

Castle Rock State Park is on one of the highest ridges in the Santa Cruz Mountains. The hike features great variety: cool, dark mixed forests, creeks and a seasonal waterfall, dry, manzanita-lined ridges, grassy hills, oak savanna, and above all, rock formations. The boulders come in amazing shapes, with curves, crevices, and caves. On weekends, climbers navigate their way up 90-degree rock faces with chalky fingers. The giant boulder that gives the park its name sits in high woodland toward the end of the hike. There are interpretive exhibits and scenic overlooks along the way.

THE RUN DOWN

Start: Saratoga Gap trailhead in the Castle Rock main parking lot on Skyline Boulevard (CA 35)
Elevation gain: 750 feet
Distance: 6.1-mile loop/lollipop
Difficulty: Moderate
Hiking time: About 3 hours
Seasons/schedule: Sunrise to sunset year-round
Fees and permits: Parking fee
Trail contact: Castle Rock State Park, 15000 Skyline Blvd., Los Gatos 95033 (408) 867-2952; www.parks .ca.gov/?page_id=538
Dog-friendly: No dogs allowed
Trail surface: Single- and some double-track dirt trail, rocky paths

between boulders, a set of stone steps with railing, a section with railing beside steep drop-off
Land status: State park
Nearest town: Los Gatos
Nat Geo TOPO! Map: Castle Rock Ridge, CA
Nat Geo Trails Illustrated Map: Skyline Boulevard #815; Big Basin, Santa Cruz #816
Other trail users: Hikers only
Special Considerations: As of 2017, there are plans to build a visitor center (with water, currently not available in the park) for Castle Rock State Park, so look for one in the next few years.

FINDING THE TRAILHEAD

On Skyline Boulevard (CA 35) go 2.5 miles south of the Saratoga Gap (CA 35 and CA 9 junction). Look for the sign to Castle Rock State Park. Turn west by the kiosk into the parking lot (overflow parking is across the highway).
GPS: N37 13.51' / W122 5.45'

Climbers in Castle Rock State Park
GREY3K

WHAT TO SEE

The trail starts creekside in shady redwood, oak, and bay woodland, with lichen-covered rocks against hillsides. Costanoan Indians used to hike this trail from their coastal villages to gather acorns produced by the park's plentiful oak trees. Rangers have found arrowheads and other faint traces of their travels through Castle Rock.

After the Civil War, farmers and dairy cattle ranchers settled in the hills around Castle Rock.

Just over a wooden bridge on the Saratoga Gap Trail, the sound of running water crescendos. An observation platform allows you to stand at the top of Castle Rock Falls and watch the water drop approximately 60 feet down onto the rocks below. This seasonal waterfall is best in spring and after storms. The trail descends through oak scrub, with sticky monkeyflowers and wild strawberries. In spring the park offers a surprising display of wildflowers. Coral bells, chickweed, hedge wood rose, and California fuchsia decorate the banks of the creek. Dryer areas host orange California poppies and Indian paintbrush, with blossoms like red sparklers that stay around through most of summer, providing perches for cabbage butterflies.

The trail rises again onto rocky ridges high above wooded ravines with spectacular views of the park and the Pacific Ocean. A safety cable helps hikers climb a set of narrow stone steps on the cliff. This rite-of-passage brings you to Goat Rock. The pockets, patterns, and protrusions of Goat Rock look like part of an alien landscape. The intricate patterns of thin ridges and small cavities in the sandstone, called stone lace and honeycomb, are the result of what geologists call "chemical weathering."

The rock formations are an intriguing sight in the park. Climbers often compare the Castle Rock boulders to those in Fontainebleau, France, though the Santa Cruz rocks, mostly less than 12 feet tall, are small in comparison. They use them to boulder—practice low-altitude maneuvers without the protection of a rope. If the boulder is high, the climbers place a landing pad on the ground below the rock. They have christened the rocks here with wonderful names like Duct Tape, the Domino, the Ecoterrorist, Parking Lot Rock, Ten Arrows, Deforestation, Lost Keys Boulder, and the Beak.

Continue past Goat Rock to an interpretive shelter that shares interesting information about park life and history. Back in the woods, you walk through the largest stand of black oak left in the Bay Area, which hosts a score of animals. Blanched boulders sit in groves of orange-red madrones against a blue sky. The popular climbing rock, Castle Rock, sits near the park entrance among trees at 3,214-foot elevation on the highest rise.

Castle Rock became a park thanks to a boy named Russell Varian. Young Russell fell in love with the big boulders. He hatched the dream to preserve the land around them as a public park for all to enjoy. As an adult he took steps to buy the land himself and donate it to the state park system. But just as he was about to buy the land in 1959, he died. His friends finished the process, purchasing 27 acres. The state officially opened it in 1968 with 513 acres. Castle Rock continues to grow. The Sempervirens Fund bought acres connected to the southwest side of the park in 2000. The park now encompasses over 5,200 acres, containing 34 miles of hiking paths.

View from Castle Rock State Park
MIGUEL VIEIRA (FLICKR.COM/
PHOTOS/MIGUELVIEIRA/)

MILES AND DIRECTIONS

0.0 START at Castle Rock's main parking lot on Skyline Boulevard. Follow Saratoga Gap Trail. The trail follows the creek (flow is seasonal) and passes over
a wooden bridge.

0.2 Pass by the trailhead to Castle Rock. (***Note:*** End of the hike brings you back
here and to the stone chateau for the hike's finale.) Continue on Saratoga
Gap Trail. Pass a memorial grove.

0.6 At a split in the trail, stay left, continuing on Saratoga Gap Trail. The fork on
the right is your return route on Ridge Trail.

0.8 Come to Castle Rock Falls and observation platform. The trail descends
through oak scrub. (***Note:*** Poison oak bushes add color in the fall—and winter too, with bare red branches. Don't touch!) Then you find yourself climbing a moderate grade into sunshine, with views of the hillsides and canyons.
The trail follows the edge of the cliff. Back by the creek, another bridge takes
you to a resting bench. If you hear gunfire, do not be alarmed. The shots are
echoing through the canyon from the Los Altos Rod and Gun Club.

1.3 Continue straight on Saratoga Gap Trail past the trailhead for the connector
path to Ridge Trail.

1.5 There's a flat rock with a rocky shelf above it hanging over the cliff by the
trail that would make a quiet place to drink water, admire the view, and
dangle your feet.

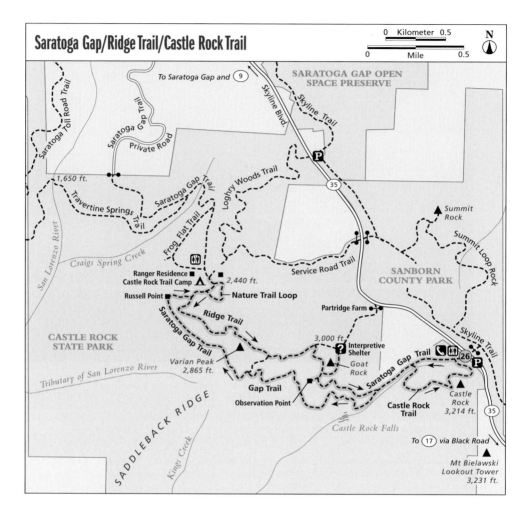

Saratoga Gap/Ridge Trail/Castle Rock Trail

0 Kilometer 0.5
0 Mile 0.5

N

To Saratoga Gap and (9)

SARATOGA GAP OPEN
SPACE PRESERVE

Saratoga Toll Road Trail

Saratoga Gap Trail

Private Road

Skyline Blvd.

Skyline Trail

1,650 ft.

Travertine Springs Trail

Saratoga Gap Trail

Loghry Woods Trail

P

35

Summit
Rock

Summit Loop Rock

San Lorenzo River

Craigs Spring Creek

Frog Flat Trail

Service Road Trail

SANBORN
COUNTY PARK

Ranger Residence
Castle Rock Trail Camp

2,440 ft.

Nature Trail Loop

Russell Point

Partridge Farm

Ridge Trail

Saratoga Gap Trail

CASTLE ROCK
STATE PARK

Tributary of San Lorenzo River

3,000 ft.

Interpretive
Shelter

Skyline Trail

Varian Peak
2,865 ft.

Goat
Rock

Saratoga Gap Trail

26

P

Gap Trail

Observation Point

Castle Rock
Trail

Castle
Rock
3,214 ft.

35

SADDLEBACK RIDGE

Kings Creek

Castle Rock Falls

To (17) via Black Road

Mt Bielawski
Lookout Tower
3,231 ft.

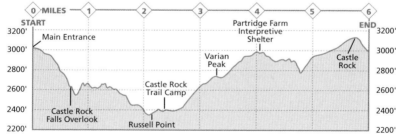

0 MILES 1 2 3 4 5 6

START

END

3200'

Main Entrance

Partridge Farm
Interpretive
Shelter

3200'

3000'

3000'

2800'

Varian
Peak

Castle
Rock

2800'

2600'

Castle Rock
Trail Camp

2600'

2400'

Castle Rock
Falls Overlook

Russell Point

2400'

2200'

2200'

2.0 The trail crosses over a cliff (a cable gets you safely across). After 2.3-miles from the trailhead, the trail heads west through a madrone grove.

2.5 Trailhead for Ridge Trail. Head uphill, bearing right, crossing over a bridge toward a picnic area.

2.6 At the trailhead for Saratoga Gap Trail, turn left to the campground and park office. You'll return to this spot after heading in the opposite direction on the self-guided nature trail loop.

2.7 Back at the split for Ridge Trail and Saratoga Gap Trail. Bear left, ascending Ridge Trail.

3.0 The trail leads to the ridge (rock-climbing boulder to the right).

3.8 Pass the trailhead for a connector trail, staying on Ridge Trail.

3.9 Emily Smith Bird Observation Point is to the right. (Side-trip: Detour to the observation point to spot raptors, ravens, and vultures, Steller's and western scrub jays, chestnut-backed chickadees, and wrentits, dark-eyed juncos, and sparrows. Bring binoculars.) Return to Ridge Trail to continue the hike.

4.0 Continue on Ridge Trail.

4.3 Come to Goat Rock. This is the backside of the rock. Turn right and detour to a scenic overlook. Return to Goat Rock.

4.4 At Goat Rock continue on Ridge Trail toward the parking lot. In about 0.1 mile reach the trailhead for the interpretive shelter, an open-air pavilion with exhibits on the different types of rock and seven types of oak found in the park. Turn left on the path to the shelter. A rock cave is on the right.

4.5 Reach the interpretive shelter. Return 0.1 mile to Ridge Trail.

4.6 Turn left on Ridge Trail to the parking lot. Take the stairs down to watch climbers challenge the face of Goat Rock. Pass other boulders. The trail once again opens up to views before heading back into woodland.

5.0 At the junction with Saratoga Gap Trail, cross the bridge heading back toward the parking lot.

5.5 At the trailhead for Castle Rock, turn right. The trail heads through a thick Douglas fir forest.

5.8 Come to Castle Rock. The trail leads around the rock and becomes fire road width.

5.9 Turn left at a trailhead for the parking lot. A single-track trail heads downhill to the starting point.

6.1 Arrive back at the parking lot.

Alternate routes: Families may enjoy the 1.3-mile lollipop loop hike through lush forest and bouldering areas to the grand vistas of 75-foot Castle Rock Falls (Saratoga Gap Trail to the falls and back on Castle Rock Trail).

Backpackers love the three-day, 25-mile hike on the Skyline-to-the-Sea Trail from Castle Rock through Big Basin and ending at Waddell Beach. Arrange for a ride home at the end, or get a shower and a comfy bed at the Costanoa Lodge and Campground.

27. PORTOLA REDWOODS STATE PARK: SLATE CREEK/ SUMMIT/IVERSON LOOP

WHY GO?

A hike in Portola Redwoods State Park takes you past an ancient 300-foot redwood tree, through first- and second-generation redwood forest, and down shady paths under mixed evergreens lined with ferns and western azaleas. The ample creeks support crawdads and steelhead trout and are central to the stories of the old lumber days in the canyon. A nature trail guides you to details in the forest. Crowds don't seem to gather on the 18 miles of trails in this off-the-beaten path state park except on the sunniest of summer weekends.

THE RUN DOWN

Start: Parking area on the road to the Campfire Center
Elevation gain: 1,465 feet
Distance: 5.4 miles
Difficulty: Moderate
Hiking time: About 2.5 hours
Seasons/schedule: Best in spring, winter, and fall; 6 a.m. to sunset year-round
Fees and permits: Parking fee
Trail contact: Portola Redwoods State Park, 9000 Portola State Park Rd., La Honda 94020; (650) 948-9098; www.parks.ca.gov/?page_id=539

Dog-friendly: No dogs allowed on trails (only on roads and in campground on leash)
Trail surface: Well-maintained dirt trail, stream crossings, nature trail, small stints on service road and main road
Land status: State park
Nearest town: La Honda
Nat Geo TOPO! Map: Mindego Hill, CA; Big Basin, CA
Nat Geo Trails Illustrated Map: Skyline Boulevard #815; Big Basin, Santa Cruz #816
Other trail users: Equestrians

FINDING THE TRAILHEAD

On Skyline Boulevard (CA 35) turn west onto Alpine Road. Go 3 miles and turn left on Portola State Park Road. Both roads are steep and winding. After paying for parking, continue past the park headquarters/office. Cross the bridge and take the first right toward the Campfire Center. Immediately on the right is parking. (If full, head back toward the park headquarters, turning right into the Tan Oak picnic area and park there.) Look for the trailhead for Slate Creek Trail and Old Tree Trail. **GPS:** N37 15.09' / W122 12.60'

WHAT TO SEE

Within Portola's rugged basin, quiet trails cross Peters Creek and Pescadero Creek and curve and climb through the canyons under the foliage of redwood, Douglas fir, live oak, madrone, and hazelnut trees. Sunlight drifts down through needles, spotlighting the leaf-carpeted forest floor. Spiderwebs glisten after fog. Shelf fungi hang on logs and rocks. Mushrooms push up through the dark soil as banana slugs inch their way across the trails (see sidebar on page 163).

On the Old Tree and Slate Creek Trails, fallen every which way are dead tree trunks in varied states of decay. Stumps are a reminder of logging days, and charred bark tells the story of the many fires to sweep through the canyon, one every sixty years or so. The last blaze to clean up the basin was in 1989. It took down the park's Shell Tree on the Sequoia Nature Trail, a 2,000 year-old-redwood that had survived some thirty fires during its long life.

The Summit Trail takes you through woodland of mostly live oaks and madrones. False Solomon's seal, trillium, and wood fern grace the hillsides. In spring the huckleberry bushes flower. Reclusive winter's wrens and American robins hop through the brush. Steller's jays and ravens squawk from branches. Gray squirrels scamper up tree trunks. Downhill, the trail returns you to the redwood basin and the Iverson Trail.

Redwood trees in Portola Redwoods
State Park
TOM SULCER

The trail takes the name of the first local settler here, Christian Iverson, a Scandinavian immigrant who worked as a Pony Express rider and shotgun guard. Iverson lived on two parcels of land on Pescadero Creek in the 1860s in a hand-split redwood cabin. The cabin stood here for over 120 years until the Loma Prieta earthquake of 1989 finally brought it down. For a long time, planks piled beside the trail served as a memorial to the site. Iverson Trail also takes you to seasonal Tiptoe Falls, with water pouring over a 6-foot shelf of rock.

On Slate Creek Trail you have the option of visiting the Page Mill site. Here the men made shingles and also cut tan oak for use in the tanneries, where slabs of dried wood were pulverized and boiled in water to make liquid tannic acid. Redwoods now grow through what was once a mill platform or tramway.

The second growth did well in the wet basin, and the beauty of the area attracted San Francisco businessman John A. Hooper. He bought the property and built a two-story summer house on Pescadero Creek around the turn of the twentieth century. In 1924 he sold 1,600 acres to his friends in the Islam Temple Shrine of San Francisco. They used it as a summer retreat until 1945 when the state purchased the parcel for a park. The visitor center and park office now occupy the Shriner's Recreation Hall. The Save the Redwoods League donated more land to create today's park, with over 2,800 acres.

The campgrounds here are a great place to spend the night. Backpack camps and many longer trails are available. Paths connect to Long Ridge Open Space Preserve and Pescadero Creek County Park. In spring and early summer, repellent to ward off mosquitoes is highly recommended. Before you leave Skyline Boulevard for the valleys below, consider visiting Methuselah, another giant ancient redwood tree (1,800 years old). The huge redwood is just off Skyline Boulevard on the east side of the road between King's Mountain Road and CA 84.

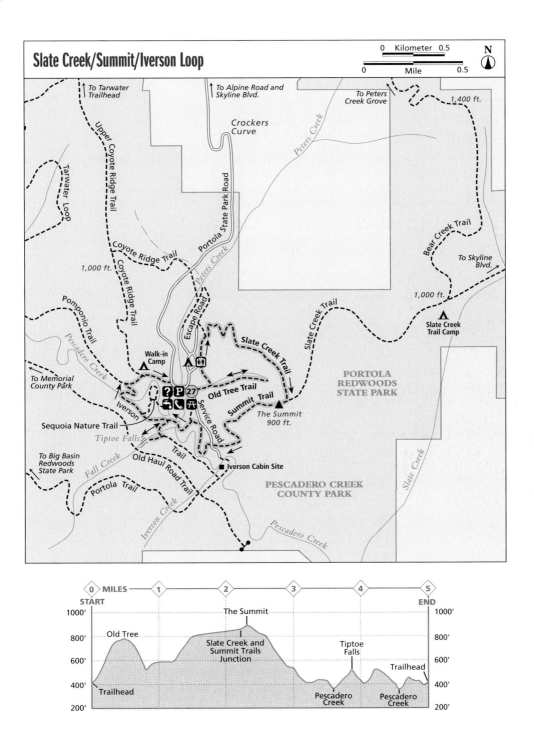

Slate Creek/Summit/Iverson Loop

To Tarwater Trailhead
To Alpine Road and Skyline Blvd.
To Peters Creek Grove
1,400 ft.

Crockers Curve

Upper Coyote Ridge Trail
Tarwater Loop
Peters Creek

Bear Creek Trail
To Skyline Blvd.

Coyote Ridge Trail
1,000 ft.
Coyote Ridge Trail
Portola State Park Road
Peters Creek

Pomponio Trail
Escape Road
Slate Creek Trail
1,000 ft.
Slate Creek Trail Camp

Pescadero Creek

Walk-in Camp
Slate Creek Trail
PORTOLA REDWOODS STATE PARK

To Memorial County Park
Iverson
27
Old Tree Trail
Summit Trail

Sequoia Nature Trail
The Summit 900 ft.

Tiptoe Falls
Trail
Iverson Cabin Site

To Big Basin Redwoods State Park
Fall Creek
Old Haul Road Trail

Slate Creek

Portola Trail
Iverson Creek
PESCADERO CREEK COUNTY PARK

Pescadero Creek

0   Kilometer   0.5
0   Mile   0.5
N

MILES   0   1   2   3   4   5
START   END

1000'   1000'
                The Summit
800'   Old Tree   800'
                Slate Creek and
                Summit Trails   Tiptoe
600'   Junction   Falls   600'
                                            Trailhead
400'   Trailhead   400'
                        Pescadero   Pescadero
200'   Creek   Creek   200'

MILES AND DIRECTIONS

0.0 START from the parking area and walk toward the Campfire Center until you see a trailhead on the left. Turn left at the trailhead for Slate Creek Trail and Old Tree Trail. At the split go straight onto Old Tree Trail.

0.3 Arrive at Old Tree. (**Note:** The Old Tree is 300 feet tall, 12 feet in diameter, and probably between 1,500 and 2,000 years old. Yet its shallow roots are only about 10 feet below the ground, connected to other trees in the area in a family system. It is among the tallest redwoods on the peninsula.) Turn around and head back the way you came.

0.5 At the trailhead for Slate Creek Trail, turn right. The single-track trail goes uphill and over a seasonal creek.

0.9 Stay right on Slate Creek Trail.

1.8 At the junction with Summit Trail, turn right on Summit. (Option: Continue another 1.4 miles on Slate Trail to check out the Page Mill site.) A single-track trail winds around switchbacks with stairs. Past the water tanks the path widens to double-track and soon ends at a service road.

2.6 Turn left on a service road. It crosses Iverson Creek and curves past Iverson's cabin site.

3.0 At the Iverson trailhead, turn right. Pescadero Creek is on the right.

3.6 Turn left to view Tiptoe Falls. Bear left to continue on Iverson Trail. The path follows the curve of the river.

3.9 Continue on Iverson Trail, taking the left fork. Cross a bridge over Pescadero Creek. (**Note:** If visiting in winter or early spring, look for spawning steelhead trout in the creek.) On the other side, the trail continues through a redwood grove.

4.2 Turn right at the junction with Pomponio Trail, staying on Iverson Trail.

4.3 At the junction with Old Haul Road and Coyote Ridge Trail, turn right, continuing on Iverson Trail.

4.4 Iverson Trail ends at the park road across from the Madrone picnic area. Turn right, walking a short distance along the park road to park headquarters.

4.5 To the left of park headquarters, follow signs to Sequoia Nature Trail.

4.7 Stay to the right, remaining on Sequoia Nature Trail.

4.8 Cross a footbridge and turn left at marker #8 to do the loop. At the trailhead for Iverson Trail, bear right toward marker #9.

5.0 Back at marker #8, bear left back the way you came, crossing the bridge and returning to the visitor center.

5.3 Turn right on the park road and walk beside it, crossing the bridge the way you drove in and turning right to the Campfire Center.

5.4 Arrive back at the parking area.

Alternate routes: For a lovely family hike, take the Sequoia Nature Trail on a 1.6-mile loop with the Iverson Trail.

BANANA SLUGS
(ARIOLIMAX COLUMBIANUS DOLICHOPHALLUS)

Almost any walk through redwood forests includes stepping around these yellow, slimy creatures. Because of the banana slug's association with the giant redwoods and its unique characteristics, Bay Area hikers have a great affinity for it. The University of California at Santa Cruz even declared the banana slug its mascot.

Some slug facts:

- The banana slug has few natural enemies.
- Its slime is anesthetic, a bit like novocaine.
- Slug slime can take away the sting from nettles.
- The banana slug has both male and female reproductive organs; when mating, banana slugs cross-fertilize.
- It has a tongue with 27,000 teeth and rasps its food.
- A slug moves about .007 miles per hour.
- A slug can stretch out eleven times its normal length.
- Slugs mark their own scent so they can find their way home after dark.
- Banana slugs were a food source for the Yurok Indians. (Yuck!)

28. PURISIMA CREEK REDWOODS OPEN SPACE PRESERVE: CRAIG BRITTON AND PURISIMA CREEK LOOP

WHY GO?

Purisima is one of the gold nuggets in the bounty of the Midpeninsula Regional Open Space District. The trails in this 4,117-acre westernmost preserve take you through deep canyons under towering redwoods with creeks gurgling and cascading between rich banks of ferns and sorrel. They traverse grassy, oak-scattered hills and ridges with inspiring views. Some of these trails follow the old mill roads of Purisima's logging past. A moderately strenuous climb is an unavoidable part of almost any hike in Purisima, except the wheelchair-accessible Redwood Trail (South parking lot).

THE RUN DOWN

Start: North Ridge trailhead at the Purisima Creek parking lot on Skyline Boulevard (can start the same loop at the end of Higgins Canyon Road or Purisima Creek Road off CA 1 just south of Half Moon Bay)
Elevation gain: 1,800 feet
Distance: 9.9-mile loop
Difficulty: Moderate due to gradual ascent
Hiking time: About 5 hours
Seasons/schedule: Half an hour before sunrise to half an hour after sunset
Fees and permits: None
Trail contact: Midpeninsula Regional Open Space District, 330 Distel

Circle, Los Altos 94022; (650) 691-1200; www.openspace.org/preserves/purisima-creek-redwoods
Dog-friendly: No dogs allowed
Trail surface: Well-maintained single- and double-track dirt trail
Land status: Open space preserve
Nearest town: Woodside and Half Moon Bay
Nat Geo TOPO! Map: Woodside, CA
Nat Geo Trails Illustrated Map: Skyline Boulevard #815
Other trail users: Mountain bikers and equestrians in summer only (hikers only on Soda Gulch)

FINDING THE TRAILHEAD

On Skyline Boulevard (CA 35), about 5 miles from CA 92 or 8 miles from CA 84 (and Alice's Restaurant), park in the Purisima Creek Redwoods Open Space (North) parking lot on the west side of the road. **GPS:** N37 27.0' / W122 20.19'

View from Whittemore Gulch Trail
MIGUEL VIEIRA (FLICKR.COM/PHOTOS/
MIGUELVIEIRA/)

WHAT TO SEE

In Spanish *purisima* means "the most pure," and this is one of those hikes that has a puri-fying quality. The Spanish named the creek and canyon to honor the Virgin Mary. But it is also the magic of the redwood trees that creates the effect. These ancient trees once dominated all of the Northern Hemisphere but are now limited to the coastal range between Monterey and southern Oregon, thriving in the cool, foggy summers and mild winters. Beside the flowing creeks several kinds of ferns prosper: sword fern, with serrated edges on its leaves; western wood fern; and the lacy bracken fern.

These meandering trails are truly a gift from the Midpeninsula Regional Open Space District, which was formed by residents of the Portola Valley who wanted to stop the development of million-dollar homes on the pristine ridge of the Santa Cruz Mountains and preserve the land for the public. Formed in 1972, today the district manages over 63,000 acres of public land in twenty-six open space preserves and continues to grow.

Previously, lumber companies owned much of the acreage, cutting down redwoods for siding, fencing, and furniture from the gold rush up to 1970. The first boom was after the gold rush, with folks settling into the new Golden West. Loggers used handsaws and axes

Forest in Purisima Creek Redwoods Preserve
MIGUEL VIEIRA (FLICKR.COM/PHOTOS/
MIGUELVIEIRA/)

to fell trees. One giant redwood took them a week to cut down, according to the park brochure. Virgin trees, some 1,000 years old or more, were as large as 20 feet in diameter.

Transportation of the lumber was difficult. Oxen dragged the logs to the creekside mills down "skid trails," roads with greased logs across them. Mill workers then blasted the logs with dynamite to split them into manageable pieces. Powered by waterwheels, the mills "gulched out" the wood, cutting them into shingles to take over the steep canyon walls to Redwood City to be shipped to San Francisco. Running the mills was expensive, so they only operated when the prices were high.

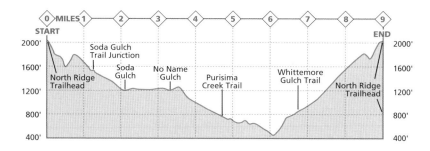

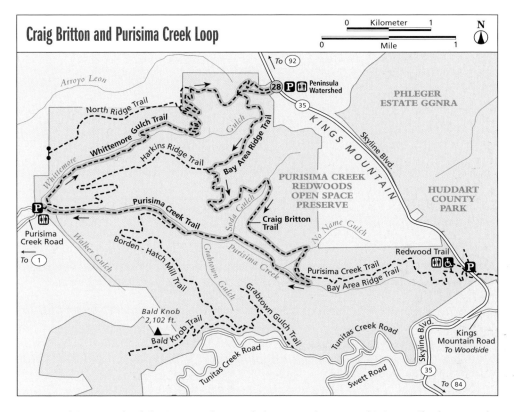

Craig Britton and Purisima Creek Loop

This particular hike is a good up–and–down workout, combining trails along creeks, through redwoods and forests of tan oak and madrone, with trails open to sunlight and canyon and coastal views. The Craig Britton Trail is an especially quiet, deep, redwood forest trail.

MILES AND DIRECTIONS

0.0 START at the parking lot and go through the gate by the restroom to the North Ridge trailhead. It will split right away. Veer right onto the hikers-only Harkins Ridge Trail.

0.5 Junction with North Ridge Trail. Continue on Harkins Ridge Trail downhill on a double-track dirt trail through a mixed woodland. Enjoy views of Half Moon Bay and Pillar Point. (**Note:** Look carefully beyond Pillar Point for the whitecaps of Mavericks, the famous surfing spot.)

1.4 Come to the trailhead for Craig Britton Trail. Turn left onto the single-track, hikers-only trail, which leads into one of the deepest parts of the redwood forest and more mixed forest.

4.0 Come to the trailhead for Purisima Creek Trail, which splits. Take the fork to the right. After crossing the creek around a bend, you next cross No-name Creek. (The clearing here is the site of Hatch Mill.) Cross Purisima Creek several times.

5.3 Pass the trailhead for Borden Hatch Mill Trail, continuing on Purisima Creek Trail. The path continues to follow the creek.

6.3 Reach the trailhead on Higgins Purisima Road. Half Moon Bay is about 5.5 miles away. Turn right and cross a bridge onto Whittemore Gulch Trail. On the other side of the bridge, go left. (Option: You can shorten the loop to around 7 miles by turning right onto Harkins Ridge Trail.) Ascend on Whittemore Gulch Trail, through redwoods, bigleaf maples, red alderberries, and Douglas firs. The trail zigzags uphill through chaparral. Beware of poison oak.

8.5 Continue on Whittemore Gulch Trail.

9.1 Whittemore Gulch Trail dead-ends at North Ridge Trail. Turn right.

9.6 Junction with Harkins Ridge Trail. Continue straight on North Ridge Trail.

9.9 Arrive back at the gate and parking lot.

Alternate routes: Families with younger children may enjoy the paved 0.25-mile Redwood Trail (accessed at the South parking lot) along with some segment of the Purisima Creek Trail.

THE PURCHASE OF PURISIMA

When acquiring the land to create this park, the Midpeninsula Regional Open Space District discovered something odd. In 1900 *Collier's* magazine had a special promotion: buy a subscription and get a parcel of land in the Santa Cruz Mountains. People ordered the magazines and the deeds were handed out. They were mostly forgotten over time. When the district contacted the descendants of the *Collier's* readers, most didn't even know they owned the land. There was good news and bad news. The good news was the land was theirs. The bad news was they were liable for all the back taxes from 1900. Given the choice, most agreed to donate their parcels to the district for a tax break.

Bonus Hikes: The Northern Santa Cruz Mountains

I. HUDDART COUNTY PARK AND PHLEGER ESTATE

WHY GO?

The best access to Phleger Estate (1,232 acres) is through Huddart County Park (973 acres), near the town of Woodside. In 1990 Mary Elena Phleger, determined to keep her family's estate intact, worked with Peninsula Open Space Trust (POST) to achieve her goal. Trails pass through a mix of second-growth redwood forests and oak woodlands, home to a variety of birds, banana slugs, and newts. Huddart Park offers forested slopes and steep, cool canyons. Both parks climb from the foothills up into the northern Santa Cruz Mountains. There are picnic areas, covered shelters, day and overnight camps, an amphitheater, and an archery club.

You can find family trails like the Chickadee Trail, or long, expert loops through both parks climbing 1,900 feet. A great 9-mile loop starts at the Crystal Springs Trail in Huddart, joins the Richards Road, and turns on the Miramonte Trail to enter Phleger Estate. The Mount Redondo Trail meets Lonely Trail. The Lonely Trail is a rigorous climb to a few hundred feet below the Kings Mountain Fire Department and Skyline Boulevard. Richards Road takes you down quickly to the Skyline Trail and Crystal Springs Trail. Crystal Springs links to the hikers-only Dean Trail. It once more intersects with Crystal Springs Trail and returns you to the start. Families might also enjoy a shorter version that includes Crystal Springs Trail.

THE RUN DOWN

Start: Crystal Springs trailhead in Huddart County Park. GPS: N37 26.26' / W122 17.31'
Elevation gain: 1,900 feet
Distance: 9-mile loop
Difficulty: Moderate
Hiking time: About 4.5 hours

Seasons/schedule: 8 a.m. to sunset year-round
Fees and permits: Parking fee
Trail contact: Huddart Park, County of San Mateo Parks Dept., 1100 Kings Mountain Rd., Woodside 94062; (650) 851-1210; http://parks

.smcgov.org/huddart-park; and Phleger Estate, Golden Gate National Recreation Area, Bldg. 201, Fort Mason, San Francisco 94123-0022; (415) 561-4323; www.nps.gov/goga/phes.htm

Dog-friendly: No dogs allowed
Trail surface: Double- and single-track dirt trail

Land status: County park and national recreation area
Nearest town: Woodside
Nat Geo TOPO! Map: Woodside, CA
Nat Geo Trails Illustrated Map: Skyline Boulevard #815
Other trail users: Equestrians

Sign in Phleger Estate
CURIOUSMIKE

J. WUNDERLICH COUNTY PARK

WHY GO?

Meadows, woodlands, flowing creeks, and an early twentieth-century horse stable are some of the features that make Wunderlich hiking fun. The 942 acres of steep mixed forest (redwoods, madrones, oaks), gulches, creeks, and open meadows can be explored on a number of well-maintained loop trails, with sections following the old logging and ranch roads. You can combine it with hiking through Huddart Park or cross Skyline Boulevard on its high ridge into El Corte de Madera Open Space Preserve. No bikes are allowed in the park, but equestrians frequent the trails.

The Alambique Trail passes the fine, large stable built by James A. Folger II (of coffee fame). The stable is still in operation here, though the Folgers' elegant summer mansion has been moved. The Alambique Trail passes through redwoods and mixed woodland. At Alambique Flat, turn right onto the Oak Trail under the dappled shade of oak woodland, popular with birds. A left onto the Meadow Trail takes you to "The Meadows," an open grassland with hawks hunting for field mice and moles. With a right on Bear Gulch, you pass through a large-scale Douglas fir grove. Stay to your left at Redwood Flat for a shady, cool walk through second- and third-growth redwoods on the aptly named Redwood Trail. A right on Bear Gulch again brings you back to the start (about 5 miles).

The park takes its name from contractor Martin Wunderlich, who bought the land from the Folgers and deeded the acreage to San Mateo County for use as a park and open space.

THE RUN DOWN

Start: Alambique trailhead in Wunderlich County Park. GPS: N37 24.40' / W122 15.40'
Elevation gain: 1,000 feet
Distance: 5-mile loop
Difficulty: Moderate
Hiking time: About 2.5 hours
Seasons/schedule: 8 a.m. to sunset year-round
Fees and permits: Parking fee
Trail contact: Wunderlich County Park, 4040 Woodside Rd., Woodside

94062; (650) 851-1210; http://parks.smcgov.org/wunderlich-park
Dog-friendly: No dogs allowed
Trail surface: Double- and single-track dirt trail
Land status: County park
Nearest town: Woodside
Nat Geo TOPO! Map: Woodside, CA
Nat Geo Trails Illustrated Map: Skyline Boulevard #815
Other trail users: Equestrians

K. WINDY HILL OPEN SPACE PRESERVE

WHY GO?

The first park of the Midpeninsula Regional Open Space District is named for its distinctive, breezy, grass-covered hilltop. But within its 1,308 acres, it has a lot more than what you see from CA 35. Besides its waving grasslands and spectacular views, you can find oak and douglas fir forests and redwoods in the canyons on the 12 miles of trails, mostly single-track. Lost Trail, Razorback Ridge (shaded with lots of switchbacks), Eagle Trail, and Hamms Gulch Trail make an enjoyable loop. Families may enjoy the Anniversary Trail, a short hike atop Windy Hill with views of the bay and surrounding valley, followed by some kite flying. Access the trails from Skyline Boulevard (CA 35)—down and up—or Alpine Road—up and back down.

THE RUN DOWN

Start: Anniversary Trail parking and picnic tables on Skyline Boulevard (CA 35). GPS: N37 21.42' / W122 14.50'; or Willowbrook/Alpine Road entrance. GPS: N37 21.53' / W122 12.56'

Elevation gain: 1,800 feet

Distance: 8.2-mile loop

Difficulty: Easy to moderate due to elevation gain

Hiking time: About 4 hours

Seasons/schedule: Half an hour before sunrise to half an hour after sunset

Fees and permits: None

Trail contact: Midpeninsula Regional Open Space District, 330 Distel Circle, Los Altos 94022-1404; (650) 691-1200; www.openspace.org/preserves/windy-hill

Dog-friendly: Dogs on leash (no dogs on Razorback Ridge and Lost Trail)

Trail surface: Single- and double-track dirt trail

Land status: Open space preserve

Nearest town: Portola Valley

Nat Geo TOPO! Map: Mindego Hill, CA

Nat Geo Trails Illustrated Map: Skyline Boulevard #815

Other trail users: Equestrians

L. RUSSIAN RIDGE OPEN SPACE PRESERVE

WHY GO?

These 3,137 acres provide a wildflower show, one of the best in the area. Its blown-grass hillsides, numerous springs creating the headwaters of Mindego and Alpine Creeks, diverse plant life, and miles of forest edge make it a popular habitat for animals, including the elusive mountain lion. It's also one of the best South Bay parks for watching raptors. Red-tailed hawks, turkey vultures, Cooper's hawks, sharp-shinned hawks, and golden eagles all soar above the 8 miles of trails. You can access the park from Skyline Boulevard (CA 35) or Alpine Road.

The suggested hike features the Ridge Trail (where there is some traffic noise) to Ancient Oaks, Charquin, and Hawk Ridge Trails. You can extend your hike by crossing CA 35 into little wooded Coal Creek Open Space Preserve (493 acres), or cross Alpine Road into Skyline Ridge Preserve. Families will enjoy the canopy of stretching oak limbs over the Ancient Oaks Trail.

THE RUN DOWN

Start: Russian Ridge Open Space Preserve parking Lot, corner of Alpine Road and Skyline Boulevard (CA 35). GPS: N37 18.55' / W122 11.19'
Elevation gain: 860 feet
Distance: 5.2-mile loop
Difficulty: Easy
Hiking time: About 2.5 hours
Seasons/schedule: Half an hour before sunrise to half an hour after sunset
Fees and permits: None
Trail contact: Midpeninsula Regional Open Space District, 330 Distel Circle, Los Altos 94022-1404; (650) 691-1200; www.openspace.org/preserves/russian-ridge
Dog-friendly: No dogs allowed

Trail surface: Single- and double-track dirt trail
Land status: Open space preserve
Nearest town: Redwood City
Nat Geo TOPO! Map: Mindego Hill, CA
Nat Geo Trails Illustrated Map: Skyline Boulevard #815
Other trail users: Equestrians and mountain bikers
Special considerations: Additional parking is located at the Caltrans Vista Point on Skyline Boulevard. You can reach Coal Creek Open Space Preserve from the vista point or farther north along Skyline Boulevard at Crazy Petes Road.

M. SKYLINE RIDGE OPEN SPACE PRESERVE

WHY GO?

Within 2,143 acres you find ridge vistas, expansive meadows, a pond for nature study, a quiet lake frequented by migrating birds, and the David C. Daniels Nature Center, open on weekends. Ten miles of trails also offer views of the Lambert Creek watershed, Butano Ridge, and Portola Redwoods State Park. Two 1-mile trails are accessible to wheelchairs and baby strollers, circling Horseshoe Lake and Alpine Pond. You can pick up a self-guided multimedia nature tour in the Daniels Nature Center for Alpine Pond and the Skyline Ridge Habitat, a 2-mile hike through a variety of habitats. The suggested trail includes the Sunny Jim Trail to the Ridge Trail around Horseshoe Lake and the Ipiwa Trail to the Pond Loop Trail around Alpine Pond.

THE RUN DOWN

Start: Russian Ridge Open Space Preserve parking lot, corner of Alpine Road and Skyline Boulevard (CA 35). GPS: N37 18.55' / W122 11.19'
Elevation gain: 765 feet
Distance: 4.1-mile figure-eight loop
Difficulty: Easy
Hiking time: About 2.5 hours
Seasons/schedule: Half an hour before sunrise to half an hour after sunset
Fees and permits: None
Trail contact: Midpeninsula Regional Open Space District, 330 Distel Circle, Los Altos 94022-1404; (650)

691-1200; www.openspace.org/preserves/russian-ridge
Dog-friendly: No dogs allowed
Trail surface: Single- and double-track dirt trail
Land status: Open space preserve
Nearest town: Redwood City
Nat Geo TOPO! Map: Mindego Hill, CA
Nat Geo Trails Illustrated Map: Skyline Boulevard #815
Other trail users: Equestrians and mountain bikers on some trails
Special considerations: Take time to go to the Daniels Nature Center.

N. MONTE BELLO OPEN SPACE PRESERVE

WHY GO?

Aptly named, Monte Bello, Italian for "beautiful mountain," is one of the district's richest parks for wildlife and diverse ecosystems. Rolling grasslands, thickly forested canyons, inspiring vistas, and the most impressive riparian habitat in the Santa Cruz Mountains constitute the 3,436 acres. Fifteen-plus miles of trails take you along Monte Bello Ridge and Black Mountain, from which you can view the whole Santa Clara Valley and Mount Hamilton. Through Stevens Creek Canyon, follow the flowing creek along the San Andreas Fault, enjoying the shade of Douglas firs. From the Stevens Creek Nature Trail, you can see Mount Umunhum and Loma Prieta, the epicenter of the 1989 earthquake. This easy, 3-mile self-guided loop with interpretive signs is perfect for families.

Trails also connect to Upper Stevens Creek County Park and down into Rancho San Antonio Open Space Preserve. The backpack camp at Black Mountain is a good first stop on a backpack trip from the valley to the coast. No dogs are allowed.

THE RUN DOWN

Start: Stevens Creek Nature trailhead, Monte Bello Open Space Preserve parking lot, 4185 Page Mill Rd., Los Altos. GPS: N37 19.33' / W122 10.43'
Elevation gain: 450 feet
Distance: 3-mile loop
Difficulty: Easy
Hiking time: About 2.5 hours
Seasons/schedule: Half an hour before sunrise to half an hour after sunset
Fees and permits: None
Trail contact: Midpeninsula Regional Open Space District, 330 Distel

Circle, Los Altos 94022-1404; (650) 691-1200; www.openspace.org/preserves/monte-bello
Dog-friendly: No dogs allowed
Trail surface: Single- and double-track dirt trail, wooden bridge
Land status: Open space preserve
Nearest town: Los Altos
Nat Geo TOPO! Map: Mindego Hill, CA
Nat Geo Trails Illustrated Map: Skyline Boulevard #815
Other trail users: Equestrians and mountain bikers

O. RANCHO SAN ANTONIO OPEN SPACE PRESERVE AND COUNTY PARK

WHY GO?

Combined, these two adjacent parks provide 4,153 acres of oak woodland, cool fern-banked ravines beside babbling creeks, soft open meadows full of lupine, poppies, and blue-eyed grass, hillsides of chaparral, and ridgetops that open to views. Along the extensive 24-mile trail system, you can create short family loops and longer, more challenging routes, including a climb to the top of Black Mountain (2,800 feet). A great family feature is Deer Hollow Farm, a working farm with pigs, goats, sheep, chickens, and other animals housed in turn-of-the-twentieth-century ranch buildings (650-903-6331).

Rancho San Antonio adjoins Hidden Villa Ranch, a nonprofit environmental education facility that has miles of lovely trails in 1,600 acres open to the public, and a hostel, a rentable lodge, and a cabin (650-949-8650). The main entrance to Hidden Villa is located on Moody Road in Los Altos Hills.

THE RUN DOWN

Start: Rancho San Antonio Open Space Preserve main entrance, 22500 Cristo Rey Dr., Cupertino. GPS: N37 19.58' W122 5.13'
Elevation gain: 400 feet (Wildcat Loop) to 2,400 feet (Black Mountain)
Distance: 3 miles to 15 miles
Difficulty: Easy to strenuous
Hiking time: Varies
Seasons/schedule: Half an hour before sunrise to half an hour after sunset
Fees and permits: None
Trail contact: Midpeninsula Regional Open Space District, 330 Distel Circle, Los Altos 94022-1404; (650) 691-1200; www.openspace.org/preserves/rancho-san-antonio
Dog-friendly: No dogs allowed
Trail surface: Single- and double-track dirt trail
Land status: Open space preserve and county park
Nearest town: Cupertino
Nat Geo TOPO! Map: Cupertino, CA
Nat Geo Trails Illustrated Map: Skyline Boulevard #815
Other trail users: Equestrians and mountain bikers on some trails

P. PESCADERO CREEK COUNTY PARK

WHY GO?

These 8,020 acres of forest and watershed land are composed of four adjacent parks: Pescadero Creek, Memorial, Heritage Grove, and Sam McDonald County Parks. Hiking trails pass creeks blackened with natural tar, trek under giant evergreens dedicated to World War I soldiers, meander in peaceful old-growth redwood forests, and pass through land donated by Sam McDonald, the descendant of a slave.

Forests consist of old- and new-growth redwood stands and mixed woodland of Douglas fir, California wax myrtle, tan oak, madrone, California bay laurel, bigleaf maple, and oak trees. Pescadero and Alpine Creeks both contain steelhead trout and silver salmon.

You can choose from short family loops like the Mount Ellen Nature Trail or many longer loops. In Pescadero Creek Park, many of the trails follow old logging roads. The 5-mile Tarwater Trail Loop gives you a sense of the park's history as the site of natural gas and oil deposits. Heritage Grove, accessible through Sam McDonald County Park, is 37 glorious acres of towering old-growth redwoods. You can reach it directly through an entrance on Alpine Road. Download a map online or pick one up at the entrance.

THE RUN DOWN

Start: Memorial County Park main entrance GPS: N37 16.34' / W122 17.28'; or Sam McDonald County Park main entrance GPS: N37 17.51' / W122 15.55'
Elevation gain: Up to 1,620 feet
Distance: 1 mile to 10-plus miles
Difficulty: Easy to strenuous due to elevation gain
Hiking time: Varies
Seasons/schedule: 8 a.m. to sunset year-round
Fees and permits: Parking fee
Trail contact: Pescadero Creek Park, County of San Mateo Parks Dept.,

9500 Pescadero Creek Rd., Loma Mar 94021; (650) 879-0238; http://parks.smcgov.org/pescadero-creek-park
Dog-friendly: No dogs allowed
Trail surface: Double- and single-track dirt trail
Land status: County park
Nearest town: Loma Mar
Nat Geo TOPO! Map: La Honda, CA
Nat Geo Trails Illustrated Map: Skyline Boulevard #815
Other trail users: Equestrians

Q. HENRY COWELL REDWOODS STATE PARK

WHY GO?

Henry Cowell is a popular park for a reason. Its 4,650 acres offer both old-growth and second-growth redwood forests and mixed evergreen forests, sand hills with marine deposits, a river with swimming holes, and the critters that thrive in this habitat: banana slugs, black-tailed deer, coyotes, bobcats, and steelhead trout.

Rail Bridge at Henry Cowell
Redwoods State Park
RUNNER1928

For a unique hike take Rincon Fire Road to the Division Dam Trail to the Big Rock Hole Trail to the Buckeye Trail to the Pipeline Trail. You'll have to cross the river four times (not advisable in higher-water months). You can swim at the Big Rock swimming hole, take in redwood groves, and admire the overlook on Pipeline Road (6.6 miles with a 1,360 change in elevation).

For more-remote hiking go to the Fall Creek Unit. You'll have 20 miles of trails to choose from in redwood canyons that feature remnants of a successful lime-processing industry. No dogs are allowed in Fall Creek.

Families will enjoy the 0.8-mile, flat, self-guided nature loop on the Redwood Grove Trail through old-growth redwoods. The oldest tree is over 1,500 years old. In the summer hike 3 miles (out and back) to the Garden of Eden swimming hole on the San Lorenzo River. Take the family into the cathedral redwoods and for a swim on Cable Car Beach by taking Pipeline Road to Rincon Fire Road to the Big Rock Hole Trail (4 miles). Check out the visitor center on the River Trail and leave time for a steam train ride on the Roaring Camp Railroad.

THE RUN DOWN

Start: Henry Cowell Redwoods State Park parking lot, Redwood Grove Loop trailhead. GPS: N37 2.26' / W122 3.49'
Elevation gain: Up to 1,360 feet
Distance: Varies
Difficulty: Easy to strenuous
Hiking time: Varies
Seasons/schedule: Sunrise to sunset year-round
Fees and permits: Parking fee
Trail contact: Henry Cowell Redwoods State Park, 303 Big Trees Park Rd., Felton 95018; (831)

335-4598; www.parks.ca.gov/?page_id=546
Dog-friendly: Dogs on leash only on some trails
Trail surface: Paved path, single- and double-track dirt trail, fire road
Land status: State park
Nearest town: Santa Cruz
Nat Geo TOPO! Map: Felton, CA
Nat Geo Trails Illustrated Map: Big Basin, Santa Cruz #816
Other trail users: Equestrians and mountain bikers on some trails

MOUNT DIABLO AND LAS TRAMPAS FOOTHILLS

Mount Diablo is the dominant natural feature of Contra Costa County, and for many who live there it symbolizes home. At sunset the mountain turns crimson, reflecting its name. With the subtlety of California seasons, Diablo is a meter. In winter the rolling green slopes reign majestically over the little city of Danville to the west and Clayton Valley to the north. Billowing clouds cover its peak. The crest may be white for a day or two after the odd cold front sifts snow down on the 3,849-foot summit. In summertime the golden mountain shows off its clumps of fine oaks on the south side, while the north remains thick with woods and scrub. Fire is a danger in the fall to the dry savanna, and every few years, charred and smoldering hillsides start the process of reseeding and recovery.

The Las Trampas hills, separating Contra Costa and Alameda Counties, present lush eastern slopes crowded with oak trees. The western faces feature hills of rock and nappy chaparral in canyons.

Mount Diablo
MIGUEL VIEIRA (FLICKR.COM/PHOTOS/MIGUELVIEIRA/)

Monocular view from the
top of Mount Diablo
DANIEL SCHWEN

Twelve million years ago, Mount Diablo and the Las Trampas ridge were under a vast ocean. As the Earth's tectonic plates moved past each other along the San Andreas Fault line, the land buckled, and a tough slab of volcanic rock rose up. The softer sediments around it washed away, forming the valleys around the peaks. Geologists suspect the mountain is still rising as landslides reshape it from time to time. Seashells are readily visible among the serpentine and sandstone rocks on Las Trampas.

For the hiker these ridges offer miles of trails and mountains to climb. You can see tumbling waterfalls, scamper up huge boulders with caves and contours, and visit historic sites, like the old coal and sand mines at Black Diamond. On Las Trampas you can visit the home of playwright Eugene O'Neill and walk the hills as he did while writing *Long Day's Journey into Night*. You can picnic in Bollinger Canyon or camp in Rock City.

There are fields of orange poppies. Wild mustard turns whole hillsides yellow. Red Indian paintbrush and lavender lupine add bursts of color, and California sagebrush perfumes the air with herb and spice. Lizards do push-ups on sunny rocks as crickets chirp the rhythm. Despite the cattle grazing that still goes on in some of the parks, there's a lot of wildlife inhabiting these hills.

29. LAS TRAMPAS REGIONAL WILDERNESS

WHY GO?

A trek in 3,882-acre Las Trampas Wilderness promises windswept ridges, rugged jigsaw rock outcroppings, dusty valleys, moist spring-fed ravines, sunny grasslands, and the dappled shade of pungent bay trees. This hike also includes two 1,000-foot climbs up Rocky Ridge and the Devil's Bowl. But you are rewarded with breezy, expansive views of the San Francisco Bay, the city skylines, the distant Delta, and majestic Mount Diablo and foothills. There is still abundant wildlife in Las Trampas today and remains of animals, plants, and geological features that tell a story that's 25 million years old.

THE RUN DOWN

Start: Bollinger Canyon Staging Area, Rocky Ridge Road trailhead
Elevation gain: 2,000 feet
Distance: 6.5-mile loop
Difficulty: Strenuous due to two long uphill sections
Hiking time: About 3.5 hours
Seasons/schedule: 5 a.m. to 10 p.m. year-round; hike early in the day in summer to avoid heat
Fees and permits: None
Trail contact: East Bay Regional Park District Headquarters, 2950 Peralta Oaks Ct., P.O. Box 5381, Oakland 94605; (510) 544-3276; www.eb parks.org/parks/las_trampas

Dog-friendly: Dogs on leash
Trail surface: Paved path, single- and double-track dirt trail
Land status: Regional wilderness
Nearest town: San Ramon
Nat Geo TOPO! Map: Las Trampas Ridge, CA
Other trail users: Equestrians on all but Sycamore Trail; mountain bikers on Upper Trail and Elderberry Trail
Special considerations: There is no drinking water available until you reach Corral Camp near the end of your hike. Bring plenty!

FINDING THE TRAILHEAD

In San Ramon, take Crow Canyon Road to Bollinger Canyon Road. Drive 4.5 miles to the end of Bollinger Canyon Road and into the Bollinger Canyon Staging Area parking lot on the left. **GPS:** N37 48.58' / W122 3.2'

WHAT TO SEE

On the Upper Trail, near the 2,024-foot summit of Las Trampas, you follow the spine of Rocky Ridge and come upon the "Indian" wind caves, sculptured by the wind and rain, colored by many lichen species, and revealing fossils. There are literally millions of

At Sycamore and Rocky Ridge Trails
MICHAEL "BINK" KNOWLES

seashells embedded in Rocky Ridge, dating back to the Pliocene era some 12 million years ago when Las Trampas was the Pacific Ocean floor.

Scattered and harder to find are the bones and teeth of fossil mammals representing a fauna around 9 million years old. Paleontologists say these remains are abundant in these hills. They have found "elephant teeth" from a four-tusked mastodon, primitive teeth belonging to four different species of camel, and, most commonly, the teeth of an extinct three-toed horse. Also here were primitive rabbits, honey badgers, archaic beavers, hyaenoid dogs, and wolverine-like carnivores. Believe it or not there were also rhinoceroses, ground sloths, and mammoths in the Pliocene Las Trampas.

Many animals live in the grassland, chaparral, woodland, and ravine habitats of current Las Trampas. On the Sycamore Trail you may glimpse garter snakes or king snakes slithering into the sagebrush (neither is dangerous to humans). You may spot jackrabbits bounding into manzanita scrub, squirrels clinging to the trunk of a bigleaf maple or buckeye tree, or California voles peeking out of burrows in the grassland. Overhead, you are bound to see hawks and turkey vultures, and perhaps even the rare golden eagle. In the ravines, especially during wetter months, you may see salamanders and newts and hear the chirping of Pacific tree frogs, the croaking of endangered red-legged frogs, and the bellow of a western toad.

Keep your eyes open for the tracks and droppings of cougars, bobcats, badgers, ringtails, foxes, and more. At dusk, dark-eyed juncos, finches, red-winged blackbirds, and hummingbirds call it a day and bats punch the clock, hunting for insects along the creeks and springs.

Wildflowers are prevalent in the springtime. One of the best displays is in rocky, steep-walled Sedum Ravine on Sycamore Trail. In mid-April the red delphinium is spectacular, and a couple of weeks later the yellow-flowered stonecrop forms bright floral mats in the upper part of the ravine.

On Rocky Ridge, Las Tampas Regional Wilderness. NICK FULLERTON (FLICKR.COM/PEOPLE/18203311@N08/)

The bison, pronghorn antelope, grizzlies, and abundant elk that have been hunted to extinction in these lands indirectly contributed to the naming of Las Trampas. Meaning "the traps" in Spanish, the name honored the native Miwok Indians' method of driving elk and deer into the steep box canyons for easier hunting.

Three Spanish brothers acquired a grant in 1844 for 17,600 acres that included much of Las Trampas. But the brothers encountered bad fortune, losing the Rancho San Ramon El Sobrante in 1858. The government took over the land. In the 1970s a group of kids organized a group called SANE (Save America's Natural Environment) and helped spearhead the preservation of the Las Trampas wilderness as parkland.

A geologic feature worth noticing on Rocky Ridge and down Elderberry Trail is the Bollinger fault line. The largest of the many faults traversing Las Trampas Wilderness, it played a crucial role in the uplift of the Rocky and Las Trampas ridges. It's probably not active today, say geologists, though some earthquakes have been recorded in its vicinity. You can observe it in the break in the slope near the crest of Rocky Ridge. Also look for green areas and seeping mountain springs. They are a dead giveaway for the fault. In August and September these areas are very apparent, appearing like oases among the baked golden grasslands and thistles.

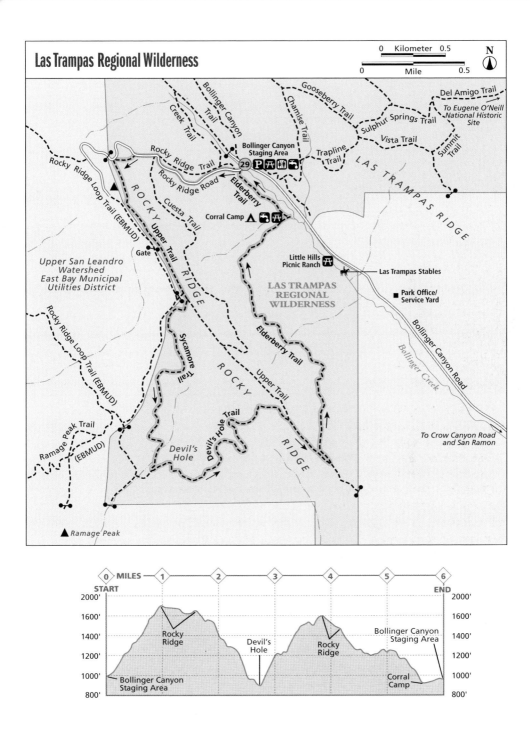

Las Trampas Regional Wilderness

0 Kilometer 0.5

0 Mile 0.5

N

Del Amigo Trail

To Eugene O'Neill
National Historic
Site

Gooseberry Trail

Bollinger Canyon Trail

Chamise Trail

Creek Trail

Sulphur Springs Trail

Vista Trail

Bollinger Canyon
Staging Area

Rocky Ridge Trail

29 P A M A

Trapline Trail

Summit Trail

LAS TRAMPAS RIDGE

Rocky Ridge Loop Trail (EBMUD)

Rocky Ridge Road

Elderberry Trail

ROCKY

Cuesta Trail

Corral Camp A

Upper Trail

Little Hills
Picnic Ranch

Las Trampas Stables

Upper San Leandro
Watershed
East Bay Municipal
Utilities District

Gate

RIDGE

LAS TRAMPAS
REGIONAL
WILDERNESS

Park Office/
Service Yard

Bollinger Canyon Road

Elderberry Trail

Rocky Ridge Loop Trail (EBMUD)

Sycamore Trail

ROCKY

Upper Trail

Bollinger Creek

Ramage Peak Trail

(EBMUD)

Devil's Hole Trail

Devil's
Hole

RIDGE

To Crow Canyon Road
and San Ramon

▲ Ramage Peak

0 MILES 1 2 3 4 5 6
START END
2000' 2000'
1600' 1600'
1400' Rocky Devil's Rocky Bollinger Canyon 1400'
Ridge Hole Ridge Staging Area
1200' 1200'
1000' Corral 1000'
Bollinger Canyon Camp
Staging Area
800' 800'

MILES AND DIRECTIONS

0.0 START at the Bollinger Canyon Staging Area. Take paved Rocky Ridge Road by walking through the gate at the northwest end of the parking lot.

0.4 Rocky Ridge Trail meets Rocky Ridge Road; junction with Cuesta Trail. Take Rocky Ridge Trail to the right, a single-track dirt path through grassland.

0.7 Junction with Upper Trail. Rocky Ridge Trail meets the road again (with a closed gate ahead). The trailhead for Upper Trail is on the left. Turn left onto the single-track trail. It becomes double-track on the ridge.

1.0 Pass the gate to East Bay Municipal Utilities District watershed land. Stay on Rocky Ridge.

1.5 Junction with Sycamore Trail. Turn right onto a single-track dirt path. Upper San Leandro Reservoir is visible in the distance, also San Francisco and Sutro Tower.

1.8 Come to the wind caves up on the ridge to the right. (**Note:** Beware of poison oak.)

1.9 Sycamore Trail leads up and over the rocky ridge. The Sycamore trailhead is on the west side. The trail heads to the right and continues through a series of hairpin turns.

2.7 Sycamore Trail crosses a creek. A cattle path crosses grasslands; stay on the trail. Across the creek is the trailhead marking Sycamore Trail.

2.8 Junction with Devil's Hole Trail. Turn left on the double-track dirt path and start climbing. The 1,000-foot ascent is moderate but continuous. Views open up to San Ramon Valley at the top.

4.0 The trail ends; junction with Upper Trail to Elderberry Trail. Turn right on double-track dirt Upper Trail.

4.4 Upper Trail ends. Turn left on double-track dirt Elderberry Trail.

6.1 Reach Corral Camp. Continue on Elderberry Trail left (northwest) to Bollinger Canyon Staging Area.

6.5 Arrive back at the Bollinger Canyon Staging Area and parking lot.

Alternate routes: If you have the time and an EBMUD permit, detour through the gate to the ridge at 0.2 mile, where you can see the first series of wind caves. No permit? Don't want to risk it? There are more wind caves on upper Sycamore Trail.

30. **MOUNT DIABLO STATE PARK: DONNER CANYON TO THE FALLS TRAIL**

WHY GO?

Mount Diablo is most often seen as dry grassland and scattered oaks on the south side, but on the less traveled north side of the mountain are shady, wooded canyons. Because they're protected from the sun most of the day, Donner, Back, and Mitchell Canyons have some of California's best wildflower shows. The seasonal waterfalls in the upper reaches of Donner Canyon, especially in Wild Oat Canyon along Falls Trail, are spectacular.

THE RUN DOWN

Start: Donner Canyon Road trailhead at Regency Gate of Mount Diablo State Park
Elevation gain: 1,630 feet
Distance: 5.9-mile loop
Difficulty: Moderate to strenuous due to elevation gain
Hiking time: About 4 hours
Seasons/schedule: Best in spring; 8 a.m. to sunset year-round
Fees and permits: None
Trail contact: Mount Diablo State Park Headquarters, Mitchell Canyon Staging Area, 96 Mitchell Canyon Rd., Clayton 94517; (925) 837-2525, www.parks.ca.gov/?page_id=517

Dog-friendly: No dogs allowed
Trail surface: Double-track dirt trail, narrow single-track trail with some rocks to traverse, downhill on mostly double-track dirt
Land status: State park
Nearest town: Clayton
Nat Geo TOPO! Map: Clayton, CA
Other trail users: Equestrians and mountain bikers on Donner Canyon and Back Creek Trails
Special considerations: Trails can be muddy after rains, but this is also the best time for the falls.

FINDING THE TRAILHEAD

On I-680 exit at Ygnacio Valley Road and go east 7.5 miles, then enter the town of Clayton. Turn right on Clayton Road and go 2.5 miles. Turn right onto Marsh Creek Road, then right onto Regency Drive and follow it until it dead-ends. There is plenty of street parking. Head south down the embankment to the Donner Canyon Road trailhead. **GPS:** N37 54.51' / W121 56.2'

WHAT TO SEE

A glistening, tree-lined creek starts this hike, along with fields of grass and wild mustard, the smell of wild sage, and glimpses of scurrying squirrels and lizards.

Falls Trail
MIGUEL VIEIRA (FLICKR.COM/
PHOTOS/MIGUELVIEIRA/)

Both Donner Creek and Back Creek flow most of the year, though they are down to a trickle in golden summer and early fall. Not long ago, and for hundreds of years, they provided a peaceful hunting camp for the Miwok Indians. In the 1860s and 1870s—the area's heyday—the surrounding valley became home to several thriving towns housing post–gold rush farmers, loggers, and coal miners. Joel Clayton, an English immigrant, discovered coal north of Clayton and founded his namesake town in 1857. But Donner and Back Canyons remained fairly quiet and peaceful. The mines were short-lived and were ghost towns by the 1880s.

The only remains of any structure on your hike are those of the Donner/Hethering-ton Cabin along Donner Creek. An eccentric landowner, Mrs. Donner (not related to the Donner Party), bought the land in the 1940s. The creek and canyon take her name. She raised sheep on the land and planted a small grove of fruit trees; apple, pear, and plum trees still thrive upslope to the right (west) of the trail. Mrs. Donner sold the building to the local sheriff's department as a hunting lodge; the hunters built the concrete slab you see, most likely as the base of a fire pit for roasting fresh venison.

The Hetheringtons purchased the land in 1952. Members of a horticulture society, the San Francisco couple spent time planting native species to restore the overgrazed land. In an effort to preserve the canyon, they sold it in 1972 to the Save Mount Diablo (SMD) organization, who turned Donner, Back, and Mitchell Canyons over to the state park. Even with the last forty years of vast development on all sides of the mountain, SMD has managed to increase the park from its original 6,788 acres to more than 89,000 acres today.

Flowers on North Peak Trail
MIGUEL VIEIRA (FLICKR.COM/
PHOTOS/MIGUELVIEIRA/)

We have a candy maker to thank for the most memorable trails on this hike: Falls Trail and Cardinet Oaks Road. In 1939 George Cardinet and his horse began hauling tools up into the canyons to construct new trails. Mr. Cardinet (maker of the U–No Bar) maintained the two trails he created for over sixty years, almost until his death in 2007 at the age of 98.

What makes his trails so memorable? In wet months and after rains, you'll see a satisfying series of sparkling waterfalls, the largest dropping 25 feet. Also, wildflowers are abundant in upper Donner and Wild Oat Canyons. Besides the usual purple California lupine, orange poppies, and fiery Indian paintbrush, you'll see the yellow Mount Diablo daisy, pink mosquito-bills, delicate white milkmaids, powder-blue grand hound's tongue, and hundreds of species of herbs, grasses, and shrubs. In the late winter the pink blossoms of the manzanitas awaken to the approaching spring.

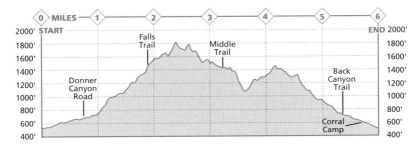

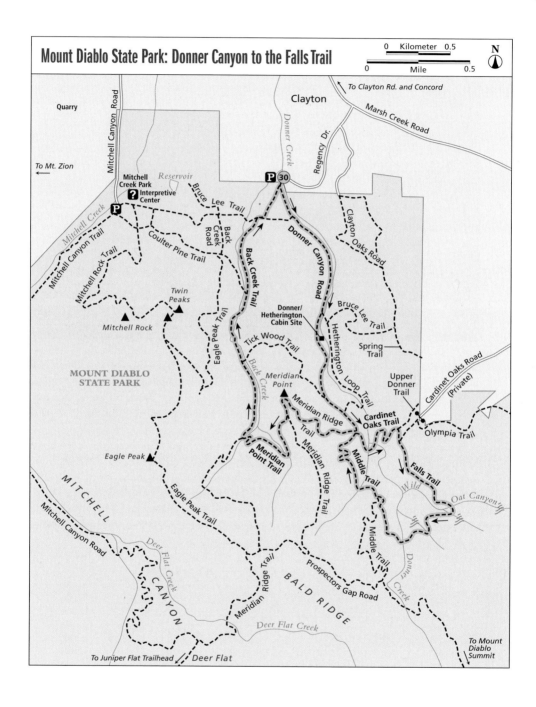

Mount Diablo State Park: Donner Canyon to the Falls Trail

MILES AND DIRECTIONS

0.0 START at the end of Regency Drive and walk past the end-of-street barrier to the fire trail below. This is Donner Canyon Road (also known as Donner Creek Fire Road), which runs perpendicular to Regency. Take Donner Canyon Road south (left).

0.1 Pass the trailhead to Bruce Lee and Back Creek Trails to Mitchell Canyon Road; stay right on Donner Canyon Road.

0.8 A single-track path goes to the Donner Cabin historic site; detour left by the creek. Continue on Donner Canyon Road to Cardinet Oaks Road.

1.2 Pass Tick Wood Trail and later Hetherington Loop Trail. Start a steady, moderate ascent.

1.4 Reach the top of the ridge, with views of Clayton, Mount Diablo foothills, and Mount Zion quarries to the west, Mitchell Rock to the south, and the northernmost part of the San Francisco Bay.

1.5 Go left on Cardinet Oaks Road. The trail crosses the creek. Head uphill again after the creek crossing on a moderate climb.

1.9 Turn right on steep, single-track Falls Trail. As the trail crests, waterfalls become visible. The first waterfall sometimes drops more than 25 feet. Depending on the season, you may cross the creek several times. The ridge drops off dramatically to the right. Moderate hiking lies beyond. The trail heads deeper into the canyon.

3.1 At Middle Trail, go right (a sign reads "To Meridian Trail 0.53 Mile")

3.7 Turn left, uphill, on Meridian Ridge Road.

4.2 Take Meridian Point Trail toward Back Creek Trail, crossing Back Creek.

4.7 The trail dead-ends on double-track Back Creek Trail; turn right, heading north.

5.1 Pass Tick Wood Trail; stay on Back Creek Trail, which follows Back Creek.

5.4 Stay right on Back Creek Trail to where it meets Donner Canyon Road (the left trail leads to Mitchell Canyon Visitor Center and Ranger Station).

5.9 Arrive back at the trailhead and Regency Drive just ahead.

Alternate routes: For a shorter hike, double back on Donner Canyon Road instead of taking Meridian to Back Creek (cuts 1 mile off the distance).

If you're hearty and have the time, climb another 2 miles up Prospectors Gap Road to the North Peak Trail to the Devil's Pulpit, the Devil's Elbow, and the Mount Diablo summit (3,849 feet).

31. BLACK DIAMOND MINES REGIONAL PRESERVE

WHY GO?

You have your choice of 70 miles of trails in this nearly 6,000-acre preserve. This hike goes through two old mining town sites, past many mine openings, and to a historic cemetery. You can see airshafts for the old coal-mining tunnels and "Jim's Place," a mysterious underground dwelling. You'll walk through mostly open grassland and some mixed evergreen forest. Black Diamond is the northernmost location of Coulter pine, black sage, and desert olive. Springtime hosts wildflowers. Leave time to tour the underground mining museum and the Hazel-Atlas Mine.

THE RUN DOWN

Start: Parking lot for Black Diamond Mines Regional Preserve

Elevation gain: 1,530 feet

Distance: 5.2-mile loop

Difficulty: Moderate, with a few short, strenuous uphill sections

Hiking time: About 3 hours (allow 4 to 5 hours if taking the tour of the Hazel-Atlas Mine)

Seasons/schedule: 8:00 a.m. to sunset year-round; avoid heat of the day in summer/fall

Fees and permits: Parking fee on weekends and holidays; fee for dogs

Trail contact: Black Diamond Mines Regional Preserve, 5175 Somersville Rd., Antioch 94509-7807, (510) 544-2750; and East Bay Regional Park District Headquarters, 2950 Peralta Oaks Ct., P.O. Box 5381, Oakland 94605; (510) 544-2750; www.ebparks.org/parks/black_diamond

Dog-friendly: Dogs on leash (except in Hazel-Atlas Mine)

Trail surface: Single-track dirt and sandstone and double-track dirt trail, paved service road

Land status: Regional preserve

Nearest town: Antioch

Nat Geo TOPO! Map: Antioch South, CA

Other trail users: Equestrians and mountain bikers on some trails

Special considerations: At the time of writing, Greathouse Visitor Center was closed for construction in the mine. The Sidney Flat Visitor Center also contains history of the park and has sign-ups for the Hazel-Atlas Mine Tour. A wildflower guide is available for download on the EBRP website, as well as a brochure with biographies of individuals buried in Rose Hill Cemetery.

FINDING THE TRAILHEAD

On CA 4 in Antioch e exit 26 for Auto Center Drive/Somersville Road. Drive south on Somersville Road (toward the hills) 3.6 miles to the parking lot and Somersville Staging Area, Black Diamond Mines Regional Preserve (in Pittsburg). Follow the signs to the Hazel-Atlas Mine. **GPS:** N37 57.33' / W121 51.47'

View from the ridge in Black Diamond
Mines Regional Preserve
NICK FULLERTON (FLICKR.COM/
PEOPLE/18203311@N08/)

WHAT TO SEE

Hiking in the Black Diamond Mines Regional Preserve, you travel through time. Your first stop is California circa 1772. The Miwok Indians had lived in this area for thousands of years, but with the arrival of European settlers in 1772, the Miwok way of life was rapidly destroyed.

The next stop is circa 1855. This preserve was once the largest coal-mining district in the state. The Mount Diablo coalfield, in operation from 1855 to 1902, gave birth to five prospering towns around twelve major mining sites: Nortonville, Somersville, Stewartville, Judsonville, and West Hartley. The Black Diamond Mine produced the weakest grade of coal: lignite (or subbituminous coal), crumbly, dull, and high in sulfur. Taken out of the Antioch Valley by train, the coal was used to run steamships and steam locomotives and to heat post–gold rush homes in the San Francisco Bay Area, Sacramento, and Stockton.

Belowground are some 100 miles of mining tunnels that produced 4 million tons of coal, amounting to $20 million during its heyday. And all this work was completed with simple equipment, by hand. Hard hats weren't yet invented. Men and boys (starting at 8 years old) worked 12-hour days. And, of course, there were accidents. Next to what is now the parking lot, you find remains of the Independent Mine. In 1873 an attached boiler room exploded, killing two men and blowing parts of the boiler a quarter mile away.

Black Diamond Mines Regional Preserve
NICK FULLERTON (FLICKR.COM/PEOPLE/18203311@N08/)

Living was tough. Babies died in epidemics; women, in childbirth; and men, of disease from years in the mines. Some were buried in Rose Hill Cemetery, and their legends are documented in the museum. There are fun myths about ghosts in the cemetery as well.

Better-grade coal found in Washington State put Black Diamond out of business in 1902, and the area cleared.

The next stop is circa 1922. The ghost towns of Somersville and Nortonville are suddenly active again. Along with coal in the abandoned mines was high-grade silica sand. Marvin Greathouse, owner of the Somersville mine area, put it back in operation to supply sand used in glassmaking by the Hazel-Atlas Glass Company in Oakland. The Nortonville mine also supplied the Columbia Steel Works in Pittsburg with foundry (casting) sand.

Competition from Belgian glass and the closing of the steel foundry ended the sand mining in 1949. But by that time, more than 1.8 million tons of sand had been mined. The towns were abandoned for good.

The Greathouse Visitor Center and the Hazel-Atlas Mine tour are must-sees, with artifacts and great old photos of the towns and their people. Tour participants also take a 400-foot walk back into the mine and see the office of the shifter (mine boss), ore chutes, and ancient geological features. Tours start every hour from noon to 4:00 p.m. on Saturday and Sunday. You can arrange a tour for an organization on weekdays by calling the park (925-757-2620).

The hike takes you past other mine openings, a powder magazine, mounds of tailings (residue of the mining process), and railroad beds, amid a variety of native and exotic plant life. Coal miners introduced the black locust, pepper tree, almond, eucalyptus, and tree of heaven. Two rare animal species dwell here—the black-shouldered kite and the Alameda striped racer.

On the narrow Chaparral Trail, partially shaded by red-barked manzanita and thickets, oaks and short pines, the trail's floor becomes soft sandstone. The Manhattan Canyon Trail is shaded by oaks. Black Diamond Trail, a wider path, requires a steady climb into grassland, but rewards you with open vistas north to the valley and west to Martinez, the bay, and the Marin Headlands. On Coal Canyon Trail, "Jim's Place" may trigger your imagination. No one knows exactly who lived here. This narrow trail takes you into a pine-shaded canyon along a creek bed.

At the bottom of the canyon, the trail is sandwiched between two tall rock faces with a pit at the bottom, site of the Nortonville Mine. The town would have stood just ahead.

With a 0.5-mile climb, smelling wild anise in late summer and fall, pass over a ridge of Rose Hill to the Protestant burial ground. You also have a great view here of the Somersville site before heading down the hill.

MILES AND DIRECTIONS

0.0 START by the park road at the parking lot for Black Diamond Mines Regional Preserve. Follow signs to Greathouse Visitor Center and Hazel-Atlas Mine. Pass a mound of tailings on the left. At Greathouse Visitor Center, take the stairs just to the right to begin the hike. Turn left toward the Hazel-Atlas Mine onto Chaparral Loop Trail.

0.1 Arrive at Hazel-Atlas Mine.

0.2 Check out the powder magazine, used to store explosives.

0.3 See the stope (chamber blasted out of sandstone by miners extracting rock for glassmaking).

0.4 Turn right to continue on Chaparral Loop Trail.

0.8 Before a bridge, turn left on Manhattan Canyon Trail, which dead-ends at Black Diamond Trail.

1.0 Turn left on Black Diamond Trail and proceed uphill.

2.1 Pass a pond on the left.

2.5 Black Diamond Trail becomes paved Black Diamond Way.

2.9 Take a short detour to the left on Cumberland Trail. Go about 0.1 mile to an air shaft (on the left before the electric wires tower). (**Note:** The air shaft, once 150 feet deep and reached here by a short tunnel, was used to keep a

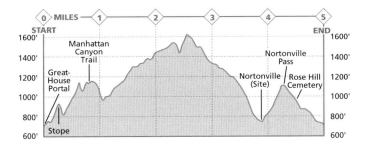

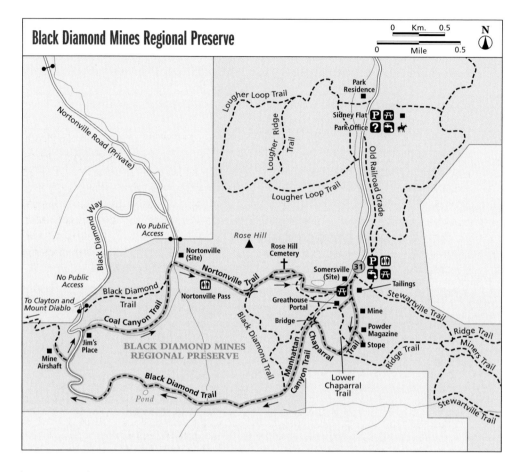

coal mine ventilated and free from dangerous gases. The marks left by miners' picks are still evident on the excavation sides.) Return to Black Diamond Way the same way you came and continue hiking north.

3.1 Look for the trailhead for Coal Canyon Trail. Turn right onto the narrow dirt footpath.

3.2 Come to Jim's Place. Follow signs to the right of the trail. Continue on Coal Canyon Trail.

3.8 Pass the covered hole of the old, vertical Nortonville Mine. Ahead is the Nortonville town site.

3.9 Turn right onto Nortonville Trail and climb the hill.

4.6 After passing over a ridge of Rose Hill, bear left to the cemetery gate. Go through the cemetery and head downhill toward the parking lot. Below is what used to be the town of Somersville.

5.2 Arrive back at the parking lot.

32. MOUNT DIABLO: ROCK CITY TO THE SUMMIT

WHY GO?

Mount Diablo, the once-sacred mountain of the Miwok Indians, continues to be sacred to today's Bay Area hikers, mountain bikers, equestrians, and nature lovers. On this hike you can scramble up boulders or search for ancient ocean fossils at Rock City; bird- and butterfly-watch and enjoy a hearty oak-laurel and gray pine forest on the Juniper Trail; identify wildflowers on the Summit Trail; learn about local history, geology, and wildlife at the Summit Museum; and take in breathtaking views of the Pacific Ocean and the snow-crested Sierra from the observatory tower at the 3,849-foot peak.

THE RUN DOWN

Start: Rock City trailhead, north of the Rock City parking and picnic area
Elevation gain: 2,885 feet
Distance: 8.5-mile double-lollipop loop
Difficulty: Moderate to strenuous due to first half being all uphill
Hiking time: About 4 hours
Seasons/schedule: 8 a.m. to sunset year-round
Fees and permits: South Gate Road vehicle entrance fee
Trail contact: Mount Diablo State Park Headquarters, 96 Mitchell

Canyon Rd., Clayton 94517; (925) 837-2525; www.parks.ca.gov/?page_id=517
Dog-friendly: No dogs allowed on trails
Trail surface: Single- and double-track dirt trail, crossing over paved road several times, short walk through paved parking lot
Land status: State park
Nearest town: Danville
Nat Geo TOPO! Map: Diablo, CA
Other trail users: Equestrians

FINDING THE TRAILHEAD

From I-680 take exit 39 for Diablo Road. Turn right on Diablo Road. Continue on Diablo Road, which becomes Blackhawk Drive. Go 4.6 miles and turn left on Mount Diablo Scenic Boulevard. Signs read "To Athenian School" and "To Mt. Diablo State Park South Gate Entrance." This becomes the South Gate Road once in the park and winds its way up the mountain. Pay the entrance fee at the kiosk and proceed to Rock City. Turn left into the Rock City camping and picnic area. Keep going until you see a street veering uphill to your left with a sign that reads "To Big Rock, Sentinel Rock and Wind Caves." Turn left and proceed to the parking lot at the end. Walk north to the end of the parking lot to start your hike on the Rock City Trail.
GPS: N37 51.0' / W121 56.2'

WHAT TO SEE

According to Miwok Indian mythology, Mount Diablo was once an island surrounded by water. From this island the creator Coyote and his assistant, Eagle-man, made the world. Coyote and his grandson, Wek-wek (Prairie Falcon-man), also created the Indian people, providing them with "everything, everywhere so they can live."

Though stories vary from tribe to tribe, all felt Mount Diablo was sacred. And you may feel this way too as you trek the 2,000 feet up to the summit over undulating grasslands, by rugged rock outcrops, and through the abundant blue oak, valley oak, and coast live oak from which the Bolbon, the Miwok tribe living closest to Mount Diablo, gathered their main staple food of acorns.

Geologically speaking, you go backward in time as you climb toward the summit. The tan-colored Rock City marine sandstone and shale date back 50 million years. The soft rocks are easily eroded to create wind caves and interesting shapes. The Summit Trail takes you back 75 million years, to the Cretaceous period. The upper part of Mount Diablo is made up of rocks as old as 190 million years. The dramatic colors of the earth around the summit are made from a combination of shale, basalt, chert, and occasional blocks of schist and green serpentinite. But it is a young mountain geologically, and an evolving one, slowly rising and pulling on the San Ramon Valley beneath it with earthquakes (every 500 years or so) caused by a thrust fault below.

When Spanish explorers Pedro Fages and Father Juan Crespi climbed the mountain in 1782, they saw rich lands to claim for Spain. In 1851, during the gold rush, deputy surveyor-general Colonel Leander Ransom and his men ascended Diablo and erected a flagpole on the summit to mark the initial point of the Mount Diablo meridian; thus began the survey of public lands in California.

The California Geological Survey Group visited the mountain in 1861, estimating that the view from the summit embraced 80,000 square miles. On a clear day you can see Lassen Peak to the north and Half Dome in Yosemite National Park to the east.

On the Summit Trail you pass the site of a first-rate hotel built in 1873 by Joseph Seavey Hall, a New Hampshire transplant. Later that year Hall opened the sixteen-room Mountain Hotel and Restaurant on the lofty ridge beside Pulpit Rock. At the summit Hall erected a telescope through which visitors could spot Mount Whitney to the south and Mount Shasta to the north. Unfortunately, money troubles forced Hall to sell his hotel, and on July 4, 1891, fire swept up the slopes from Morgan Territory and destroyed the observatory.

In 1912 landowner R. N. Burgess built new toll roads all the way to Diablo's summit (North Gate and Mount Diablo Scenic Boulevard, completed in 1915). He also had plans for a tower hotel, Torre de Sol, on the summit, backed and publicized by William Randolph Hearst. But with World War I, Hearst lost interest, and Burgess's company went bankrupt.

This allowed for 630 acres on the top to become Mount Diablo State Park in 1921. In 1927 Frederick Law Olmsted, champion of US parks, recommended acquisition of 6,000 acres at Mount Diablo to "amplify" the state park at the summit. Thanks to the Save

Fiddlenecks (*Amsinckia* sp.) on
Mount Diablo North Peak Trail
MIGUEL VIEIRA (FLICKR.COM/
PHOTOS/MIGUELVIEIRA/)

Mount Diablo organization, protected open space has expanded by tens of thousands of acres since the 1970s.

In the 1930s the Civilian Conservation Corps constructed campgrounds and picnic areas, marked hiking trails, and built park residences, dams, and the rustic stone summit building you can still enjoy.

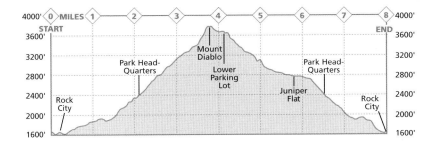

HIKE 32   **203**

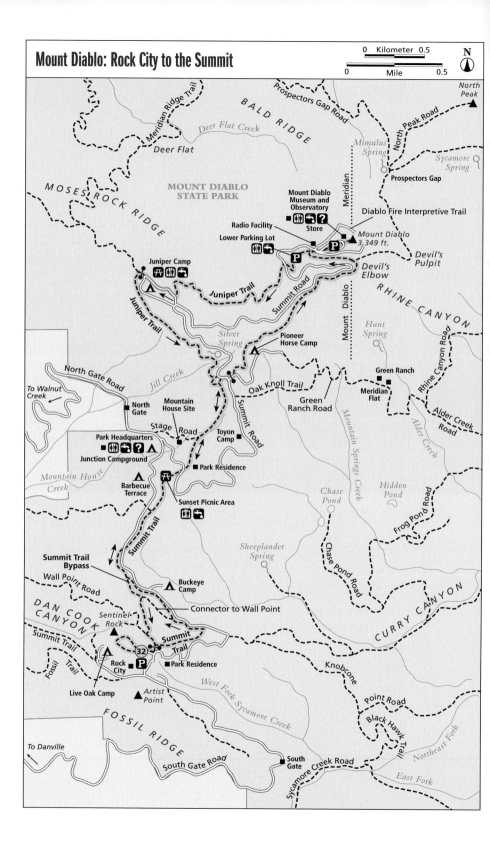

Mount Diablo: Rock City to the Summit

0 Kilometer 0.5
0 Mile 0.5

N

Prospectors Gap Road

BALD RIDGE

North Peak

Deer Flat Creek

Deer Flat

MOSES ROCK RIDGE

Meridian Ridge Trail

MOUNT DIABLO STATE PARK

Mimulus Spring

Sycamore Spring

Meridian

North Peak Road

Prospectors Gap

Mount Diablo Museum and Observatory

Diablo Fire Interpretive Trail

Radio Facility

Store

Lower Parking Lot

Mount Diablo 3,349 ft.

Devil's Pulpit

Juniper Camp

Devil's Elbow

RHINE CANYON

Juniper Trail

Juniper Trail

Summit Road

Mount Diablo

Hunt Spring

Silver Spring

Pioneer Horse Camp

North Gate Road

Jill Creek

Oak Knoll Trail

Green Ranch

Meridian Flat

Rhine Canyon Road

To Walnut Creek

North Gate

Mountain House Site

Stage Road

Summit Road

Toyon Camp

Green Ranch Road

Alder Creek Road

Alder Creek

Park Headquarters

Junction Campground

Park Residence

Mountain House Creek

Barbecue Terrace

Sunset Picnic Area

Mountain Springs Creek

Chase Pond

Hidden Pond

Frog Pond Road

Summit Trail

Sheeplander Spring

Chase Pond Road

Summit Trail Bypass

Wall Point Road

Buckeye Camp

DAN COOK CANYON

Sentinel Rock

Connector to Wall Point

Summit Trail

CURRY CANYON

Summit Trail

32

Fossil Trail

Rock City

Park Residence

Knobcone

Live Oak Camp

Artist Point

West Fork Sycamore Creek

Point Road

Black Hawk Trail

FOSSIL RIDGE

Northeast Fork

To Danville

South Gate Road

South Gate

Sycamore Creek Road

East Fork

MILES AND DIRECTIONS

0.0 START at the north end of the parking lot for Rock City in Mount Diablo State Park. Start the hike on the single-track dirt trail to Sentinel Rock. The trail goes through natural-rock Little Rock amphitheater. Take the trail behind a cave and stay left.

0.1 Climb a rock to see Sentinel Rock to the west and get your bearings. Take an unmarked trail with a poison oak warning to head in the right direction. The trail will take you over rocks with stairs carved out in places. It is a moderately strenuous hike. (**Note:** There are numerous trails that lead to Sentinel Rock.)

0.2 At Sentinel Rock, climb to the top with the help of railings and enjoy the view. Head back toward the Rock City parking lot. The trail to the right leads around rocks, staying on soft ground. (**Note:** Beware of poison oak.)

0.4 Take any trail through Rock City toward the main road.

0.5 On the bend in the road just past Rock City, across from an employee residence, there are two trailheads on the left. Pass the first (Wall Point Road to Macedo Ranch) and take the second one—double-track, multiuse Summit Trail—to the summit parking lot (3.7 miles).

0.6 Pass another employee residence and the Horseshoe picnic area; the road is on the right.

0.8 Make a sharp left turn and continue on Summit Trail.

1.2 Junction of Summit Trail Bypass. Stay right on Summit Trail, which becomes single-track.

1.8 Cross paved Summit Road to stay on Summit Trail, which becomes a double-track dirt trail again. The state park heliport is along the trail. Pass the junction to Barbecue Terrace Road, staying on Summit Trail for a moderate climb. To the left is North Gate Road.

2.1 The Sunset picnic area is on the left. The double-track trail becomes a paved road past the picnic area, meeting Summit Road at a crosswalk. Cross the road and continue on Summit Trail, now a paved road (also a driveway for an employee residence). Pass the house; Summit Trail once again becomes a double-track dirt trail, mostly shady.

2.3 Come to the Mountain House junction. The ranger station is to the left 0.2 mile. The fork to the right is Summit Trail (1.9 miles to the top from here). The Mountain House site is just before the junction between the two trails (path leading to the ranger station is part of the original stagecoach road). Continue on Summit Trail; Mountain House Creek is on the right (dry in summer).

2.6 Junction with Juniper Trail; stay on Summit Trail. It will soon become single-track, hikers only.

2.7 Pass a water tank, Pioneer Horse Camp, and an interpretive sign about the Alameda whipsnake. Summit Trail heads up left, becoming double-track dirt again. It ascends into single-track trail in less than 0.2 mile. The summit museum is visible above.

3.5 Trail meets Summit Road. Follow paved Summit Road about 20 feet to where Summit Trail continues to the right, starting as a double-track gravel road.

Winter blue oak woodlands
on Mount Diablo
MIGUEL VIEIRA (FLICKR.COM/
PHOTOS/MIGUELVIEIRA/)

3.6 Summit Trail to the left becomes a single-track dirt path again.

3.7 Reach the Devil's Elbow. The trail meets Summit Road again. There are two trailheads; stay left on Summit Trail (the other is Prospector's Gap, which leads to Donner Canyon and Clayton).

4.0 The trail meets Summit Road again. The lower Summit parking lot is to the left. Turn right and stay right on the paved road less than 0.1 mile. To the left is the trailhead for Summit Trail that leads to a single-track trail to the Summit parking lot and museum.

4.2 Arrive at the Mount Diablo summit and museum. Return to the trailhead for Summit Trail to the lower parking lot.

4.4 The trail comes out at the lower parking lot. Walk straight across the lot to its end to the trailhead for Juniper Trail to Juniper Camp.

4.6 Cross the road on the crosswalk and proceed up the road to the right about 70 feet to continue on Juniper Trail. The trail heads downhill.

5.6 Juniper Camp. Walk along paved Juniper Campground Road, past campsites, to where the road curves. There, take a double-track dirt road. About 100 yards down is a gate and the trailhead for Deer Flat Creek Road. At the gate turn left onto single-track dirt Juniper Trail. About 100 yards later the path splits; stay right.

5.8 Stay on Juniper Trail (a single-track, hikers-only, dirt path). Below are buildings of Diablo Ranch and the park headquarters at the junction of North and South Roads. Juniper and chaparral grow thick here, then the trail opens up into hillside grassland. Cross a small wooden bridge over Jill Creek (dry in summer).

6.5 The trail meets a gravel parking lot; cross it and restart Juniper Trail on the other side. About 20 feet later, stay to the left on the trail.

6.7 Junction with Summit Trail. Turn right, going south downhill on double-track dirt Summit Trail.

7.0 At the junction, Mountain House Creek is now on the left. Take the left fork, Summit Trail.

7.2 Pass an employee residence onto paved road, cross the road, and pass the Sunset picnic area on the right. The trail is back to double-track dirt.

7.3 Cross the road on the crosswalk and continue on Summit Road. A sign reads "To South Gate Road."

7.9 Junction with Summit Trail Bypass. Take the bypass, turning right on a single-track trail with great views of Rock City.

8.1 Junction with a connector to Wall Point Road. Turn right on the single-track connector trail.

8.3 Dead-end at Wall Point Road. Turn left on double-track dirt Wall Point Road.

8.4 The trail meets the road right at the curve above Rock City where you started on Summit Trail. Head up into Rock City Camp on any trail; turn right on the paved road marked Little Rock Picnic Area. At the end of the gravel turnaround area, take the stone steps, climb another set, and pass through the Little Rock amphitheater. Follow the rock steps back to the parking lot.

8.5 Arrive back at the parking lot.

Alternate routes: Young families might enjoy a romp around Rock City then a drive to the peak for the Mary Bowerman Trail (under a mile), a guided nature trail.

THE ALAMEDA WHIPSNAKE

Mount Diablo's rocky, brush-covered slopes provide habitat preferred by both the Alameda whipsnake and its favorite prey, the western fence lizard. Not often seen, this wary snake hibernates in a rock crevice or rodent burrow during the winter months. It also escapes the summer's intense heat underground. Because most of its natural habitat in Alameda and Contra Costa Counties has been destroyed by development, only three sizable populations of the Alameda whipsnake still exist. This harmless snake has been listed as a California endangered species and is now protected by law. Habitat preservation is the key to its survival.

Bonus Hikes: Mount Diablo and Las Trampas Foothills

R. LAS TRAMPAS REGIONAL WILDERNESS: THE EUGENE O'NEILL LOOP

WHY GO?

This hike is a literary adventure, walking in reflection through the Las Trampas Regional Wilderness, focused on the thoughts and property of one man: playwright Eugene O'Neill. The great American playwright moved into the "corduroy hills" with his wife, Carlotta, in 1936 and there wrote some of his best-known plays including *Long Day's Journey Into Night.* You'll see their Spanish colonial home, called the Tao House, built on 158 acres with the money from the Nobel Prize, awarded him earlier that year (Tao is a philosophy and means "the right way of life").

Start hiking from either the Danville or Alamo trailheads. This hike suggests a loop encompassing Virgil, Madrone, Amigo, and Williams Trails. Tour the house and grounds (reservations required; call 925-838-0249). To make the day even more memorable, bring one of his plays and stop now and then in a shady knoll to read some lines aloud to contemplate with fellow hikers. This is quite a different way to hike, challenging O'Neill's notion: "We all are more or less the slaves of conventions, or of discipline, or of a rigid formula of some sort."

THE RUN DOWN

Start: Toward the end of Camille Lane in Alamo on the Madrone Trail. GPS: N37 49.55' / W122 1.34'
Elevation gain: 480 feet
Distance: 3.5-mile loop
Difficulty: Easy
Hiking time: 4 to 5 hours (with house tour)

Seasons/schedule: Wednesday through Sunday (except holidays) year-round
Fees and permits: None
Trail contact: East Bay Regional Park District Headquarters, 2950 Peralta Oaks Ct., P.O. Box 5381, Oakland 94605; (510) 544-3276; www.ebparks.org/parks/las_trampas

Dog-friendly: Dogs on leash (but not at Tao House)
Trail surface: Single- and double-track dirt trails
Land status: Regional wilderness and national historic site
Nearest town: Danville

Nat Geo TOPO! Map: Las Trampas Ridge, CA
Other trail users: Equestrians
Special considerations: For Tao House reservations, call (925) 838-0249; www.nps.gov/euon/index.htm.

The Eugene O'Neill National Historic Site COURTESY OF HISTORIC AMERICAN LANDSCAPES SURVEY (HALS)

S. **MOUNT DIABLO STATE PARK: WALL POINT—PINE CANYON LOOP**

WHY GO?

This loop offers yet another perspective of Mount Diablo and its foothills from a less frequented trailhead. A good climb rewards with lovely views of the textured and oak-dotted hills. Mostly open to the sun, it is best in the early part of the day or during cooler months. In springtime you can spot multiple rare lilies among the grasses.

Take Wall Point Road to Secret Trail to BBQ Terrace Road to Stage Road to Dusty Road and back to Wall Point and the Macedo Ranch Staging Area.

THE RUN DOWN

Start: Macedo Ranch Staging Area, end of Green Valley Road, Alamo. GPS: N37 51.47' / W121 58.46'
Elevation gain: 900 feet
Distance: 6.1-mile loop
Difficulty: Moderate due to elevation gain
Hiking time: About 3 hours
Seasons/schedule: Sunrise to sunset year-round; avoid heat of the day in summer/fall
Fees and permits: Parking fee

Trail contact: Mount Diablo State Park Headquarters, Mitchell Canyon Staging Area, 96 Mitchell Canyon Rd., Clayton 94517; (925) 837-2525; www.parks.ca.gov/?page_id=517
Dog-friendly: No dogs allowed
Trail surface: Mostly double-track with 1 single-track dirt trail
Land status: State park
Nearest town: Alamo
Nat Geo TOPO! Map: Diablo, CA
Other trail users: Equestrians and bikers

Valley oaks in Pine Canyon
MIGUEL VIEIRA (FLICKR.COM/PHOTOS/MIGUELVIEIRA/)

T. JOHN MUIR NATIONAL HISTORIC SITE: MOUNT WANDA

WHY GO?

This hike is a celebration of John Muir, who started the formation of the National Park Service and the modern conservation movement. In these 326 acres of hills, grassland, and oak groves, John Muir walked with his daughters, Wanda and Helen, reflecting on the natural world, which he valued not only for economic gain, but for its beauty and healing powers. Not touched by grazing, the nature trail is quite pretty. After your hike, drive ¼ mile to the John Muir House parking lot to tour the house, the orchards, and grounds (with a docent or cell phone–guided tour). It was at this house that he wrote most of his 300 magazine articles and twelve books. Also on the grounds, check out the Martinez Adobe, with bilingual exhibits about the 1775 Juan Bautista de Anza National Historic Trail.

THE RUN DOWN

Start: For Mount Wanda, park at the Caltrans Park and Ride lot at the corner of Franklin Canyon Rd. and Alhambra Ave. GPS: N37 59.21'/ W122 7.46'

Drive 0.25 mile to the John Muir house parking lot on Alhambra Avenue. GPS: N37 59.31' / W122 7.51'
NOTE: You can walk from one to the other, but busy Alhambra Avenue has no sidewalks, so this is not recommended if you have small children.
Elevation gain: 500 feet
Distance: 3-mile lollipop loop
Difficulty: Easy to moderate due to initial elevation gain
Hiking time: About 1.5 hours
Seasons/schedule: Sunrise to sunset year-round; visitor center 10 a.m.

to 5 p.m. year-round, except some holidays
Fees and permits: None
Trail contact: John Muir National Historic Site, 4202 Alhambra Ave., Martinez 94553; (925) 228-8860; www.nps.gov/jomu/index.htm
Dog-friendly: Dogs on leash
Trail surface: Paved sidewalk, double-track dirt trail
Land status: National historic site
Nearest town: Martinez
Nat Geo TOPO! Map: Briones Valley, CA
Other trail users: Bikers and equestrians on fire road only
Special considerations: The only restrooms and water are at the visitor center.

Alternate routes: For more hiking, continue from the Muir house onto the California Riding and Hiking Trail onto the Franklin Ridge Loop in the Carquinez Strait Regional Shoreline (1,415 acres of bluffs and shoreline). Visit www.ebparks.org/parks/carquinez for more information.

The grounds of John Muir's house with
Mount Wanda in the background

U. BRUSHY PEAK REGIONAL PRESERVE

WHY GO?

Brushy Peak Loop Trail, opened in 2008, tours some of the 1,833-acre preserve of this Native American sacred land. These hills were the center of a network of ancient trade routes that linked Bay Area Ohlones, Bay Miwoks, and Northern Valley Yokuts, once the scene of multiple camps of visiting tribes, trading feasts, and ceremonial events. During the gold rush, the caves and rocky outcrops of Brushy Peak were a favorite retreat of the legendary Mexican bandit Joaquin Murietta. The hike follows the contours of the hills and is almost all open grassland with views of the Altamonte windmills, ridgelines, and towns below and hosting some spring wildflowers. You also pass through some scrubland and one small oak woodland near the top. The ponds are a breeding ground for western toads and Pacific tree frogs and other amphibians. Avoid hiking in the summer heat.

THE RUN DOWN

Start: Laughlin Ranch Staging Area, north end of Laughlin Road, Livermore. GPS: N37 44.52'/ W121 42.33'
Elevation gain: 1,030 feet
Distance: 5.4-mile loop
Difficulty: Moderate due to elevation gain
Hiking time: About 3 hours
Seasons/schedule: 8 a.m. to sunset year-round
Fees and permits: None
Trail contact: East Bay Regional Park District Headquarters, 2950 Peralta Oaks Ct., P.O. Box 5381, Oakland 94605; 888-EBPARKS (888-327-2757), option 3, ext. 4512

Dog-friendly: Dogs on leash
Trail surface: Double-track and single-track dirt trail
Land status: Regional preserve
Nearest town: Livermore
Nat Geo TOPO! Map: Altamont, CA; Bryon Hot Springs, CA
Other trail users: Mountain bikers
Special considerations: Brushy Peak is a sacred Native American site and can only be accessed through a guided tour. Contact Livermore Area Recreation and Park District (LARPD) directly at (925) 373-5700 for information.

Alternative route: Also from Brushy Peak Regional Park, you can take a shuttle to the Vasco Caves Regional Preserve, which can only be hiked with naturalist-led interpretive tour groups because of its amazing combination of rare, state- and federally listed plant and wildlife species, fragile rock outcrops, and Native American archaeological sites. Call ahead for a reservation at 888-EBPARKS (888-327-2757), press option 2; www.ebparks.org/parks/vasco.

THREE RIDGES: SAN PABLO, THE OAKLAND/BERKELEY HILLS, AND SUNOL RIDGE

Right above bustling cities and dense suburbs are three ridgetops, home to parks and open space preserves full of natural beauty and history, and punctuated with bodies of water. In the basins between the ridges a hiker can find solitude exploring areas that are among the East Bay's best-kept secrets.

Who would think that above the city "that puts the There in There,"—Oakland, California—you can find quiet, enchanting hills that were once covered with ancient, giant redwoods. After loggers downed the forest, much of the area gave way to development, but thousands of acres have survived to support native wildlife and remind us of our past.

You can find variety as well. While Redwood Park and Joaquin Miller Park host gurgling creeks, second-generation redwoods, and cool, shady trails, Robert Sibley Volcanic Regional Preserve offers geological exploration with dikes, mudflows, and lava flows. Huckleberry Botanic Regional Preserve is an ecological jewel with a native plant population found nowhere else.

Nearby Briones Regional Park offers sweeping grasslands with ridgetop tarns and a view of San Pablo Bay and the Carquinez Straits.

Water is key to the drama on the Sunol Ridge. In early spring, Little Yosemite splashes down over gray boulders. The wildflower display is unmatched anywhere else in the East Bay. Backpackers can hike past all this into the Ohlone Regional Wilderness to spend the night under the stars and finish off with a cool dunk in Lake Del Valle.

On the San Pablo Ridge between Wild Cat Canyon and Claremont Canyon is a family favorite, Tilden Regional Park. A study in combining recreation and preservation, Tilden offers wooded canyons, view trails, and a nature preserve, along with pony rides, a steam train, a working farm, and a beautiful old carousel. It also has Anza Lake, a favorite swimming and fishing hole.

While most of these parks are part of the well-run East Bay Regional Park District, the East Bay Municipal Utilities District (EBMUD) owns a lot of open space around these ridges, too. And here's the secret: To hike on EBMUD lands, you have to get a permit for a nominal fee. The process is simple, but because of it, few people walk the 55 miles of trails in the watershed, open to the public since 1973.

33. TILDEN REGIONAL PARK: FROM JEWEL LAKE TO WILDCAT PEAK

WHY GO?

For seventy-five years, Bay Area families have come to Tilden Regional Park to learn about nature, to play, and to create memories. You will likely see wildlife on your way up Wildcat Peak: a speckled egg on the trail dropped from a nest, squirrels hopping through the trees, a banana slug. The view from Wildcat Peak is breathtaking, including the San Francisco Bay and the Lamorinda areas. Pass through Rotary Peace Grove, then enjoy a self-guided nature hike on the Jewel Lake Trail on your way back to the well-equipped Environmental Education Center (EEC).

THE RUN DOWN

Start: Tilden Nature Area on Central Park Road, behind the Environmental Education Center at the Laurel Canyon trailhead
Elevation gain: 610 feet
Distance: 3.8-mile loop
Difficulty: Moderate due to a couple short but strenuous uphill sections
Hiking time: About 2 hours
Seasons/schedule: 5 a.m. to 10 p.m. year-round; EEC open Tuesday through Sunday
Fees and permits: None
Trail contact: East Bay Regional Park District Headquarters, 2950 Peralta Oaks Ct., P.O. Box 5381, Oakland 94605; 888-EBPARKS (888-327-2757), option 3, ext. 4562; www.ebparks.org/parks/tilden
Dog-friendly: No dogs in nature study area; on leash elsewhere
Trail surface: Single-track dirt path crossing several sturdy bridges, double-track dirt, fire road, boardwalk
Land status: Regional park
Nearest town: Berkeley
Nat Geo TOPO! Map: Richmond, CA; Briones Valley, CA
Other trail users: Hikers only; equestrians on Wildcat Creek Trail
Special considerations: Bring lettuce to feed the animals in Little Farm. See the "Attractions in Tilden" sidebar in this chapter for more.

FINDING THE TRAILHEAD

From the CA 24 exit onto Fish Ranch Road, at a four-way stop sign, turn right on Grizzly Peak Road; signs read "To Tilden." Turn right on Golf Course Drive. Take a right on Shasta Road, then right on Wild Canyon Road. Turn right on Central Park Drive, the main entrance to Tilden Regional Park. Follow signs to the Tilden Nature Area and Little Farm.

Great blue heron on Jewel Lake
BECKY MATSUBARA (FLICKR.COM/
PHOTOS/BECKYMATSUBARA/)

From I-80 take the Buchanan Street/Albany exit, turning right onto Buchanan. After Buchanan Street crosses San Pablo, the name changes to Marin. Stay on Marin until you reach Spruce at a four-way stop sign. Turn left on Spruce and go approximately 2 miles. After you cross Grizzly Peak Road, take a quick left down Canon Drive. At the bottom turn left on Central Park Drive to the parking lot.
GPS: N37 54.32' / W122 15.57'

WHAT TO SEE

Tilden is a wilderness and outdoor playground, the heart of the East Bay Regional Park District (EBRPD). In 1934 it was part of the first land acquisition for wilderness preservation in the San Francisco Bay Area. It is named in honor of Charles Lee Tilden. Part of the first graduating class of the University of California–Berkeley and the first EBRPD president, Tilden helped found the park system.

In Tilden you can feed barnyard animals, ride a train or an antique carousel, stroll through a botanical garden, go golfing, or swim or fish in a lake.

Near the trailhead is the Little Farm, a community-created project designed to expose urban children to farm animals. The current Environmental Education Center (EEC) opened in 1974, replacing the cluster of buildings used by the Civilian Conservation Corps (CCC) in the 1930s. The CCC cleared many of the trails here and built the stone signs, drinking fountains, and restrooms you see today. Buy or borrow the self-guiding trail booklet from the EEC for the Jewel Lake Trail.

On summer weekends you see a lot of people here. This is the most frequented park in the East Bay. But most visitors do not venture far past the man-made attractions and picnic areas. You can still find breathing space and a pleasing bit of wilderness in the 2,079 acres of canyons and hills (with 39 miles of trails).

The protected nature area featured in this hike (740 acres) is accessible to hikers only and home to readily seen wildlife and native and exotic plants. It rambles through creekside woodlands, eucalyptus groves, grasslands, and coastal scrubland.

The Laurel Canyon Trail offers the shade of two large eucalyptus groves, several small groves of conifers, a dense oak and bay woodland, mature coastal brush, rich creek vegetation, grassland, and areas of coyote brush. The rare Oakland mariposa lily (*Calochortus umbellatus*) grows here. Trickling Laurel Creek is a major tributary of Wildcat Creek, home to native steelhead trout. The riparian woodland supports arroyo willow trees and white alder. Sword and wood ferns add to the lushness of the scene.

It's a steady, moderately strenuous trek uphill that brings you to the Wildcat Peak Trail, a ridge trail where you can admire westward views. A surprising and pleasant sight along this sunny trail is the garden of redwoods in the Rotary Peace Grove. The one hundred giant sequoias are monuments to individuals who have made a notable contribution to the advancement of international understanding, peace, and goodwill.

The detour to Wildcat Peak (1,250 feet) is worth the short, steep trek, with 360-degree views that show off both the natural beauty and man-made splendor of the area.

Heading back down on the peak trail, you are likely to see native wildflowers: bright orange California poppies, lupine, wild hyacinth, buttercups, and mallow. Serenading you are songbirds like the bushtit, northern mockingbird, song sparrow, western meadowlark, and American goldfinch. If you don't see jackrabbits, black-tailed deer, bobcats, foxes, or long-tailed weasels in person, look for their tracks or scat (examples are in the EEC).

On the Jewel Lake Trail, numbered wooden markers correspond to the self-guided trail booklet. Learn about the spicy bay trees and all their uses. The bays were planted here in honor of Joshua Barkin, an eastern factory worker turned California naturalist who worked in Tilden for twenty years. Douglas fir, incense cedar, and Monterey pines also came to Tilden as memorial plantings. Standing on the boardwalk above Jewel Lake, see if you can spot western pond turtles among the cattails.

MILES AND DIRECTIONS

- **0.0** START from the parking lot for Tilden Nature Area. Walk across the bridge to the Environmental Education Center (EEC).
- **0.1** If open, visit the EEC, then go around the building to the right next to the Little Farm to reach the Laurel Canyon trailhead.
- **0.2** Pass over a service road. Continue straight on Laurel Canyon Trail.
- **0.5** Cross over a double-track road, heading down it about 50 feet to the left for the continuation of Laurel Canyon Trail. (**Note:** Watch out for poison oak beside the trail.)

From Jewel Lake to Wildcat Peak

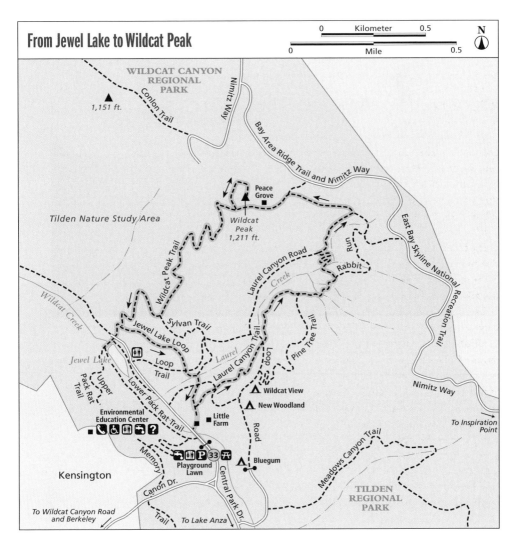

0   Kilometer   0.5

0   Mile   0.5

N

WILDCAT CANYON REGIONAL PARK

1,151 ft.

Conlon Trail

Nimitz Way

Bay Area Ridge Trail and Nimitz Way

Peace Grove

Tilden Nature Study Area

Wildcat Peak 1,211 ft.

Wildcat Peak Trail

Laurel Canyon Road

Creek

Rabbit Run

East Bay Skyline National Recreation Trail

Sylvan Trail

Wildcat Creek

Jewel Lake Loop

Loop Trail

Laurel

Laurel Canyon Trail

Loop

Pine Tree Trail

Jewel Lake

Upper Pack Rat Trail

Lower Pack Rat Trail

Wildcat View

New Woodland

Nimitz Way

Environmental Education Center

Little Farm

Road

To Inspiration Point

Memory

Playground Lawn

33

Bluegum

Meadows Canyon Trail

Kensington

Canon Dr.

Central Park Dr.

TILDEN REGIONAL PARK

To Wildcat Canyon Road and Berkeley

Trail

To Lake Anza

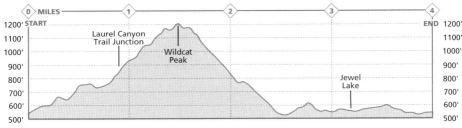

MILES

0   1   2   3   4

START

1200'

1100'

Laurel Canyon Trail Junction

1000'

Wildcat Peak

900'

800'

Jewel Lake

700'

600'

500'

END 1200'

1100'

1000'

900'

800'

700'

600'

500'

The view west from the top of Tilden Regional Park
BRIANRICECA

0.8 Stay on Laurel Canyon Trail as you pass the trailhead for Pine Tree Trail. Several more bridges pass over Laurel Creek.

0.9 The trail splits. Turn left on Laurel Canyon Trail. The path heads downhill, then up switchbacks.

1.0 Turn right on Laurel Canyon Road, a double-track trail heading up to Wildcat Peak Trail.

1.2 At the Y, go left onto Wildcat Peak Trail. It becomes single-track before becoming a wider dirt road. You hit a strenuous but short uphill section.

1.4 Keep to the left, continuing on Wildcat Peak Trail.

1.6 Arrive at the sequoias of Rotary Peace Grove.

1.7 Turn left toward Wildcat Peak, another strenuous but short uphill section.

1.8 Come to Wildcat Peak (1,250 feet). Enjoy the great views from the observation area—west: Bay Bridge, San Francisco, Marin Headlands, Berkeley Marina; north: Point Richmond, refineries of Martinez; east: San Pablo Dam Reservoir, Mount Diablo; south: Oakland, Alameda. Go back the way you came, returning to Wildcat Peak Trail.

1.9 Turn right on Wildcat Peak Trail. A sign reads To Nature Area. It's downhill from here.

2.8 The trail splits. Go right to Jewel Lake Trail.

3.1 Cross Wildcat Creek Trail to Jewel Lake.

3.2 Arrive at Jewel Lake. From here head back the way you came, across Wildcat Canyon Trail.

3.3 Turn right on Jewel Lake Trail. This part of the loop heads back to the EEC. Use the self-guided trail booklet along the trail.

3.6 Pass over Loop Road, continuing on Jewel Lake Trail back to the EEC, passing some service areas.

3.8 Arrive back at the EEC.

Alternate routes: Young families may enjoy the 1.3-mile loop made from Wildcat Creek Trail, Loop Road, and around Jewel Lake (Lower Packrat Trail and around Jewel Lake is less than a mile).

A two-car hike can take you from the Inspiration Point parking lot in Tilden along the Bay Area Ridge Trail through Sibley Regional Park and Huckleberry Preserve, ending at the Skyline Gate in Redwood Regional Park (9.3 miles).

ATTRACTIONS IN TILDEN

Tilden Park's merry-go-round (and snack bar) was built in 1911 by European artisans employed at the Hershell Spillman Company of Tonawanda, New York, and has been here since 1948 (on the National Register of Historic Places). It features fifty-nine hand-carved horses and other animals as well as a pipe organ. In December it's decorated with holiday lights and ornaments.

The Brazilian Room was built as part of the Brazilian Pavilion at the San Francisco World's Fair of 1939 on Treasure Island (halfway across the Bay Bridge) and given by the Brazilian government as a gift of friendship. Used to entertain World War II soldiers for parties and high teas, it is currently one of the most popular wedding sites in the Bay Area. A bronze statue of Tilden is out front.

The Regional Parks Botanic Garden was founded in 1940. The 20-acre site botanically represents the whole state of California. Blooms are best January through June.

Lake Anza opened to the public in 1939 with an aquatic sports carnival featuring synchronized swimmers. You can take a splash or fish for largemouth bass, bluegill, sunfish, and channel catfish (fishing license required).

The Tilden Golf Course, constructed by the CCC in 1937, is an eighteen-hole public course.

The steam train is the Redwood Valley Railway (RVR), popularly known as the "Little Train." Constructed in 1952, it is one of the most authentic miniature steam trains in the United States. It was built at a scale of 5 inches to 1 foot and burns oil. The 1.25-mile ride is on narrow slopes and gives brief views of San Pablo Bay.

34. BRIONES REGIONAL PARK

WHY GO?

Briones Regional Park offers long, ambling walks through grassy hills spotted with oak trees and a couple lagoons; views of distant towns, landmarks, and neighboring parkland; and a contrasting dense, damp woodland. Hawks, eagles, and turkey vultures circle above the canyons. Black-tailed deer love to munch on brush in the deeper canyons. There are several small creeks lined with ferns and shrubs, and patches of sun-loving wildflowers grow along most of the trails. The landscape changes seasonally from summer gold to winter green, and gives you a taste of California's Spanish ranch past.

THE RUN DOWN

Start: Parking lot of Briones Regional Park

Elevation gain: 820 feet

Distance: 7-mile loop

Difficulty: Moderate due to uphill and steep downhill sections

Hiking time: About 3.5 hours

Seasons/schedule: 8 a.m. to sunset year-round

Fees and permits: Parking fee; fee for dogs

Trail contact: East Bay Regional Park District Headquarters, 2950 Peralta Oaks Ct., P.O. Box 5381, Oakland

94605; 888-EBPARKS (888-327-2757), option 3, ext. 4508; www.ebparks.org/parks/briones

Dog-friendly: Dogs on leash

Trail surface: Packed double-track and single-track dirt trail with one manageable creek crossing

Land status: Regional park

Nearest town: Orinda

Nat Geo TOPO! Map: Briones Valley, CA

Other trail users: Equestrians and mountain bikers, hikers only on Bear Creek Trail

FINDING THE TRAILHEAD

From CA 24 take the Orinda/Moraga exit and turn left at the light onto Camino Pablo. Two lanes merge into one. About a mile later turn right on Bear Creek Road. Travel past the Briones Reservoir, past Happy Valley Road. Turn right into Briones Regional Park, Bear Creek Staging Area. (Note the cement retaining wall on the left. The Abrigo Valley trailhead is on the right in the parking lot. **GPS:** N37 55.37'/ W122 9.28'

WHAT TO SEE

For nearly 200 years the land that is now Briones Regional Park has provided grass for grazing cattle, which replaced the herds of elk and antelope reported by early settlers. Since the land grants of the Spanish in the early 1800s, livestock have shaped this landscape. The annual grasses are Spanish, carried as seeds by the cattle. The stepped hillsides

Briones in fog
NICK FULLERTON (FLICKR.COM/
PEOPLE/18203311@N08/)

are a result of cows creating paths to new grass. After the rains the trails can be badly rutted from hooves, creating an uneven surface for hiking boots. And, of course, you should watch out for cow pies.

But if you look carefully, you can also see a Georgia O'Keeffe painting in the Briones scenery: long valleys between subtle and smooth rolling hills of grassland and scattered oaks. Those round, grassy hills dominate the park—pastoral green in winter and late spring, golden in summer and fall, radiating the heat of California sunshine and creating a scene of old western ranch land.

The park is named for Felipe Briones, the original Spanish grant holder of this land. In 1829 young Briones fell in love with a waterfall and built a home near what is now the Bear Creek entrance to the park. The retired Spanish soldier cultivated the land and kept a few hundred cattle and horses, supporting a family of eighteen.

Occasionally native Californians tried to reclaim their land. In 1839 a group stole nearly all the saddle horses belonging to Captain Ygnacio Martinez, Briones's neighbor to the north. The captain's son, Don Jose Martinez, and eight or ten other neighbors, including Briones, went in pursuit of them. They succeeded in recovering the animals, but Felipe Briones was struck by an arrow and killed. In 1842 his widow, Maria Manuela Valencia Briones, claimed the grant and continued to ranch here. And so it continued for fifty years.

Briones in spring
NICK FULLERTON (FLICKR.
COM/PEOPLE/18203311@N08/)

In 1906 there was a water shortage in the growing East Bay. The People's Water Company began purchasing land in San Pablo and Bear Creek to create a watershed. Lake Chabot (1875), the San Pablo Dam and Reservoir (1919), Upper San Leandro Reservoir (1926), and finally the Briones Reservoir (1964) were built for this purpose. It all became parkland in 1957.

Passing through green-painted cattle gates, the wide Abrigo Valley Trail brings you into an area lined with bays, oaks, and maples. The trail rises steeply in places. Look for indications of landslides. These sparse hillsides of loose soil are prone to this natural phenomenon, as is the entire Lamorinda area.

The park still leases some grazing land for cows, goats, and sheep. The rule with cows is to just walk on past them; the docile animals will likely move out of your way as you approach. But never stand directly behind a cow, which could kick if frightened.

The Sindicich Lagoons, protected natural pond habitats, are fenced to keep out rogue cattle. They replenish themselves from a spring below. White egrets and blue herons stop here to rest. In the fall, dragonflies twirl over the water. In the spring, California newts lay their eggs here.

On the Crescent Ridge Trail, you pass the Briones Archery Club Range, where you find pit toilets, picnic tables, and shelters with places for quivers and bows.

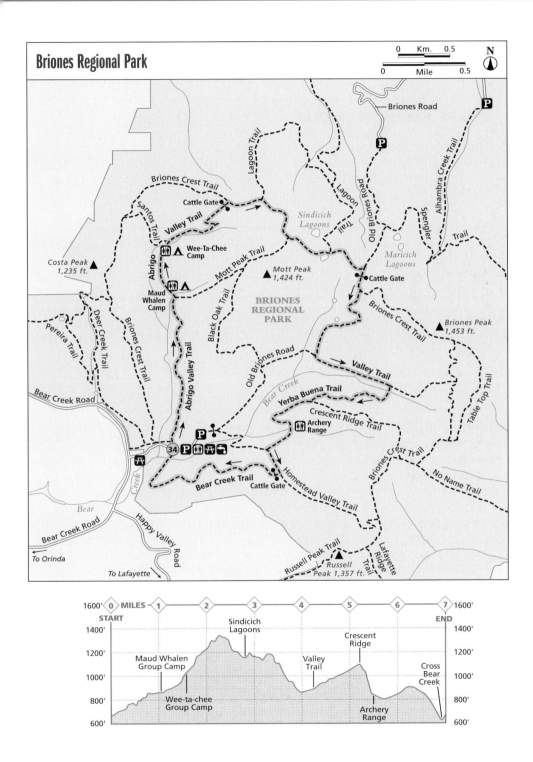

Briones Regional Park

0 Km. 0.5

0 Mile 0.5

N

Briones Road

P

Briones Crest Trail

Cattle Gate

Santos Trail

Valley Trail

Lagoon Trail

Lagoon Trail

Old Briones Road

Sindicich Lagoons

Maricich Lagoons

Alhambra Creek Trail

Spengler Trail

P

Wee-Ta-Chee Camp

Abrigo

Costa Peak 1,235 ft.

Maud Whalen Camp

Mott Peak Trail

Mott Peak 1,424 ft.

Cattle Gate

Briones Crest Trail

Briones Peak 1,453 ft.

Black Oak Trail

BRIONES REGIONAL PARK

Deer Creek Trail

Pereira Trail

Briones Crest Trail

Old Briones Road

Bear Creek

Valley Trail

Abrigo Valley Trail

Yerba Buena Trail

Crescent Ridge Trail

Table Top Trail

Bear Creek Road

Archery Range

34 P

Bear Creek Trail

Cattle Gate

Homestead Valley Trail

Briones Crest Trail

No Name Trail

Bear

Bear Creek Road

Happy Valley Road

Creek

To Orinda

To Lafayette

Russell Peak Trail

Russell Peak 1,357 ft.

Lafayette Ridge Trail

1600' 0 MILES 1 2 3 4 5 6 7 1600'

START END

1400' 1400'

Sindicich Lagoons

1200' Crescent Ridge 1200'

Maud Whalen Group Camp

Valley Trail

Cross Bear Creek

1000' 1000'

Wee-ta-chee Group Camp

800' Archery Range 800'

600' 600'

Bear Creek Trail, the only single-track, hikers–only trail in Briones, is a wonderful finale. It takes you up and down through thick woods and an underbrush of ferns, mosses, and flowering brush.

MILES AND DIRECTIONS

0.0 START at the Abrigo Valley trailhead. Take the trail past the Oak Grove picnic area to a cattle gate.

0.1 Go through the cattle gate, staying on Abrigo Valley Trail.

1.0 Stay on Abrigo Valley Trail past the Mott Peak Trail turnoff. Group Camp Maud Whalen is on the right.

1.4 Wee-Ta-Chee Camp is on the right over the bridge. Continue on Abrigo Valley Trail.

2.1 Go through a cattle gate and turn left on Briones Crest Trail.

2.3 Stay on Briones Crest Trail as you pass the first trailhead for Lagoon Trail.

3.0 Pass the smaller Sindicich Lagoon on the right. Just past the pond on Briones Crest Trail, take a left on Lagoon Trail to see the larger Sindicich Lagoon.

3.1 Arrive at the larger Sindicich Lagoon. Go back the way you came to Briones Crest Trail.

3.2 From Lagoon Trail, take a left back onto Briones Crest Trail to continue along the ridge headed east.

3.4 Turn right on Old Briones Road.

3.5 Stay on Old Briones Road, passing through another cattle gate. It is downhill for a while.

4.1 Take a left on Valley Trail.

4.7 Take a right on Yerba Buena Trail, which leads back up into the wooded hillsides.

5.3 Go right on Crescent Ridge Trail. A steep downhill section brings you to the archery club. Continue on Crescent Ridge Trail.

5.9 Turn left on Homestead Valley Trail. You can see the next trailhead just ahead in 0.1 mile.

6.0 Turn right on Bear Creek Trail. The single-track trail leads through a wildlife-populated woodland habitat. (***Note:*** Beware of poison oak.)

6.9 Cross the creek. (***Note:*** There's no bridge, but it's a short leap over unless you are trekking after unusually heavy rains.) Climb the stairs on the opposite bank, up a couple switchbacks, past a kiosk to the parking lot.

7. 0 Back at parking lot.

Alternate routes: Families can take the 2-mile Bear Creek Loop by taking Bear Creek and returning on the Seaborg Trail.

35. ROBERT SIBLEY VOLCANIC REGIONAL PRESERVE

WHY GO?

This greatly loved 660-acre park includes trails through Monterey pines and blue gum eucalyptus, and grassland hillsides with views looping around Round Top Peak. A mere 1,761 feet, people still refer to Round Top as a mountain, perhaps in respect to its eruptive past. Remaining are the walls of the caldera, old river gravels, basalt lava flows, and varicolored "redbeds"—layers of oxidized iron explored worldwide for fossils. Remains have been found of mastodons, hipparions, camels, and prong-bucks in the old quarries here. Now these quarry sites contain picturesque rock labyrinths.

THE RUN DOWN

Start: Sibley Park Main Staging Area
Elevation gain: 500 feet
Distance: 3.6-mile loop, with some detours
Difficulty: Easy, with some moderate slopes
Hiking time: About 2 hours
Seasons/schedule: 5 a.m. to 10 p.m. year-round
Fees and permits: None
Trail contact: East Bay Regional Park District Headquarters, 2950 Peralta Oaks Ct., P.O. Box 5381, Oakland 94605; 888-EBPARKS (888-327-2757), option 3, ext. 4554; www.eb parks.org/parks/sibley
Dog-friendly: Dogs on leash

Trail surface: Mostly well-packed dirt trail that varies in width, some loose gravel, paved path
Land status: Regional preserve
Nearest town: Oakland and Berkeley
Nat Geo TOPO! Map: Oakland East, CA
Other trail users: Hikers and equestrians only, bikers on Volcanic Trail and last section of Round Top Loop Trail
Special considerations: There is an outdoor interpretive center, flush toilets, and drinking water at the start. The park trail guide available at the trailhead includes a self-guided tour of Round Top's geological journey. A wildflower guide is available online.

FINDING THE TRAILHEAD

From CA 24 take the Fish Ranch Road exit just east of the Caldecott Tunnel. Continue 0.8 mile to Grizzly Peak Boulevard. Turn left and go 0.24 mile on Grizzly Peak to Skyline Boulevard. Turn left on Skyline and proceed to Robert Sibley Volcanic Regional Preserve, Main Staging Area on the left.
GPS: N37 50.51' / W122 12.4'

WHAT TO SEE

From its beginning, Robert Sibley Volcanic Regional Preserve's story is one of fire.

Ten million years ago, a freshwater lake extended from what is now Tilden Park north to San Leandro Reservoir and south and east to Lafayette. Within these waters a fiery volcano thrust itself upward on the western shores. It spewed lava, took a break for a dozen or a few hundred years for sediment to fill in, then gushed again. During its active period, the volcano released at least eleven lava flows, with two explosive episodes of epic proportions. One violent eruption likely equaled that of Mount Saint Helens in Washington. This breath of fire helped shape the area's ridges and formed the mound known as Round Top. Today you can see the alternating volcanic and sedimentary layers that were folded, tilted, crumpled, and tossed about by millions of years of earthquake activity. Welcome to California.

Rock quarries north of the peak have made geologic features even more visible. Years of commercial gouging by the land's previous owner, the Kaiser Corporation, exposed old lava flows, mudflows, volcanic dikes, vents, and cinder piles.

You'll find two official labyrinths in the old quarry beds, both on marked trails, but with some wandering, you can find more. The first rock labyrinth was created by artist Helena Mazzariello in 1989 as a gift to fellow hikers. She modeled it after ancient labyrinths on the island of Crete in the Mediterranean and used it as a meditation device (consider bringing an offering to add to the altar in the center).

Spring green in Sibley

Through the cattle gate
on Volcanic Trail

In the twentieth century, Round Top was witness to fire many times. Author and journalist Herman Whitaker stood on the peak of Round Top on April 19, 1906, the day after the San Francisco earthquake and watched flames engulf the city on the bay, describing what he saw for *Harper's* magazine.

In 1910 millionaire Frank Havens founded the Mahogany Eucalyptus and Land Company that forever changed the look of the area, and was eventually the cause of more fire. His ill-conceived idea was to cover the crests of the Oakland–Berkeley Hills with great forests of fast-growing Australian eucalyptus trees. They are, he proclaimed, "the most valuable tree on the face of the globe," tough, dense, strong, and hard.

He built Skyline Boulevard and planted eucalyptus by the millions along the 14-mile stretch from North Berkeley to what is now Redwood Park. But Havens had not verified his claim. In 1913 he invited a forester to test-mill a few of the trees. That's when he learned the terrible truth: The blue gum eucalyptus he had planted was worthless. The species of eucalyptus the Australians used for lumber were so slow growing that the trees could not be harvested until they were several hundred years old.

The abandoned eucalyptus woodland went untended for decades, until Round Top was covered with an impenetrable jungle. The year 1923 saw a disastrous fire, made worse by the oily, hot-burning eucalyptus. That same year the East Bay Hills Fire Protection Committee built an official fire lookout on Round Top.

In 1973 loggers downed many of the Australian transplants. This allowed bay trees, Monterey pines, coyote brush, and poison oak to grow. But the resilient eucalyptus made a comeback.

On Sunday, October 20, 1991, winds in excess of 65 miles per hour gusted through the dangerously dry Oakland hills. An unseen ember found a parched eucalyptus tree. It burst into flames, and fire raced down from the crest of the Oakland–Berkeley Hills. The East Bay hills firestorm killed twenty-five people and destroyed 3,469 homes, with an estimated loss of $1.5 billion.

An attempt was made to remove more eucalyptus trees from the area after that. But as you'll see, the spunky eucalyptus grove around Round Top has grown back again, despite another brushfire in August 1998.

MILES AND DIRECTIONS

0.0 START at the Robert Sibley Volcanic Regional Preserve entrance on Skyline Boulevard. Facing the visitor center, walk to the right of it. To the right of a paved path is the trailhead for Bay Area Ridge Trail. Take this single-track dirt path.

0.2 Stay on Bay Area Ridge Trail as you cross over a paved road that leads to Round Top.

0.4 Again cross over the paved road. Within about 30 feet the path will split again. Take the fork to the left, Round Top Loop Trail, which leads around the eastern side of Round Top.

0.6 The burned and cut logs here are probably a result of the August 1998 fire.

0.9 Go through a cattle gate.

1.0 Come to views, a railing, and marker #4. (This corresponds to #4 on the Self-Guided Tour of Round Top Volcanoes.) View the largest of the quarry pits. Turn around and return to the double-track trail; take the trail to the left for a diversion into the quarry.

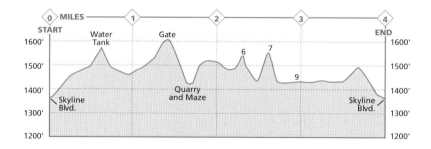

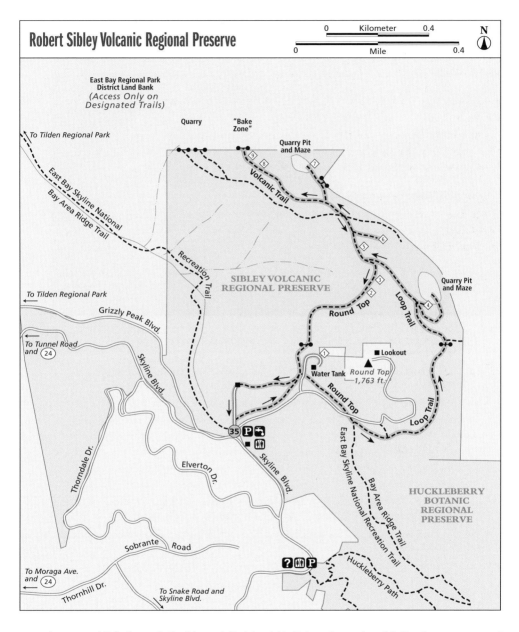

Robert Sibley Volcanic Regional Preserve

0 — Kilometer — 0.4
0 — Mile — 0.4

N

East Bay Regional Park
District Land Bank
*(Access Only on
Designated Trails)*

Quarry

"Bake
Zone"

Quarry Pit
and Maze

To Tilden Regional Park

East Bay Skyline National
Bay Area Ridge Trail

Volcanic Trail

Recreation Trail

SIBLEY VOLCANIC
REGIONAL PRESERVE

To Tilden Regional Park

Grizzly Peak Blvd.

Quarry Pit
and Maze

Round Top

Loop Trail

To Tunnel Road
and 24

Skyline Blvd.

Lookout

Round Top
1,763 ft.

Water Tank

35 P

Round Top

Loop Trail

East Bay Skyline National Recreation Trail

Thorndale Dr.

Elverton Dr.

Skyline Blvd.

Bay Area Ridge Trail

HUCKLEBERRY
BOTANIC
REGIONAL
PRESERVE

Sobrante Road

To Moraga Ave.
and 24

Thornhill Dr.

To Snake Road and
Skyline Blvd.

Huckleberry Path

1.1   Walk through the Mazzariello labyrinth. Return to marker #4. Continue on
Round Top Loop Trail, heading northwest.

1.2   Go straight on Volcanic Trail.

1.3   Site #5 on the tour; "redbeds" are on the right.

Welcome to Robert Sibley
Volcanic Regional Preserve

1.4   Take a detour to the right to see site #6: sandstone from the age of the dinosaurs.

1.5   The trail splits. Stay on Volcanic Trail, the trail on the right, going straight ahead.

1.6   Veer to the right to see the smaller quarry and site #7.

1.7   Arrive at the small quarry, marker #7. Turn around and head back to where the trail veered.

1.8   To see sites #8 and #9, keep going northwest on Volcanic Trail.

2.1   Cross a cattle gate. Go through to view "bake zones," bands of red, oxidized rocks rich in fossils.

2.3   View the "bake zones" on the right. Turn around and head back through the cattle gate and back to Volcanic Trail. Pass sites #6 and #5 again.

3.0   Turn right on Round Top Loop Trail, which heads around the western side of Round Top.

3.1   Site #3 is on the left. Site #2 comes up shortly after.

3.4   Walk about 10 feet or so on a paved road. To the left are two dirt paths. Take the upper, single-track path.

3.5   Come to a viewing platform with interpretive plaques and benches. Enjoy views of Grizzly, Chaparral, and Volmer Peaks. Continue on the paved path on the opposite side of the viewing area from where you entered.

3.6   Arrive back at the visitor center.

36. HUCKLEBERRY BOTANIC REGIONAL PRESERVE

WHY GO?

The self-guided nature trail guide available at the trailhead makes for some fun learning and discovery along this loop trail through the 235-acre preserve. You descend a canyon under bays and oaks and hear the trickling of seasonal San Leandro Creek below. Follow the ridge on a narrow footpath through dense shrubs, mostly huckleberries. Short side trails take you up to bald vistas, home to rare manzanitas and hosting soothing pastoral views of the surrounding foothills.

THE RUN DOWN

Start: Staging area on Skyline Boulevard
Elevation gain: 870 feet
Distance: 2.4-mile loop
Difficulty: Easy
Hiking time: About 1.5 hours
Seasons/schedule: 5 a.m. to 10 p.m. year-round
Fees and permits: None
Trail contact: East Bay Regional Park District Headquarters, 2950 Peralta Oaks Ct., P.O. Box 5381, Oakland 94605; 888-EBPARKS (888-327-2757), option 3, ext. 4532; www.eb parks.org/parks/huckleberry

Dog-friendly: Dogs not allowed, except on Skyline National Trail
Trail surface: Well-maintained, serpentining, narrow dirt path, a short set of stairs
Land status: Regional preserve
Nearest town: Oakland
Nat Geo TOPO! Map: Oakland East, CA
Other trail users: Hikers only
Special considerations: Take the self-guided botanic interpretive tour (revised in January 2018) and check out the wildflower photo guide available on the website: www .ebparks.org/parks/huckleberry.

FINDING THE TRAILHEAD

From Mountain Boulevard in the Montclair Village district of Oakland, go up Snake Road until it dead-ends at Skyline Boulevard. Turn left (northwest) on Skyline Boulevard. In 0.4 mile the Huckleberry Botanic Regional Preserve parking lot is on your right. **GPS:** N37 50.34' / W122 11.50'

WHAT TO SEE

A stroll along Huckleberry Botanic Regional Preserve's winding, narrow pathway, surrounded by dense, flowering shrubs, is like a walk through a medieval maze. It provides seclusion and offers a botanical adventure on an almost entirely single-track trail.

Lush Loop Trail

The self-guided nature path guide, available at the trailhead, describes the plant life you see at the markers. The information is fascinating (even for non–green thumbs). Featured are the pliable western leatherwood, the pioneering brittleleaf manzanita, and the sticky-berried pallid manzanita. Extremely rare, you cannot find them anywhere else in the world but in these Bay Area foothills.

The park guide calls Huckleberry Preserve "an island of time . . . what's left of a time gone by." Not a part of the Spanish land grant system in the late 1700s, like surrounding areas, this canyon was saved from the grazing cattle that brought so many drastic changes to the landscape.

The ancient rock strata below the foliage once lay at the bottom of a deep ocean basin. It contains remains of microscopic diatoms and simple marine life. Subjected to uplift and folding, the bedrock now stands exposed as hard, brittle bands of chert and shale with soil low in nutritional value. Manzanitas like these conditions.

With the complex topography of the area, Huckleberry has its own Mediterranean-type climate: warm, dry summers and cool, wet winters. Dense ocean fogs sometimes coat the place in summer, lasting for days. This creates moisture for the local plant life during a time when rainfall is rare.

Late summer and fall is berry season, and birds are abundant. The animals have their pick of juicy berries: Thimbleberries, osoberries, California coffeeberries, elderberries, and dwarf snowberries grow beside the fruitful huckleberries.

But it's not all peace and love among the plant life here. In the preserve you are witness to botanical warfare. The resilient huckleberry bushes are slowly taking over the manzanita, aided by the shade of live oaks and bay laurels that have moved into the area. You can see indications of this conflict throughout the park.

The Huckleberry area was purchased in 1936 by the newly formed East Bay Regional Park District. Previously owned by the East Bay Municipal Utilities District, the hills still serve as a watershed for San Leandro Creek. The park became a preserve in the 1970s.

On the loop you first descend into a canyon through a mature bay forest. Take a whiff of the pungent bays (five times more potent than the commercial spice). You can also hear running water from San Leandro Creek, where rainbow trout were first identified as a species. The narrow trail follows the ridge in the shade of the trees beside banks of ferns. On the Skyline Trail, oaks dominate and the trail is a bit dryer. The upper Huckleberry

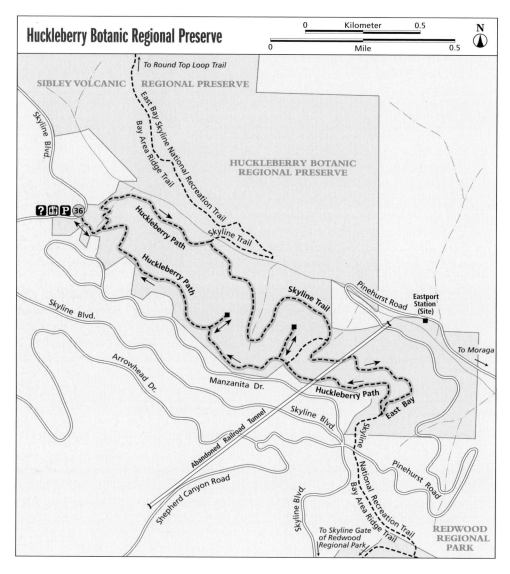

Huckleberry Botanic Regional Preserve

0   Kilometer   0.5

0   Mile   0.5

N

To Round Top Loop Trail

SIBLEY VOLCANIC   REGIONAL PRESERVE

East Bay Skyline National Recreation Trail

Bay Area Ridge Trail

Skyline Blvd.

HUCKLEBERRY BOTANIC
REGIONAL PRESERVE

Huckleberry Path

Skyline Trail

Huckleberry Path

Skyline Trail

Pinehurst Road

Eastport
Station
(Site)

Skyline Blvd.

Arrowhead Dr.

Manzanita Dr.

Huckleberry Path

East Bay

To Moraga

Abandoned Railroad Tunnel

Skyline Blvd.

Shepherd Canyon Road

Skyline National Recreation Trail
Bay Area Ridge Trail

Pinehurst Road

Skyline Blvd.

To Skyline Gate
of Redwood
Regional Park

REDWOOD
REGIONAL
PARK

Path, going back toward the trailhead, hosts wonderfully thick plant life, occasionally creating a low canopy overhead. Beware of poison oak that grows right beside the trail.

In sharp contrast, there is one strip of land through the middle of Huckleberry that is owned by the Pacific Gas and Electric Company. You can't miss it, with its giant steel towers and electricity and telephone service lines. Thankfully you pass it quickly.

On the last part of the trail, you find short diversions up to sandy manzanita barrens. The peaceful, open views include Flicker Ridge, Las Trampas Ridge, and the rise of Mount Diablo.

Viewpoint on Upper Loop Trail

WHAT IS A REGIONAL PRESERVE?

A regional preserve is an area of at least 100 acres with a suitable staging area that must include either a significant historical/cultural resource or a natural feature of scientific importance. This last can be a rare or endangered plant or animal species and its supporting ecosystem, significant fossils or geological features, or unusual topographic features.

MILES AND DIRECTIONS

0.0 START at the Huckleberry Botanic Regional Preserve trailhead on Skyline Boulevard in the staging area/parking lot.

0.4 Bear right for the loop.

0.9 Bear left to extend the Huckleberry loop with part of Skyline National Trail.

1.3 Turn right, back onto Huckleberry Path.

1.6 Stay straight. The path heading to the right is the shortcut from where you just came from.

1.7 Take this 0.3-mile diversion up to a manzanita barren to see rare California coastal plant life and a good view of Mount Diablo.

1.9 Take another 0.3-mile diversion with three markers for the Huckleberry self-guided botanic interpretive tour.

2.4 Arrive back at the parking lot.

Alternate routes: Families may want to take the shorter 1.7-mile loop, staying on the Huckleberry Path loop by turning right at the junction with the Skyline Trail.

The well-marked paths of Huckleberry Botanic Regional Preserve

37. REDWOOD REGIONAL PARK: STREAM TRAIL, FROM EAST RIDGE TO WEST RIDGE

WHY GO?

This ridge and canyon hike offers dramatic changes in scenery, light, and even temperature. An easy first mile follows a road-wide dirt path among pines, oaks, and eucalyptus, exposed to sun, with views of the foothills and Mount Diablo. Winding down Prince Road, the scenery changes, shaded by bay and madrone trees. Suddenly you find yourself in the seclusion of a thriving redwood grove, walking beside Redwood Creek, with banks full of ferns and water-loving plants. The trail then heads back up to evergreens and views again.

THE RUN DOWN

Start: Skyline Gate Staging Area on Skyline Boulevard
Elevation gain: 760 feet
Distance: 4-mile loop
Difficulty: Moderate
Hiking time: About 2 hours
Seasons/schedule: 5 a.m. to 10 p.m. year-round
Fees and permits: None
Trail contact: East Bay Regional Park District Headquarters, 2950 Peralta Oaks Ct., P.O. Box 5381, Oakland 94605; 888-EBPARKS (888-327-2757), option 3, ext. 4553; www.eb parks.org/parks/redwood
Dog-friendly: Dogs permitted

Trail surface: Road-wide dirt trail, double- and single-track dirt trail, several easy creek crossings
Land status: Regional park
Nearest town: Montclair Village of Oakland
Nat Geo TOPO! Map: Oakland East, CA
Other trail users: Mountain bikers and equestrians
Special considerations: You can print out the Wildflower Photo Guide of Redwood Regional Park on their website. Watch for poison alongside the trail. Facilities at the trailhead include pit toilets, water for canines and humans, and biodegradable bags for dog waste.

FINDING THE TRAILHEAD

From Mountain Boulevard in the Montclair district of Oakland, turn uphill on Snake Road. It winds around through neighborhoods, becoming Shepherd Canyon Road. At the road's end, turn right on Skyline Boulevard. In about 0.5 mile, turn into the parking lot on your left. **GPS:** N37 49.54' / W122 11.14'

WHAT TO SEE

You might never know, as you hike through serene Redwood Regional Park, that this was once the backdrop for mass destruction, fires, lynchings, manhunts, and vindictive justice laid down by rifle-toting lumberjacks. Before that it was a magnificent land of giants. The 1,830-acre park also hosted farms, orchards, and ranches for ninety years. Today a peaceful getaway amid suburban foothills and urban sprawl, the park proves the resilience of nature, sporting few indications of its dramatic past.

The 150-foot coastal redwoods you see in the park today are second and mostly third generation. Their ancient mothers were so tall that sea captains sailing into the San Francisco Bay used them as navigational landmarks from 16 miles away, where the

Stream Trail turns to meet Tres Sendas Trail at the base of the canyon.

West Ridge Trail

Pacific meets the Golden Gate. A report in 1893 measured stumps as wide as 33.5 feet in diameter. If this account is correct, the redwoods may have been the largest living things on earth.

Luis Maria Peralta, a Spanish settler who owned a nearby rancho, kept logging to a minimum, recognizing the grand beauty of this forest that was home to grizzly bears, mountain lions, rattlesnakes, and hundreds of California condors, now nearly extinct.

But after the gold rush, settlers recognized the profit to be had by lumber. Ten saw-mills set up shop here. With each mill employing up to one hundred men, shantytowns sprang up around them. The loggers, mostly jump-ship sailors, were hard-drinking, oath-swearing, feared men. Several times they formed their own retributive posses, emerging from the forest to hang horse and cattle thieves. In 1854 they mounted a nighttime manhunt in the woods for twenty-five felons who had escaped from San Quentin Prison Camp. Most were shot on sight.

By 1860 commercial logging had clear-cut the entire forest. Even the undergrowth was burned away, leaving a charred sea of stumps.

A second wave of logging took place after the 1906 San Francisco earthquake, when the second-growth redwoods (approximately fifty years old) as well as the stumps from the first-generation trees were logged. Redwood Park became parkland in 1939.

Starting your hike on the wide East Ridge Trail, you share the first mile with bicyclists, equestrians, runners, and undoubtedly dogs romping happily off-leash. This is one of the most dog-friendly trails in the area.

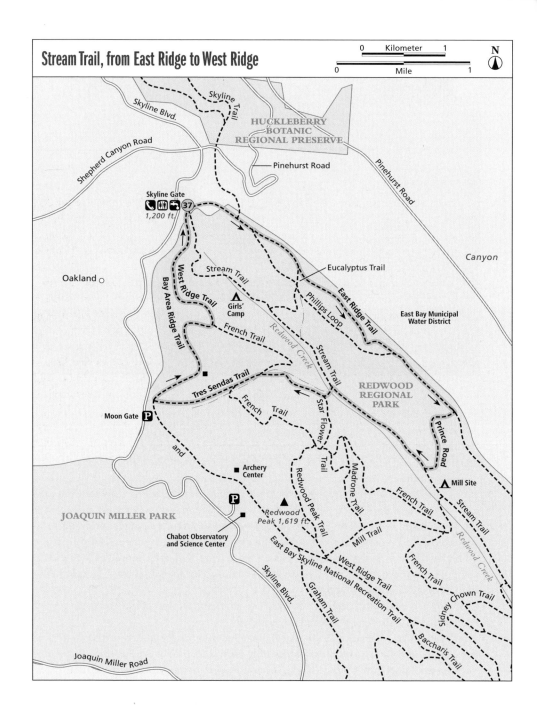

Stream Trail, from East Ridge to West Ridge

0 Kilometer 1
0 Mile 1

N

Skyline Trail

Skyline Blvd.

Shepherd Canyon Road

HUCKLEBERRY BOTANIC REGIONAL PRESERVE

Pinehurst Road

Pinehurst Road

Canyon

Skyline Gate
1,200 ft.
37

Stream Trail

Eucalyptus Trail

Oakland

West Ridge Trail

Bay Area Ridge Trail

Girls' Camp

Phillips Loop

East Ridge Trail

East Bay Municipal Water District

Redwood Creek

French Trail

Stream Trail

Tres Sendas Trail

French Trail

Star Flower Trail

REDWOOD REGIONAL PARK

Moon Gate

and

Prince Road

Archery Center

Mill Site

JOAQUIN MILLER PARK

Redwood Peak Trail

Madrone Trail

French Trail

Stream Trail

Chabot Observatory and Science Center

Redwood Peak 1,619 ft.

Mill Trail

French Trail

East Bay Skyline National Recreation Trail

West Ridge Trail

Sidney Chown Trail

Skyline Blvd

Graham Trail

Redwood Creek

Baccharis Trail

Joaquin Miller Road

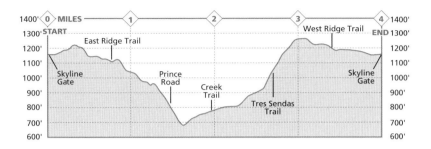

Pines, coast live oaks, and aromatic blue gum eucalyptus border the trail on the ridge. Rabbits, red squirrels, and quail may appear out of the grasses. Starflowers, lupine, leatherwood, and cleavers grow alongside the path. Three-quarters of a mile in is a great view of the rolling hills and woodland that makes up Chabot Regional Park, the Las Trampas foothills, and Mount Diablo.

Prince Road was named for Thomas and William Prince, who established a steam-driven sawmill here in 1852. The landscape around the road darkens in the thicker forest, adding red-barked madrone and California bay trees to the mix. It feels a bit like falling into Alice's rabbit hole.

The seasonal Redwood Creek beside the Stream Trail has its place in history as a tributary of San Leandro Creek, where the world-famous rainbow trout was first identified as a distinct species. When the water is too low to support the fish, you may see frogs or salamanders. Masses of ladybugs (*Hippodamia convergens*) cluster along the creek in late autumn through winter.

Tres Sendas (Three Paths) Trail continues your journey through the woods. The West Ridge Trail, a portion of the 31-mile East Bay Skyline National Recreation Trail that runs along the Coast Range, opens once again to sky and expansive views.

MILES AND DIRECTIONS

0.0   START at the Skyline Gate Staging Area; take the East Ridge Trail to the far left.

0.75 Enjoy the great view of Mount Diablo.

1.3   Turn right on Prince Road (you pass Eucalyptus Trail and Phillips Loop first).

1.7   Bear right where the path meets Stream Trail. (**Note:** For restrooms, water, and picnic tables, turn left and walk 1 mile, then double back.)

2.1   Stream Trail heads up right. Stay left around the bend onto Tres Sendas Trail. (**Note:** If you want picnic tables, water, or restrooms, proceed up Stream Trail another 0.5 mile to Girls' Camp.)

2.5   Tres Sendas Trail crosses the creek and branches right and left. Bear right to a steep uphill. Pass French Trail.

3.0   Tres Sendas Trail meets West Ridge Trail. Turn right.

4.0   Arrive back at the Skyline Gate Staging Area and parking lot.

Alternate routes: For a great shorter hike, start down the Stream Trail to Tres Sendas to West Ridge (2.7 miles). The route passes Girls' Camp (with facilities) and the winter ladybug gathering site.

Families will also enjoy the loop hike in Roberts Regional Park from Chabot Space and Science Center past the archery range through the Redwood Bowl to the playground and lawn area and former site of the giant navigational redwoods (plaque #962 near the Madrone picnic area). Take Roberts Ridge Trail, Graham Trail, and Access Road (1.7 miles).

Ladybugs gathered beside the Stream Trail, Redwood Regional Park

38. JOAQUIN MILLER PARK: SEQUOIA BAYVIEW TRAIL AND BIG TREES LOOP

WHY GO?

A wide trail winds through native coast redwoods (*Sequoia sempervirens*), opening up to views before returning into the shade and coolness of the redwoods.

THE RUN DOWN

Start: Sequoia Bayview Trail trailhead on Skyline Boulevard
Elevation gain: 290 feet
Distance: 2-mile loop
Difficulty: Easy
Hiking time: About 1 hour
Seasons/schedule: Sunrise to sunset year-round
Fees and permits: None
Trail contact: Oakland Parks and Recreation, Joaquin Miller Park Ranger Station, 3590 Sanborn Dr., Oakland 94602; (510) 615-5566; www2.oaklandnet.com/government/o/opr/s/Parks/JoaquinMiller/index.htm
Dog-friendly: Dogs on leash
Trail surface: Double-track and a little single-track dirt trail
Land status: City park
Nearest town: Oakland
Nat Geo TOPO! Map: Oakland East, CA
Other trail users: Bikers and equestrians

FINDING THE TRAILHEAD

From CA 13 South take the Joaquin Miller Road/Lincoln Avenue exit. Turn left onto Monterey Boulevard, then turn left (east) up the hill on Joaquin Miller Road. Turn left onto Skyline Boulevard. The Sequoia Bayview Trail trailhead is on your left in about 0.4 mile (10800 Skyline Blvd., Oakland) Park along the road. **GPS:** N37 48.28' / W122 10.40'

WHAT TO SEE

Named for the colorful nineteenth-century poet and frontiersman Joaquin (nee Cincinnatus Hiner) Miller, this park is a favorite in the city of Oakland. Miller, known as the "Poet of the Sierras," bought 70 acres of grassy hillside in 1886 just below the redwood grove where this hike takes place. He called his home "the Hights," planted up to 75,000 Monterey cypress, olive, and eucalyptus trees on the property, and remained there until his death in 1913. His whitewashed home, beside Joaquin Miller Road, along with his funeral pyre where his ashes were scattered, is a California Historic Landmark. The City of Oakland purchased The Hights in 1919 and turned it into parkland.

Bay laurel leaves

The Sequoia Bayview Trail, named for the native coast redwoods (*Sequoia sempervirens*) that dominate the trail, is one of the most popular in Joaquin Miller Park. A wide path weaves through a cool, dim canyon of redwoods and oaks, bay trees, and madrones, past a couple of hillside creeks. These creeks are part of the Sausal Creek Watershed.

The trail opens up to views of downtown Oakland, the bay, and San Francisco. Along the way you see many varieties of fern, including western sword ferns, along with trailing blackberries and evergreen huckleberries. Look for little lavender western star flowers, yellow French bloom, and miner's lettuce. There are many varieties of fungi as well. Where the trail opens to sunlight, orange bush monkeyflowers are common. There are over 200 species of native plants here, as well as the invading species like those planted by Miller. Rare natives include star tulip, pallid manzanita, and leatherwood. Pungent nonnatives include fennel, acacia, and eucalyptus trees. Joaquin Miller Park hosts California's state grass, purple needle grass, and the state flower, the California golden poppy.

Big Trees Trail takes you past the largest redwoods in the park, which helps make up for the noise of cars on nearby Skyline Boulevard. Though satisfyingly tall, these are second- and more probably third-generation trees, having grown from the mother roots after the mass logging post–gold rush and post-1904 San Francisco earthquake.

Because the trails are popular with dog-walkers, you may have to hike closer to dawn or dusk to see the shyer wildlife—the gray fox, deer, and California quail that make this home. Towhees, scrub jays, Cooper's hawks, wild turkeys, and lizards may make an appearance.

Though this is a short hike, you can take these trails to many others in both Joaquin Miller Park and Redwood Regional Park to make longer loops and explore the park further.

MILES AND DIRECTIONS

0.0 START at the Sequoia Bayview Trail trailhead.

0.3 Pass the Sunset Trail. Stay on Sequoia Bayview Trail.

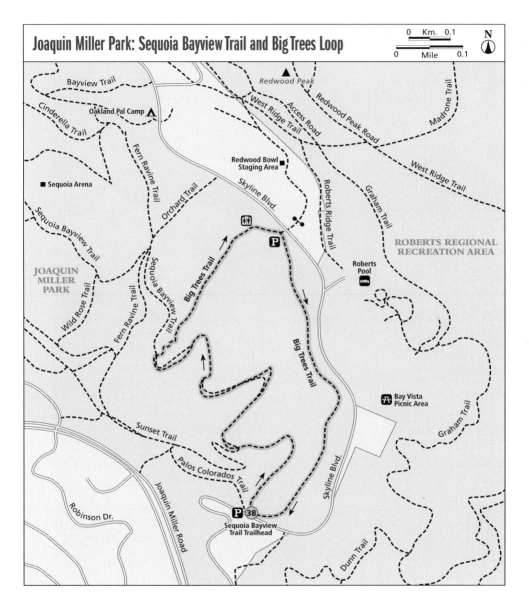

Joaquin Miller Park: Sequoia Bayview Trail and Big Trees Loop

0 Km. 0.1
0 Mile 0.1

N

- 0.9 Turn right (east) onto Big Trees Trail.
- 1.2 Pass restrooms.
- 1.3 Reach the Glen trailhead and the parking lot on Skyline Boulevard. Stay on Big Trees Trail.
- 2.0 Arrive back at the Sequoia Bayview Trail trailhead.

Sequoia Bayview Trail

Alternate routes: For a historical and lovely path through Oakland's hills and city parks, start at Dimond Canyon Park in the Fruitvale district and head all the way up through Joaquin Miller to Roberts Recreational Area and Redwood Regional Park to the Bay Area Ridge Trail. See www.oaklandtrails.org for more info.

39. **ANTHONY CHABOT REGIONAL PARK**

WHY GO?

The 5,067-acre Anthony Chabot Regional Park offers walks by burbling creeks, through groves of eucalyptus, redwood, and oaks, over hills alive with swaying grasses, and along the rim of the well-loved Lake Chabot. The terrain ranges from gentle to rugged, with flat uplands, steep-sided ravines, and the deep, narrow Grass Canyon. Elevation ranges from 235 feet at Lake Chabot to about 1,200 feet at Vulture's View. The area reflects the small but mighty Anthony Chabot, who helped create and preserve the area as you see it today.

THE RUN DOWN

Start: Goldenrod trailhead at the Clyde Woolridge Staging Area, Skyline Boulevard and Grass Valley Road
Elevation gain: 850 feet
Distance: 8.1 miles out and back
Difficulty: Moderate
Hiking time: About 4 hours
Seasons/schedule: 5 a.m. to 10 p.m. year-round
Fees and permits: None
Trail contact: East Bay Regional Park District Headquarters, 2950 Peralta Oaks Ct., P.O. Box 5381, Oakland 94605; 888-EBPARKS (888-327-2757), option 3, ext. 4502; www.eb parks.org/parks/anthony_chabot

Dog-friendly: Dogs on leash
Trail surface: First double-track then single-track dirt trail
Land status: Regional park
Nearest town: San Leandro and Castro Valley
Nat Geo TOPO! Map: Oakland East, CA; Las Trampas Ridge, CA; Hayward, CA
Other trail users: Equestrians and mountain bikers on Goldenrod Trail and Jackson Grade
Special considerations: There are no facilities at the trailhead, but you can find a drinking fountain by detouring uphill to the right on Goldenrod Trail.

FINDING THE TRAILHEAD

From I-580 take the Keller Street exit and follow Keller up the hill. Keller Street dead-ends at Skyline Boulevard. Turn right onto Skyline. At the end is the Clyde Woolridge Staging Area for Anthony Chabot Regional Park.
GPS: N37 45.12' / W122 7.4'

WHAT TO SEE

Before the first Europeans arrived in 1769, Chabot Park was home to the native Jalquin people. There was no lake then, no eucalyptus trees. Giant redwoods populated the

The trailhead at the Clyde
Woolridge Staging Area
KEN SOREY

northern end of the park. The growl of a grizzly bear sometimes rumbled through the canyon.

The vegetation of Chabot changed with the coming of the Spanish, who introduced grazing animals and hunted to extinction the tule elk and California grizzly. Victorian and twentieth-century Californians also influenced the land, removing grazing animals, suppressing wildfires, logging redwood trees, planting and logging eucalyptus trees, and creating Lake Chabot as a water supply for Oakland.

As you head down the Jackson Grade, brush and woodland become delightfully denser, especially on moist east-facing slopes. Above the monkeyflowers and eucalyptus, vultures circle the canyon. Wild blackberries, live oaks, buckeyes, a few Monterey pines, and young redwoods share the grove.

Just before the old Stone Bridge, probably built by the Civilian Conservation Corps (CCC) in the 1930s, the single-track Cascade Trail disappears into thick brush and healthy creekside trees. In spring and early summer, lupine, Indian paintbrush, fairy bells, and geraniums grow along the dappled path. Clover and wild strawberries provide ground cover. Fifteen types of ferns and horsetails sprawl on the banks, including maidenhair, lady fern, bird's foot fern, and the common sword and wood ferns. Bigleaf maples, sweet cherry, madrone, black walnut, and black cottonwoods shade much of the path. Grass Valley Creek trickles beside you, bursting into cascades in early spring.

The southern part of the Columbine Trail hosts more sun-loving flowers. Diverse native wildflowers take bloom among the Spanish grasses, especially in spring. As you make your way south on the trail, you enter seamlessly what was once called Rancho San Lorenzo, owned by Don Guillermo Castro.

Lake Chabot

Castro received the grant to the southern half of the park in 1843, part of his 27,722-acre rancho. He put cattle on the land, and the hides of the cattle put money in his pocket. But it didn't stay there long. Don Castro was a gambler, and a pretty bad one. To pay losses from one unlucky game after the next, he started selling off portions of his land. Piece by piece, his ranch shrank.

By 1864 Castro had lost his land holdings to Faxen Dean Atherton, a businessman who sold off parcels to those interested in the agrarian life. The largest of the ranches within what is now Chabot Regional Park was the Grass Valley Ranch, where you begin the hike. But just a few years later, the land was consolidated again, this time into a watershed to provide a reliable source of water for the rapidly growing Oakland area.

Amateur engineer, businessman, and philanthropist Anthony Chabot and his associates had built Lake Temescal in 1868. The supply was not nearly enough during the frequent drought years. To combat this, Chabot secured water rights to San Leandro Creek (limiting it as a spawning ground for native rainbow trout) and began to acquire land in the narrow gorge around the creek. In 1875 he completed the San Leandro Dam, creating Lake Chabot, the mainstay of the East Bay's water supply for forty years. You can see the dam from the beginning of the Columbine Trail; 115 feet high, made of earth fill, the structure is now a designated historic landmark.

In 1952 the park district turned 3,100 acres of Chabot, then called Grass Valley Regional Recreation Area, into parkland. In 1965 Grass Valley was renamed the Anthony Chabot Regional Park, and in that same year Lake Chabot went on "standby" status as a drinking water reservoir and became a center for boating and fishing.

MILES AND DIRECTIONS

0.0 START at the Clyde Woolridge Staging Area parking lot at the Goldenrod trailhead. Go left on Goldenrod Trail.

0.1 The trail splits. Take Jackson Grade to the right toward Cascade Trail.

0.4 Around a bend is the stone bridge. The trailhead for Cascade Trail is before the bridge on the right, clearly marked. (**Note:** Watch for poison oak.) The trail is mostly level. Grass Valley Creek is below on the left.

1.9 Cascade Trail becomes Columbine/Cascade Trail. Keep straight. The trail heads downhill after Columbine and Cascade merge, going deeper into the canyon and woods. The creek is on the left of the trail.

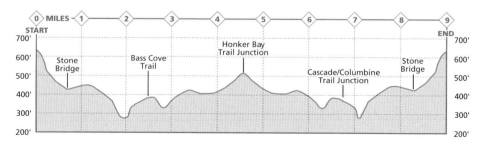

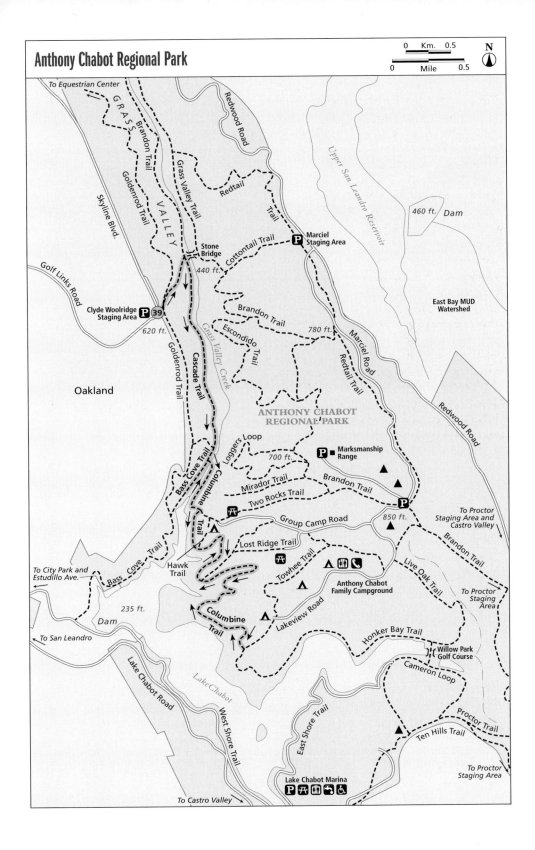

Anthony Chabot Regional Park

0 Km. 0.5
0 Mile 0.5

N

To Equestrian Center

GRASS VALLEY

Brandon Trail

Goldenrod Trail

Skyline Blvd.

Grass Valley Trail

Redwood Road

Redtail Trail

Upper San Leandro Reservoir

460 ft. Dam

Golf Links Road

Cottontail Trail

Marciel Staging Area

Stone Bridge

440 ft.

Clyde Woolridge Staging Area

39

620 ft.

Goldenrod Trail

Cascade Trail

Grass Valley Creek

Brandon Trail

Escondido Trail

780 ft.

Marciel Road

East Bay MUD Watershed

Redwood Road

Oakland

ANTHONY CHABOT REGIONAL PARK

Redtail Trail

Loggers Loop

700 ft.

Marksmanship Range

Bass Cove Trail

Columbine Trail

Mirador Trail

Two Rocks Trail

Brandon Trail

850 ft.

To Proctor Staging Area and Castro Valley

Group Camp Road

Brandon Trail

Bass Cove Trail

Lost Ridge Trail

Hawk Trail

Towhee Trail

Live Oak Trail

To Proctor Staging Area

To City Park and Estudillo Ave.

Anthony Chabot Family Campground

235 ft.

Dam

Columbine Trail

Lakeview Road

To San Leandro

Honker Bay Trail

Willow Park Golf Course

Lake Chabot Road

Cameron Loop

West Shore Trail

Lake Chabot

East Shore Trail

Proctor Trail

Ten Hills Trail

To Proctor Staging Area

Lake Chabot Marina

To Castro Valley

Lake Chabot

2.3 Cross the creek. (***Note:*** In wetter seasons like late winter and early spring, the creek may flood the trail here, but it tends to be shallow, and branches and rocks make for easy crossing.)

2.4 Trailhead for Bass Cove Trail. Go left, staying on Columbine Trail.

3.4 Keep straight on Columbine Trail for a view of Lake Chabot Marina. (***Bailout:*** If you have had enough, this is a turnaround and picnic stop. A short walk on Group Camp Road Trail to the left takes you to group camps, restrooms, and drinking water.)

4.1 Columbine Trail meets Honker Bay Trail. Turn around and head back the way you came.

6.2 Turn right on Cascade/Columbine Trail (Bass Cove Trail is to the left).

6.7 Continue straight on Cascade Trail. (***Option:*** Head left up Columbine to Goldenrod, which is a double-track trail along a golf course and neighborhood houses.)

7.7 Cascade Trail runs into Jackson Grade and the stone bridge. Turn left, heading west up Jackson

8.1 Jackson Grade meets Goldenrod Trail. Continue the short distance to arrive back at the parking lot of the Clyde Woolridge Staging Area.

Alternate routes: You can turn this into a loop by turning from Columbine north onto Two Rocks Trail and then west on Brandon Trail back to the stone bridge.

For a two-car hike, park one at the Lake Chabot Marina and take Columbine to Bass Cove Trail (3.3 miles). Picnic or fish at the lake.

Young families may best enjoy walking Bass Cove Trail from the marina or the paved West Shore Trail lakeside.

40. **SUNOL REGIONAL WILDERNESS**

WHY GO?

This loop in the 6,859-acre wilderness starts by bridging and paralleling Alameda Creek. Up through tranquil wooded canyons, you pass Indian Joe Cave Rocks to grassy slopes covered with California poppies, lupine, and wild mustard in spring and views of Lake Del Valle and the Ohlone Wilderness. Little Yosemite offers misting water cascading over boulders in the gorge in early spring. Traverse a ridge and head down a canyon with weathered green serpentine and sandstone outcrops, through oak woodland, back to the start.

THE RUN DOWN

Start: Indian Joe Nature Trail marker, by the bridge near the Sunol Regional Wilderness Visitor Center
Elevation gain: 800 feet
Distance: 6-mile loop
Difficulty: Moderate
Hiking time: About 3.5 hours
Seasons/schedule: Best in spring for falls and wildflowers; 8 a.m. to sunset year-round
Fees and permits: Parking fee on weekends and holidays; fee for dogs
Trail contact: Sunol Regional Wilderness Visitor Center, 1895 Geary Rd., Sunol 94586; (510) 544-3249; and East Bay Regional Park District Headquarters, 2950 Peralta Oaks Ct., P.O. Box 5381, Oakland 94605; 888-EBPARKS (888-327-2757), option 3, ext. 4559; www.eb parks.org/parks/sunol
Dog-friendly: Dogs on leash

Trail surface: Single-track dirt path, double-track dirt trail, short gravel fire road
Land status: Regional wilderness
Nearest town: Sunol
Nat Geo TOPO! Map: La Costa Valley, CA
Other trail users: Hikers only on Indian Joe Creek Trail and Canyon View Trail; equestrians and mountain bikers on Cave Rocks and Camp Ohlone Roads
Special considerations: Borrow or buy a self-guided nature trail booklet at the visitor center to identify markers on the Indian Joe Nature Trail (wildflower identification kits and bird lists are also available). You can also download a pictorial wildflower guide from the park's website. Note that the park is subject to closure or restriction during the wildfire season.

FINDING THE TRAILHEAD

 From I-680 exit at Calaveras Road/CA 84, just south of the town of Pleasanton. Turn left onto Calaveras Road and proceed to Geary Road, which leads directly into the park. **GPS:** N37 30.56' / W121 49.57'

Oak grove in Sunol Regional Wilderness
MIGUEL VIEIRA (FLICKR.COM/PHOTOS/MIGUELVIEIRA/)

WHAT TO SEE

The combination of landscapes here—riparian, woodland, and grassland—and abundant plant and wildlife provide for a fun day in Sunol, especially during the springtime, when you are sure to see dozens of species of wildflowers, birds, and butterflies, and maybe a cow feeding its calf up on the hill. Look for foothill yellow-legged frogs around Little Yosemite, among the alders and grassy tussocks. Even when the falls slow to a trickle, the creek is fun for rock-hopping and exploration.

Sunol has had many human inhabitants as well. Naturalists have found bedrock mortars used by the Costanoan Indians for pounding acorns. In 1839 this park, along with 48,000 acres, most of the south-central portion of Alameda County, was granted as Rancho el Valle de San José to Antonio Mariá Suñol, the Bernal brothers, and Antonio Pico. They released cattle and sheep onto the land. The gold rush brought squatters onto the land in 1848. When California became a state in 1850, much of the land became government property, and large parcels of the ranch were sold off to settlers.

In 1865 Pat and Mary Ann Geary purchased 160 acres from the US government for $2.50 an acre. The Gearys' homesite was next to Indian Joe Creek, about a half mile upstream from where it joins Alameda Creek. All that remains of their cabin is a pile of flat stones. Needing help to build the ranch, the Gearys hired some Native Americans recently released from San Quentin Prison, most of whom had been jailed for stealing horses. Indian Joe was among this group, although he had been sent there for stabbing a fellow Indian. Joe lived in a milk storage shed located upstream from the Geary home. He continued to live beside the creek that would take his name until he died in the early 1950s.

The Gearys eventually acquired 1,500 acres and became prominent dairy farmers, providing milk and butter for the San Francisco market. They had eleven children. In 1895

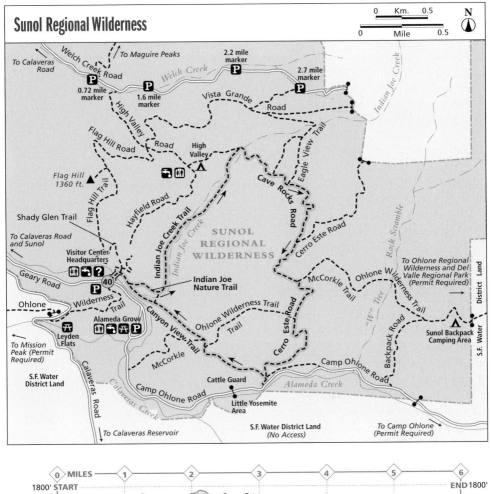

Sunol Regional Wilderness

To Calaveras Road
To Maguire Peaks
Welch Creek Road
2.2 mile marker
2.7 mile marker
0.72 mile marker
1.6 mile marker
Welch Creek
Vista Grande Road
High Valley
Flag Hill Road
Road
High Valley
Eagle View Trail
Flag Hill 1360 ft.
Shady Glen Trail
Hayfield Road
Cave Rocks
Flag Hill Trail
To Calaveras Road and Sunol
Indian Joe Creek Trail
Indian Joe Creek
Cerro Este Road
Rock Scramble
SUNOL REGIONAL WILDERNESS
Visitor Center Headquarters
Geary Road
Indian Joe Nature Trail
McCorkle Trail
To Ohlone Regional Wilderness and Del Valle Regional Park (Permit Required)
Ohlone Wilderness Trail
Ohlone Wilderness Trail
Alameda Grove
Canyon View Trail
Ohlone Wilderness Trail
Cerro Este Road
"W" Tree
Backpack Road
District Land
Leyden Flats
Sunol Backpack Camping Area
To Mission Peak (Permit Required)
McCorkle
Cerro Este Road
S.F. Water District Land
Camp Ohlone Road
Calaveras Road
Camp Ohlone Road
Cattle Guard
Alameda Creek
Calaveras Creek
Little Yosemite Area
Camp Ohlone Road
To Calaveras Reservoir
S.F. Water District Land (No Access)
To Camp Ohlone (Permit Required)
S.F. Water District Land

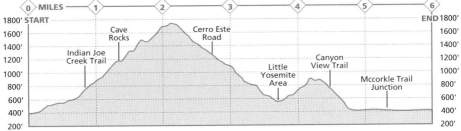

the oldest son, Maurice, built the house and Old Green Barn now used by the park as the visitor center and nature center (rebuilt after a 1954 fire). The road you travel in on, Geary Road, was laid by Pat Geary with some help from neighbors. They constructed the whole thing with picks and shovels.

Somewhere between Geary Road and Alameda Creek used to be the Rosedale School. The superintendent, Mr. A. A. Moore, named the school in honor of his wife, Rose. At its peak, Rosedale School had thirty students in eight grades, but enrollment declined until, in 1908, it was closed down.

To give you an idea of how much water used to flow in Alameda Creek, Rosedale's school year was arranged around the flow of water. Students had only the month of June for summer break because the school was closed from Christmas until April, when the creek was too high to cross.

Before the Calaveras Dam was built (to provide water for San Francisco), Alameda Creek carried enough water to support large runs of steelhead trout, salmon, and Sacramento pike. Tule elk roamed this area (last one killed in 1872), along with grizzly bears (last one killed in 1888), many deer, coyotes, mountain lions, and foxes. The deer and coyotes, made sparse by hunting, have been reestablished.

The East Bay Regional Park District purchased 3,863 acres from the last private owner, Willis Brinker (a contractor for the original San Francisco airport, the Mint, and part of the Bay Bridge) to establish the Sunol Regional Wilderness in 1962.

MILES AND DIRECTIONS

0.0 START at the Indian Joe Nature Trail marker. To reach the trailhead, facing the park buildings, walk behind them and left until you see a bridge crossing the creek. The bridge starts the hike on Indian Joe Nature Trail. After the bridge turn right and follow along the bank of Alameda Creek. Stay on Indian Joe Nature Trail past Hayfield Road.

0.2 After crossing over the creek, come to the trailhead for Indian Joe Creek Trail. Take a left onto the single-track trail, which leads uphill. (**Note:** Watch for poison oak.)

0.4 Stay on Indian Joe Creek Trail past the junction with Canyon View Trail. This trail takes you through all three of the main botanical communities in Sunol Valley: riparian (river side), oak woodland, and grassland. During the next 0.9 mile, you go through a cattle gate and cross the creek. (**Note:** If it's running, you will cross the creek a few times.) The trail gets steeper toward the top.

1.3 Pass the junction for Hayfield Road, staying on Indian Joe Creek Trail. Come to an open area of sagebrush and grass and a large rock outcropping. At the top of Indian Joe Creek Trail, the terrain begins to change from oak woodland to grassland.

1.6 Indian Joe Creek Trail dead-ends onto Cave Rocks Road. Turn right on the double-track dirt trail. The path continues uphill. This trail allows equestrians and mountain bikers.

1.9 Junction with Eagle View Road. Turn right, staying on Cave Rocks Road, which continues uphill gradually.

2.6 Reach the Cerro Este overlook, with the Del Valle Reservoir in the distance. Soon after is the trail marker for Cerro Este Road toward McCorkle Trail and Little Yosemite (1.6 miles to Little Yosemite from here). Head downhill on double-track dirt Cerro Este Road. Pass cattle ponds (ranchers still lease grazing rights here).

View from Sunol Regional Wilderness's Flag Hill Trail
MIGUEL VIEIRA (FLICKR.COM/PHOTOS/MIGUELVIEIRA/)

3.0 Junction with McCorkle Trail. Stay on Cerro Este Road toward Little Yosemite.

3.8 Junction with Canyon View Trail. Stay on Cerro Este Road, continuing to Little Yosemite.

3.9 Cerro Este dead-ends at Camp Ohlone Road, a dirt and gravel service road. Turn right. The Little Yosemite area starts here. Continue on just past Little Yosemite to a cattle gate.

4.2 Turn around at the cattle gate and head back to Cerro Este Road the way you came.

4.5 Turn left on Cerro Este Road and walk about 0.2 mile to Canyon View Trail, just past a water trough.

4.7 Trailhead for Canyon View Trail. Turn left on Canyon View Trail, which follows a cattle fence through a grassland corridor on a single-track trail. The trail flattens out and goes along the ridge, where it drops off steeply to the left (with Camp Ohlone Road below). After the ridge the trail heads over a hill (where you may run into cows), then downhill through a wooded canyon.

5.3 Junction with McCorkle Trail; stay on Canyon View Trail. The trail may be slightly eroded by hooves and rainwater, but is usually well maintained and dry.

5.7 Canyon View Trail becomes Indian Joe Nature Trail. Continue straight on Indian Joe Nature Trail.

5.9 Junction with Indian Joe Creek Trail. Continue straight, following Alameda Creek (on the left) to the bridge and park headquarters. Cross the bridge.

6.0 Arrive back at the trailhead near the visitor center.

Alternate routes: Families will enjoy the 1-mile self-guided Indian Joe Nature Trail. Get booklets at the visitor center.

Take an easy 2.6-mile loop hike to Little Yosemite and Alameda Creek; take Canyon View Trail to Camp Ohlone Road and back to the start on McCorkle Trail.

This is also your gateway to the Ohlone Wilderness for backpacking. A 20-mile trip goes to Lake Del Valle.

Bonus Hikes: Three Ridges: San Pablo, the Oakland/ Berkeley Hills, and Sunol Ridge

V. MISSION PEAK REGIONAL PRESERVE

WHY GO?

When people think of mountains to climb in the Bay Area, they don't always think of Mission Peak, but perhaps they should. Shaped by the shifting of the earth, with quakes along the Hayward fault and landslides down its steep faces, nature is still sculpting this 2,517-foot mountain.

There are four ways to climb to the summit. The shortest, but steepest, starts at the end of Stanford Avenue. The Hidden Valley Trail is a calf-burning climb, better in winter because it has few trees. Slightly longer, but a more gradual ascent through wildflowers and some woodland, the trail begins at Ohlone College on Mission Boulevard. A seldom-used path starts at Sunol Regional Wilderness and requires a wilderness permit (available at the park headquarters). This 11-mile round trip follows a gentle route west to the peak. The fourth route is from the Ed Levin County Park in Milpitas and follows the Bay Area Ridge Trail around 12 miles from Santa Clara County into Contra Costa.

The mountain is either bathed in sun or white-capped for short days in winter. Your reward, besides a great workout, are views of Mount Hamilton, Mount Diablo, Mount Tamalpais, the Santa Cruz Mountains, Silicon Valley, San Francisco, and, if it's really clear, the Sierra Nevada to the northeast (clearest views are after rains).

THE RUN DOWN

Start: Ohlone College, 43600 Mission Blvd., Fremont, behind the tennis courts, YSC trailhead on Pine Street. GPS: N37 31.39' / W121 54.52'
Elevation gain: 2,100 feet
Distance: 6.2 miles up and back
Difficulty: Strenuous due to elevation gain to peak
Hiking time: About 3.5 hours
Seasons/schedule: 6 a.m. to 10 p.m. year-round; avoid heat of the day in summer/fall
Fees and permits: Parking fee at Ohlone College (unless on break or holiday)

Trail contact: 43600 Mission Blvd., Fremont 94539; (510) 544-3246; www.ebparks.org/parks/mission
Dog-friendly: Dogs on leash
Trail surface: Double-track dirt trail
Land status: Regional park
Nearest town: Fremont
Nat Geo TOPO! Map: Niles, CA
Other trail users: Bikers and equestrians
Special considerations: Carry lots of water for you and your dog and wear sunscreen.

Approaching Mission Peak on the Ohlone Wilderness Trail
MIGUEL VIEIRA (FLICKR.COM/PHOTOS/MIGUELVIEIRA/)

W. COYOTE HILLS REGIONAL PARK

WHY GO?

On the bay by the Dumbarton Bridge, the Coyote Hills Regional Park is a sanctuary for all kinds of wetland birds, wild pheasants, raptors—and for hikers and bicyclists as well. You can experience wind-swept grasslands with wildflowers in spring and close-up views of the San Francisco Bay. The paved Bayview Trail skirts Red Hill by the marshes and bay levees, which are fun to explore. Red Hill offers views of the Santa Cruz Mountains to the west and the East Bay hills inland. The Tuibin Trail, Chochenyo Trail, and the trails over the boardwalks show off the marshes where white egrets and great blue herons feed at the water's edge.

Check out the visitor center and reproduced Ohlone tule house and learn the history and ecology of the area, as well as about the salt flat operations. The waters to the west and south of Coyote Hills are part of the Don Edwards San Francisco Bay National Wildlife Refuge. The Shoreline, No Name, Apay Way, and Alameda Creek Trails provide access to the refuge. Apay Way leads to the refuge visitor center via a bridge over CA 84. The Alameda Creek Trail stretches 12 miles south to Niles Canyon.

Families might enjoy a visit to nearby Ardenwood Historic Farm after the stroll, especially in the fall to pick out a pumpkin.

THE RUN DOWN

Start: Coyote Hills Regional Park parking lot, Quail trailhead. GPS: N37 33.6' / W122 5.8'
Elevation gain: Varies
Distance: Varies
Difficulty: Varies
Hiking time: Varies
Seasons/schedule: 5 a.m. to 10 p.m. year-round
Fees and permits: Parking fee at visitor center (free at parking lot)

Trail contact: Coyote Hills Regional Park, 8000 Patterson Ranch Rd., Fremont 94555; 888-EBPARKS (888-327-2757), option 3, ext. 4519; www.ebparks.org/parks/coyote_hills
Dog-friendly: No dogs allowed
Trail surface: Paved fire road, double- and single-track dirt trail
Land status: Regional park
Nearest town: Fremont
Nat Geo TOPO! Map: Newark, CA
Other trail users: Bikers

California poppy about to bloom

X. CLAREMONT CANYON REGIONAL PRESERVE

WHY GO?

The climb up the Stonewall Panoramic Trail is a popular calf-burner, located behind the historic Claremont Hotel near the University of California at Berkeley. Passing eucalyptus trees and into grassy hillsides, the views are worth it. There are only two trails in the 205 acres of preserve. Gwin Canyon Trail is the other. But you can continue on the the Stonewall Trail along the ridge, connecting with the university's Ecological Study Area trail system and all the way up to Grizzly Peak.

THE RUN DOWN

Start: Trailhead on Stonewall Road, off Claremont Avenue, in Oakland. GPS: N37 51.46' / W122 14.39'
Elevation gain: 700 feet
Distance: 1.6 miles out and back
Difficulty: Strenuous due to rapid elevation gain
Hiking time: About 1.5 hours
Seasons/schedule: 5 a.m. to 10 p.m. year-round
Fees and permits: None
Trail contact: East Bay Regional Park District Headquarters, 2950 Peralta Oaks Ct., P.O. Box 5381, Oakland 94605; 888-EBPARKS (888-327-2757), option 3, ext. 4516; www.ebparks.org/parks/claremont_canyon#map
Dog-friendly: Dogs on leash
Trail surface: Double-track dirt trail
Land status: Regional preserve
Nearest town: Oakland and Berkeley
Nat Geo TOPO! Map: Oakland East, CA
Other trail users: Hikers only
Special considerations: Muddy after heavy rains

Y. TILDEN REGIONAL PARK— GREATER TILDEN

WHY GO?

Charles Lee Tilden Regional Park straddles the boundary between Alameda and Contra Costa Counties in the hills above Berkeley. If you're hiking with your dog, the nature area is off-limits, but in the rest of Tilden you have miles of trails in canyon and ridge terrain to keep your feet and your pet happy. A full loop around the park starting at the steam train swings by Lake Anza, the Brazilian Room, the golf course, the botanic garden, and two peaks offering expansive vistas: Vollmer Peak (1,905 feet) and Grizzly Peak (1,795 feet). Vollmer can be reached on the Bay Area Ridge Trail, also part of the Skyline National Trail. You can enjoy 2 miles of views on the ridge, although the dirt path is road-wide and allows bike and horse traffic.

A 7-mile loop, it includes treks on Curran, Selby, and Grizzly Peak Trails and takes 3.5 hours, not including stops at the sites, so bring lunch and plan for a whole day.

THE RUN DOWN

Start: Depending on the loop, start at the steam train, Lone Oak picnic site, Lake Anza parking lot, or Inspiration Point; GPS: Redwood Valley Railway: N37 52.57'/W122 13.21'; GPS: Lake Anza: N37 53.45'/ W122 15.5'
Elevation gain: Varies
Distance: Varies
Difficulty: Easy to strenuous
Hiking time: Varies
Seasons/schedule: 5 a.m. to 10 p.m. year-round
Fees and permits: None

Trail contact: East Bay Regional Park District Headquarters, 2950 Peralta Oaks Ct., P.O. Box 5381, Oakland 94605; 888-EBPARKS (888-327-2757), option 3, ext. 4562; www.eb parks.org/parks/tilden
Dog-friendly: Dogs on leash
Trail surface: Mostly single-track and double-track dirt trail
Land status: Regional park
Nearest town: Berkeley
Nat Geo TOPO! Map: Richmond, CA; Briones Valley, CA
Other trail users: Mountain bikers

Z. BRIONES RESERVOIR

WHY GO?

The Bear Creek Trail (3 miles) traverses the south slopes of Briones Reservoir, moderately steep in places, mostly forested. At the Bear Creek Staging Area, enter the gate on the left and cross the creek to the Bear Creek Trail. (Turning left would take you to the Briones Regional Park gate.) Turn right and head along the reservoir through the tree farm to the shore. A dirt fire road follows the shoreline, then winds gradually higher up the slope, where it becomes a narrow path. With a brief stint on a service road, you are back on the serene single-track trail, home to rabbits, foxes, and deer, which you are likely to see along this undisturbed path. The only drawback is the faint sound of occasional traffic from Bear Creek Road and some horse droppings on the narrow trail. At the Overlook Staging Area (a good place to drop a shuttle car for a group hike), you find a restroom. The trail continues on, following the lake's edge to the dam and down the grassy slope alongside the spillway to the junction with Oursan Trail.

Oursan Trail (9.4 miles) is a long, fairly easy, dog-friendly trail through high, often windy meadows that descends lakeside again, skirting the northern shores of Briones Reservoir. It returns to the Bear Creek Staging Area.

THE RUN DOWN

Start: Either at the Bear Creek Staging Area (left side of Bear Creek Road between Happy Valley Road and the Briones Regional Park entrance) or at the Briones Overlook Staging Area (on Bear Creek about a mile before the regional park, coming from Camino Pablo). GPS: N37 54.48'/ W122 12.9'
Elevation gain: Up to 1,500 feet
Distance: Varies, up to 13.2 miles all the way around the reservoir
Difficulty: Moderate due to uphill and steep downhill sections
Hiking time: Varies
Seasons/schedule: Sunrise to sunset year-round

Fees and permits: Briones Reservoir requires a permit (available online) from East Bay Municipal Utilities District (EBMUD); (510) 287-0459; www.ebmud.com/recreation/buy-trail-permit. Maps also are available online.
Trail contact: East Bay Regional Park District Headquarters, 2950 Peralta Oaks Ct., P.O. Box 5381, Oakland 94605; 888-EBPARKS (888-327-2757), option 3, ext. 4508; www.ebparks.org/parks/briones
Dog-friendly: Dogs on leash on Oursan Trail only
Trail surface: Packed double-track and single-track dirt trail

Land status: Municipal district watershed
Nearest town: Orinda
Nat Geo TOPO! Map: Briones Valley, CA
Other trail users: Hikers only

Special considerations: Trails in this watershed interconnect with paths into the regional park area, around San Pablo Reservoir, and all the way to Inspiration Point in Tilden.

TRAILS LESS TRAVELED—EBMUD LAND

Living in a busy and populated area, Bay Area hikers are frequently looking for the trail less traveled. Because it requires a permit, EBMUD land contains some of those trails. EBMUD maintains about 80 miles of trails on 27,000 acres of watershed lands. The area stretches from Castro Valley in the south to Pinole Valley in the north. Maps are available for the North Watershed and South Watershed areas, and there is lovely land surrounding reservoirs and creeks to explore. To learn more, get maps, and purchase your daily or annual permit, go to www.ebmud.com/recreation/east-bay/east-bay-trails/. Some of the Peninsula Watershed is opening to hikers as well.

With the diversity of Bay Area parklands and open spaces, you can readily find some unique features, characteristics, and activities while hiking. Here are a few categories that might be of interest:

	BEST HIKES FOR BEACH-GOERS	HIKES THROUGH HISTORY	CALF-BURNER CLIMBS	BEST HIKES FOR ANIMAL AND BIRD LOVERS	BEST HIKES FOR REDWOODS
POINT REYES					
1. Point Reyes National Seashore: Mount Wittenberg and Bear Valley to the Sea Loop	•		•	•	
2. Point Reyes National Seashore: Tomales Point				•	
3. Point Reyes National Seashore: Lighthouse and Chimney Rock Trails				•	
4. Point Reyes National Seashore: Palomarin Trailhead to Alamere Falls	•			•	
5. Tomales Bay State Park: Heart's Desire Beach to Shell Beach	•	•			
6. Samuel P. Taylor State Park: To the Top of Barnabe Peak			•		•
BONUS HIKES: POINT REYES					
A. Point Reyes National Seashore: Inverness Ridge					
B. Kule Loklo & the Earthquake Trail		•			
MOUNT TAMALPAIS AND ITS FOOTHILLS					
7. Muir Woods: Bootjack Trail to Dipsea Trail Loop					•
8. Phoenix Lake: Tucker and Bill Williams Trails					
9. Steep Ravine Loop to Stinson Beach	•				
10. Mt. Tamalpais: East Peak Loop		•			
11. Marin Headlands: Miwok Trail to Point Bonita	•	•		•	

	BEST HIKES FOR BEACH-GOERS	HIKES THROUGH HISTORY	CALF-BURNER CLIMBS	BEST HIKES FOR ANIMAL AND BIRD LOVERS	BEST HIKES FOR REDWOODS
MOUNT TAMALPAIS AND ITS FOOTHILLS (CONTINUED)					
12. Marin Municipal Water District: Kent Trail along Alpine Lake		•		•	•
13. Mount Burdell Open Space Preserve			•		
14. Ring Mountain Open Space Preserve					
BONUS HIKES: MOUNT TAMALPAIS AND ITS FOOTHILLS					
C. China Camp State Park: Shoreline-Bayview Loop Trail					
D. Cataract Trail					
SAN FRANCISCO AND THE BAY					
15. Angel Island State Park: Mt. Livermore	•	•			
16. Golden Gate National Recreation Area: San Francisco's Lands End	•	•			
17. Sweeney Ridge: San Francisco Bay Discovery Site		•			
18. San Bruno State Park: Summit Loop Trail			•		
BONUS HIKES: SAN FRANCISCO AND THE BAY					
E. Golden Gate Park		•			
F. The Presidio: Lovers' Lane and the Ecology Trail		•			
SAN MATEO COUNTY COASTLINE					
19. Pescadero Marsh Trail				•	
20. Butano State Park				•	•
21. Año Nuevo State Park				•	
22. McNee Ranch at Montara State Beach	•		•		
23. James V. Fitzgerald Marine Reserve: The Tide Pool Loop	•			•	
24. San Pedro Valley County Park					
BONUS HIKES: SAN MATEO COASTLINE					
G. Mori Point	•				
H. Crystal Springs Regional Trail					

	BEST HIKES FOR BEACH-GOERS	HIKES THROUGH HISTORY	CALF-BURNER CLIMBS	BEST HIKES FOR ANIMAL AND BIRD LOVERS	BEST HIKES FOR REDWOODS
THE NORTHERN SANTA CRUZ MOUNTAINS					
25. Big Basin Redwoods State Park: Berry Creek Falls Trail Loop					•
26. Castle Rock State Park: Saratoga Gap/Ridge Trail/Castle Rock Trail					
27. Portola Redwoods State Park: Slate Creek/Summit/Iverson Loop					•
28. Purisima Creek Redwoods Open Space Preserve: Craig Britton and Purisima Creek Loop					•
BONUS HIKES: THE NORTHERN SANTA CRUZ MOUNTAINS					
I. Huddart County Park and Phleger Estate			•		•
J. Wunderlich County Park					•
K. Windy Hill Open Space Preserve					
L. Russian Ridge Open Space Preserve				•	
M. Skyline Ridge Open Space Preserve				•	
N. Monte Bello Open Space Preserve					
O. Rancho San Antonio Open Space Preserve and County Park					
P. Pescadero Creek County Park					•
Q. Henry Cowell Redwoods State Park					•
MOUNT DIABLO AND LAS TRAMPAS FOOTHILLS					
29. Las Trampas Regional Wilderness			•		
30. Mount Diablo State Park: Donner Canyon to the Falls Trail			•		
31. Black Diamond Mines Regional Preserve		•			
32. Mount Diablo: Rock City to the Summit			•		

	BEST HIKES FOR BEACH-GOERS	HIKES THROUGH HISTORY	CALF-BURNER CLIMBS	BEST HIKES FOR ANIMAL AND BIRD LOVERS	BEST HIKES FOR REDWOODS
BONUS HIKES: MOUNT DIABLO AND LAS TRAMPAS FOOTHILLS					
R. Las Trampas Regional Wilderness: The Eugene O'Neill Loop		•			
S. Mount Diablo State Park: Wall Point–Pine Canyon Loop			•		
T. John Muir National Historic Site: Mount Wanda		•			
U. Brushy Peak Regional Preserve				•	
THREE RIDGES: SAN PABLO, THE OAKLAND/BERKELEY HILLS, AND SUNOL RIDGE					
33. Tilden Regional Park: From Jewel Lake to Wildcat Peak				•	
34. Briones Regional Park					
35. Robert Sibley Volcanic Regional Preserve					
36. Huckleberry Botanic Regional Preserve					
37. Redwood Regional Park: Stream Trail, from East Ridge to West Ridge				•	•
38. Joaquin Miller Park: Sequoia Bayview Trail and Big Trees Loop					•
39. Anthony Chabot Regional Park					
40. Sunol Regional Wilderness					
BONUS HIKES: THREE RIDGES: SAN PABLO, THE OAKLAND/BERKELEY HILLS, AND SUNOL RIDGE					
V. Mission Peak Regional Preserve			•		
W. Coyote Hills Regional Park		•		•	
X. Claremont Canyon Regional Preserve			•		
Y. Tilden Regional Park—Greater Tilden					
Z. Briones Reservoir				•	

Angel Island State Park: Mt. Livermore, 85

Año Nuevo State Park, 119

Anthony Chabot Regional Park, 249

Big Basin Redwoods State Park: Berry Creek Falls Trail Loop, 145

Black Diamond Mines Regional Preserve, 196

Briones Regional Park, 222

Briones Reservoir, 267

Brushy Peak Regional Preserve, 214

Butano State Park, 113

Castle Rock State Park: Saratoga Gap/Ridge Trail/Castle Rock Trail, 152

Cataract Trail, 83

China Camp State Park: Shoreline-Bayview Loop Trail, 82

Claremont Canyon Regional Preserve, 265

Coyote Hills Regional Park, 262

Crystal Springs Regional Trail, 141

Golden Gate National Recreation Area: San Francisco's Lands End, 90

Golden Gate Park, 105

Henry Cowell Redwoods State Park, 182

Huckleberry Botanic Regional Preserve, 233

Huddart County Park and Phleger Estate, 169

James V. Fitzgerald Marine Reserve: The Tide Pool Loop, 129

Joaquin Miller Park: Sequoia Bayview Trail and Big Trees Loop, 245

John Muir National Historic Site: Mount Wanda, 211

Kule Loklo & the Earthquake Trail, 35

Las Trampas Regional Wilderness, 186

Las Trampas Regional Wilderness: The Eugene O'Neill Loop, 208

Marin Headlands: Miwok Trail to Point Bonita, 60

Marin Municipal Water District: Kent Trail along Alpine Lake, 66

McNee Ranch at Montara State Beach, 124

Mission Peak Regional Preserve, 260

Monte Bello Open Space Preserve, 177

Mori Point, 140

Mount Burdell Open Space Preserve, 71

Mount Diablo: Rock City to the Summit, 201

Mount Diablo State Park: Donner Canyon to the Falls Trail, 191

Mount Diablo State Park: Wall Point—Pine Canyon Loop, 210

Mt. Tamalpais: East Peak Loop, 54

Muir Woods: Bootjack Trail to Dipsea Trail Loop, 37

Pescadero Creek County Park, 181

Pescadero Marsh Trail, 108

Phoenix Lake: Tucker and Bill Williams Trails, 43

Point Reyes National Seashore: Inverness Ridge, 32

Point Reyes National Seashore: Lighthouse and Chimney Rock Trails, 12

Point Reyes National Seashore: Mount Wittenberg and Bear Valley to the Sea Loop, 2

Point Reyes National Seashore: Palomarin Trailhead to Alamere Falls, 17

Point Reyes National Seashore: Tomales Point, 7

Portola Redwoods State Park: Slate Creek/Summit/Iverson Loop, 158

Presidio, The: Lover's Lane and the Ecology Trail, 106

Purisima Creek Redwoods Open Space Preserve: Craig Britton and Purisima Creek Loop, 164

Rancho San Antonio Open Space Preserve and County Park, 180

Redwood Regional Park: Stream Trail, from East Ridge to West Ridge, 239

Ring Mountain Open Space Preserve, 76

Robert Sibley Volcanic Regional Preserve, 227

Russian Ridge Open Space Preserve, 173

Samuel P. Taylor State Park: To the Top of Barnabe Peak, 27

San Bruno Mountain State Park: Summit Loop Trail, 100

San Pedro Valley County Park, 135

Skyline Ridge Open Space Preserve, 176

Steep Ravine Loop to Stinson Beach, 48

Sunol Regional Wilderness, 255

Sweeney Ridge: San Francisco Bay Discovery Site, 95

Tilden Regional Park: From Jewel Lake to Wildcat Peak, 216

Tilden Regional Park—Greater Tilden, 266

Tomales Bay State Park: Heart's Desire Beach to Shell Beach, 22

Windy Hill Open Space Preserve, 172

Wunderlich County Park, 171

Sunset from Point Pinole
NICK FULLERTON (FLICKR.COM/PEOPLE/18203311@N08/)